ENGLISH / CHINESE

英文 / 中文

THIRD CANADIAN EDITION

OPD

OXFORD PICTURE DICTIONARY

ENGLISH / CHINESE

英文 / 中文

THIRD **CANADIAN** EDITION

OXFORD

PICTURE

DICTIONARY

Jayme Adelson-Goldstein

Norma Shapiro

OXFORD

UNIVERSITY PRESS

OXFORD
UNIVERSITY PRESS

Oxford University Press is a department of the University of Oxford.
It furthers the University's objective of excellence in research, scholarship,
and education by publishing worldwide. Oxford is a registered trade mark of
Oxford University Press in the UK and in certain other countries.

Published in Canada by
Oxford University Press
8 Sampson Mews, Suite 204,
Don Mills, Ontario M3C 0H5 Canada

www.oupcanada.com

Copyright © Oxford University Press Canada 2017

The moral rights of the author have been asserted

Database right Oxford University Press (maker)

First Edition published in 1999
Second Edition published in 2010

Oxford Picture Dictionary 3e was originally published in 2016.
This reprint published by arrangement with Oxford University Press for
sale/distribution in Canada only and not for export therefrom.
© Oxford University Press 2016

Library and Archives Canada Cataloguing in Publication

Adelson-Goldstein, Jayme, author
    Oxford picture dictionary. English/Chinese = Ying wen/Zhong wen /
Jayme Adelson-Goldstein, Norma Shapiro. – Third Canadian edition.

Title in English only ; with text in English and Chinese.
ISBN 978-0-19-902711-8 (softcover)

1. Picture dictionaries, Chinese. 2. Picture dictionaries, English. 3. Chinese
language–Dictionaries–English. 4. English language–Dictionaries–Chinese.
5. Dictionaries. I. Shapiro, Norma, author II. Title.

PL1455.A44 2016   495.13'21   C2016-903853-X

Oxford University Press is committed to our environment.
Wherever possible, our books are printed on paper which comes
from responsible sources.

Printed and bound in the United States of America

1 2 3 4 — 20 19 18 17

ACKNOWLEDGMENTS

Translated by: Techno-Graphics & Translations, Inc.
Illustrations by: Lori Anzalone: 13, 70-71, 76-77; Joe "Fearless" Arenella/Will Sumpter:
196; Argosy Publishing: 66-67 (call-outs), 108-109, 114-115 (call-outs), 156, 196, 205,
206-207, 215; Barbara Bastian: 4, 15, 208; Philip Batini/AA Reps: 50; Thomas Bayley/
Sparks Literary Agency: 162; Sally Bensusen: 217, 220; Peter Bollinger/Shannon
Associates: 14-15; Higgens Bond/Anita Grien: 232; Molly Borman-Pullman: 118, 119;
Jocelyne Bouchard: 208; Mark Duffin: 7, 37, 61, 94, 238, 239, 240, 241; Jim Fanning/
Ravenhill Represents: 80-81; Mike Gardner: 10, 12, 17, 22, 134, 116-117, 145-146, 179,
225, 234-235; Garth Glazier/AA Reps: 106, 111, 120; Dennis Godfrey/Mike Wepplo:
214; Steve Graham: 126-127, 230; Julia Green/Mendola Art: 231; Donna Guilfoyle: 4,
13, 15, 26, 40, 41, 142, 156, 166, 167, 173, 184, 208, 212, 221, 222; Glenn Gustafson:
9, 27, 48, 76, 100, 101, 119, 134-135, 138, 159, 165, 197; Barbara Harmon: 218-219,
221; Ben Hasler/NB Illustration: 94-95, 101, 174, 188, 198-199; Betsy Hayes: 136,
140, 143; Matthew Holmes: 75; Stewart Holmes/Illustration Ltd.: 204; Janos Jantner/
Beehive Illustration: 5, 13, 82-83, 124-125, 132-133, 152-153, 166-167, 168, 169, 174,
175, 182-183, 192, 193; Ken Joudrey/Munro Campagna: 52, 68-69, 187; Bob Kaganich/
Deborah Wolfe: 10, 40-41, 123; Steve Karp: 237, 238; Mike Kasun/Munro Campagna:
224; Graham Kennedy: 27; Marcel Laverdet/AA Reps: 23; Jeffrey Lindberg: 33, 42-43,
92-93, 135, 164-165, 176-177, 186; Dennis Lyall/Artworks: 208; Chris Lyons/Lindgren
& Smith: 203; Alan Male/Artworks: 216, 217; Jeff Mangiat/Mendola Art: 53, 54, 55, 56,
57, 58, 59, 66-67; Adrian Mateescu/The Studio: 200-201, 238-239; Karen Minot: 28-29;
Paul Mirocha/The Wiley Group: 206, 222-223; Peter Miserendino/P.T. Pie Illustrations:
208; Lee Montgomery/Illustration Ltd.: 4; OUP Design: 20-21; Roger Motzkus: 235;
Laurie O'Keefe: 112, 222-223; Daniel O'Leary/Illustration Ltd.: 8-9, 26, 34-35, 78, 137,
138-139, 244; Vilma Ortiz-Dillon: 16, 20-21, 60, 98-99, 100, 217; Terry Pazcko: 46-47,
148-149, 156, 194, 233; David Preiss/Munro Campagna: 5; Pronk & Associates:
204-205; Tony Randazzo/AA Reps: 160, 240-241; Mike Renwick/Creative Eye: 128-129;
Mark Riedy/Scott Hull Associates: 48-49, 79, 142, 157; Jon Rogers/AA Reps: 114; Jeff
Sanson/Schumann & Co.: 84-85, 246-247; Ben Shannon/Magnet Reps: 11, 64-65, 90,
91, 96, 97, 121, 147, 170-171, 172-173, 180-181, 245; Lynn Shwadchuck: 22, 121, 140,
141, 142, 20; Reed Sprunger/Jae Wagoner Artists Rep.: 18-19, 238-239; Studio Liddell/
AA Reps: 27; Angelo Tillary: 108-109; Samuel Velasco/5W Infographics: 10, 11, 12, 13,
15, 48, 49, 80-81 (design), 110, 112, 113, 138, 143, 146, 156, 159, 210, 211, 212-213;
Ralph Voltz/Deborah Wolfe: 50-51, 130-131, 144, 158, 163, 185, 190, 191, 207 (top left),
215 (bot. left), 242-243; Jeff Wack/Mendola Art: 24, 25, 86-87, 102-103, 136-137, 237;
Brad Walker: 104-105, 154-155, 161, 226-227; Wendy Wassink: 112-113; John White/
The Neis Group: 209; Eric Wilkerson: 32, 140; Simon Williams/Illustration Ltd.: 2-3,
6-7, 30-31, 36, 38-39, 44-45, 72-73, 141, 178, 184; Lee Woodgate/Eye Candy Illustration:
228-229; Andy Zito: 62-23; Craig Zuckerman: 14, 88-89, 114-115, 122-123, 206-207.

Cover Design: Studio Montage
Chapter icons designed by Anna Sereda

Commissioned studio photography for Oxford University Press done by Dennis
Kitchen Studio: 37, 61, 72, 73, 74, 75, 95, 96, 100, 189, 194, 195, 232.

*The publishers would like to thank the following for their kind permission to reproduce
photographs:* 20-21 (calendar) dikobraziy/Shutterstock; 31 (flowers photo) Digital
Vision/OUP; 48 (apartment interior) Sindre Ellingsen/Alamy Stock Photo; 61
(oven) gerenme/Getty Images, (table) Stefano Mattia/Getty Images, (window)
nexus 7/Shutterstock, (shower) FOTOGRAFIA INC./Getty Images, (dishes) Nika Art/
Shutterstock, (kitchen counter/sink) zstock/Shutterstock; 94 (watch) WM_idea/
Shutterstock; 98 (cotton texture) Saksan Maneechay/123RF, (linen texture)
daizuoxin/Shutterstock, (wool texture) riekephotos/Shutterstock, (cashmere
texture) ovb64/Shutterstock, (silk texture) Anteromite/Shutterstock, (leather
texture) Victor Newman/Shutterstock; 99 (denim) Jaroslaw Grudzinski/123RF,
(suede) KPG Payless2/Shutterstock, (lace) Nataliia Melnychuk/Shutterstock, (velvet)
Neirfy/Shutterstock, (corduroy) Eldad Carin/Shutterstock, (nylon) B Calkins/
Shutterstock; 141 (Pentagon) Don S. Montgomery/Corbis; 156 (bus transfer) © TTC,
(bus ticket) © City of Winnipeg, (Presto card) © Metrolinx; 208 (women win the
right to vote) City of Edmonton Archives EA-10-2070, (train) Tim Dixon, Locomotive
1392 is owned and operated by the Alberta Railway Museum in Edmonton, Alberta,
(Halifax Explosion) Public Archives of Nova Scotia, (Great Depression) Library and
Archives Canada, (WWII) Library and Archives Canada, (Constitution Act) Robert
Cooper/Library and Archives Canada/e008300499, (WWI) ASSOCIATED PRESS; 212
(thoughtful woman) Di Studio/Shutterstock; 213 (people in uniform) Rawpixel.com/
Shutterstock; 232 (tent) Hurst Photo/Shutterstock, (campfire) wolv/Getty Images;
244 (flute) cowardlion/Shutterstock, (clarinet) Vereshchagin Dmitry/Shutterstock,
(oboe) Matthias G. Ziegler/Shutterstock, (bassoon) Rodrigo Blanco/Getty Images,
(saxophone) Ocean/OUP, (violin) Ocean/OUP, (cello) Stockbyte/Getty Images, (bass)
the palms/Shutterstock, (guitar) Photodisc/OUP, (trombone) seen/Shutterstock,
(trumpet) Photodisc/OUP, (tuba) Ingram/OUP, (French horn) Venus Angel/
Shutterstock, (piano) liangpv/Getty Images, (xylophone) Yuri Kevhiev/Alamy Stock
Photo, (drums) lem/Shutterstock, (tambourine) Vereshchagin Dmitry/Shutterstock,
(keyboard) George Peters/Getty Images, (accordion) Stockbyte/Getty Images, (organ)
C Squared Studios/Getty Images, (harmonica) Goran Bogicevic/Alamy Stock Photo.

*The publisher would like to thank the following for their permission to reproduce
copyrighted material:*
4, 40: SIN card source: Service Canada website (servicecanada.gc.ca). Reproduced
with the permission of the Minister of Public Works and Government Services,
2016. 26, 82, 134, 156: Bank note images used and altered with permission of the
© Bank of Canada. L'utilisation et la modification des images de billets de banque
ont été autorisées par la © Banque du Canada. 40: Permanent Resident Card and
Citizenship Certificate reproduced with the permission of the Minister of Public
Works and Government Services Canada, 2016. 120: Health card courtesy of New
Brunswick Department of Health, Medicare Operations. 136–137: ™Priority Courier,
Xpresspost and Lettermail are trademarks of Canada Post Corporation. 141: New
Brunswick flag courtesy of Communications New Brunswick. 174: National Center
for O*NET Development. O*NET OnLine. Retrieved November 23, 2015, from
https://www.onetonline.org/. 191: Microsoft Word® is a registered trademark of
Microsoft Corporation. Screen shot reprinted with permission from Microsoft
Corporation. 191: Microsoft Excel® is a registered trademark of Microsoft
Corporation. Screen shot reprinted with permission from Microsoft Corporation.
191: Microsoft PowerPoint® is a registered trademark of Microsoft Corporation.
Screen shot reprinted with permission from Microsoft Corporation. 210: Microsoft
icons reprinted by permission of Microsoft.

This third edition of the Oxford Picture
Dictionary is lovingly dedicated to the
memory of Norma Shapiro.

Her ideas, her pictures, and her stories
continue to teach, inspire, and delight.

Acknowledgments

The publisher and authors would like to acknowledge the following individuals for their invaluable feedback during the development of this program:

Nawal Abbas, Lawrence Tech University, MI; **Dr. Macarena Aguilar**, Cy-Fair College, TX; **Penny Aldrich**, Durham Technical Community College, NC; **Deanna Allen**, Round Rock ISD, TX; **Angela Andrade-Holt**, Western Nevada College, NV; **Joseph F. Anselme**, Atlantic Technical Center, FL; **Stacy Antonopoulos**, Monterey Trail High School, CA; **Carol Antunano**, The English Center, FL; **Irma Arencibia**, Thomas A. Edison School, NJ; **Stephanie Austin**, CBET Program Moreland School District, CA; **Suzi Austin**, Alexandria City Public School Adult Program, FL; **Carol Beebe**, Niagara University, NY; **Patricia S. Bell**, Lake Technical Center, FL; **Derick Bonewitz**, College of Lake County, IL; **Emily Box,** Granite Peaks Learning Center, UT; **Diana Brady-Herndon**, Western Nevada College, NV; **Jim Brice**, San Diego Community College District, CA; **Theresa Bries**, Black Hawk College, IL; **Diane Brody**, St. John's Lutheran Church; **Mindy Bruton**, Abilene ISD, TX; **Caralyn Bushey**, Montgomery College TESOL Certificate Program, MD; **Phil Cackley**, Arlington Education and Employment Program (REEP), VA; **Frieda Caldwell**, Metropolitan Adult Education Program, CA; **Anne Marie Caney**, Chula Vista Adult School, CA; **Lynda Cannon**, Ashland Community and Technical College, KY; **Lenore Cardoza**, Brockton Public Schools Adult Learning Center, MA; **Victor Castellanos**, Covina Public Library, CA; **Marjorie Castillo-Farquhar**, Community Action/Austin Community College, TX; **Patricia Castro**, Harvest English Institute, NJ; **Paohui Lola Chen**, Milpitas Adult School, CA; **Alicia Chicas**, The Hayward Center for Education & Careers (Adult School), CA; **Michelle Chuang**, East Side Adult Education, CA; **Lori Cisneros**, Atlantic Vo-Tech, FL; **Joyce Clapp**, Hayward Adult School, CA; **Stacy Clark**, Arlington Education and Employment Program (REEP), VA; **Melissa Cohen**, Literacy New Jersey - Middlesex Programs, NJ; **Dave Coleman**, LAUSD District, CA; **Edith Cowper**, Wake Technical Community College, NC; **Leslie Crawley**, The Literacy Center; **Kelli Crow**, City College San Francisco Civic Center, CA; **Nancy B. Crowell**, Southside Programs for Adults in Continuing Education, VA; **Doroti da Cunha**, Hialeah-Miami Lakes Adult Education Center, FL; **Brenda Custodio**, Ohio State University, OH; **Dory Dannettell**, Community Educational Outreach, CO; **Paula Da Silva-Michelin**, La Guardia Community College, NY; **Peggy Datz**, Berkeley Adult School, CA; **Cynthia L. Davies**, Humble I.S.D., TX; **Christopher Davis**, Overfelt Adult Center, CA; **Laura De Anda**, Margaret Aylward Center, CA; **Tyler Degener**, Drexel University College of Medicine, PA; **Jacquelyn Delaney**; **Mariana De Luca**, Charlotte-Mecklenburg Public Schools, NC; **Georgia Deming**, Johnson County Community College (JCAE), KS; **Beverly De Nicola**, Capistrano Unified School District, CA; **Irena Dewey**, US Conversation; **Frances Tornabene De Sousa**, Pittsburg Adult Education Center, CA; **Matthew Diamond**, The University of Texas at Austin, TX; **Beatriz Diaz**, Miami-Dade County Public Schools, FL; **Druci Diaz**, Program Advisor, Adult & Career Services Center Hillsborough County Public Schools, FL; **Natalya Dollar**, North Orange County Community College District, CA; **Marion Donahue**, San Dieguito Adult School, CA; **Nick Doorn**, International Education Services, MI; **Mercedes Douglass**, Seminole Community College, FL; **Joan Dundas**, Brock University, ON (Canada); **Jennifer Eick-Magán**, Prairie State College, IL; **Jenny Elliott**, Montgomery College, MD; **Paige Endo**, Mt. Diablo Adult Education, CA; **Megan Ernst**, Glendale Community College, CA; **Elizabeth Escobar**, Robert Waters School, NJ; **Joanne Everett**, Dave Thomas Education Center, FL; **Jennifer Fadden**, Arlington Education and Employment Program (REEP), VA; **Cinzia Fagan**, East Side Adult Education, CA; **Jacqui Farrell**, Literacy Volunteers on the Green, CT; **Ross Feldberg**, Tufts University, MA; **Sharyl Ferguson**, Montwood High School, TX; **Emily Finch**, FCI Englewood, CO; **Dr. Robert Finkelstein**, Willammette Dental, OR; **Janet Fischer**, Lawrence Public Schools - Adult Learning Center, MA; **Dr. Monica Fishkin**, University of Central Florida, FL; **Jan Foley**, Wilbur Wright College - City Colleges of Chicago, IL; **Tim Foster**, Silver Valley Adult Education Center, CA; **Nancy Frampton**, Reedley College, CA; **Lynn A. Freeland**, San Dieguito Union High School District, CA; **Sally A. Fox**, East Side Adult Education, CA; **Cathy Gample**, San Leandro Adult School, CA; **Hillary Gardner**, Center for Immigrant Education and Training, NY; **Elizabeth Gibb**, Castro Valley Adult and Career Education, CA; **Martha C. Giffen**, Alhambra Unified School District, CA; **Elgy Gillespie**, City College San Francisco, CA; **Lisa Marcelle Gimbel**, Community Learning Center, MA; **Jill Gluck**, Hollywood Community Adult School, CA; **Richard Goldberg**, Asian American Civic Association, MA; **Carolyn Grebe**, The Hayward Center for Education & Careers (Adult School), CA; **Carolyn Grimaldi**, LaGuardia Community College, NY; **Cassell Gross**, Intercambio, CO; **William Gruenholz**, USD Adult School, CA; **Sandra G. Gutierrez**, Hialeah-Miami Lakes Adult Education Center, FL; **Conte Gúzman-Hoffman**, Triton College, IL; **William J. Hall**, M.D. FACP/FRSM (UK); **Amanda Harllee**, Palmetto High School, FL; **Kathy Harris**, Portland State University, OR; **Kay Hartley**, Fairfield-Suisun Adult School, CA; **Melissa Hassmanm**, Northwest Iowa Community College, IA; **Mercedes Hearn**, Tampa Bay Technical Center, FL; **Christyann Helm**, Carlos Rosario International Public Charter School, WA; **Suzanne Hibbs**, East Side Adult Education, CA; **Lindsey Himanga**, Hiawatha Valley ABE, MN; **Marvina Hooper**, Lake Technical College, FL; **Jill A. Horohoe**, Arizona State University, AZ; **Roxana Hurtado**, Miami Dade Adult, FL; **Rachel Johnson**, MORE Multicultural School for Empowerment, MN; **Randy Johnson**, Hartford Public Library, CT; **Sherry Joseph**, Miami Dade College, FL; **Elaine Kanakis**, The Hayward Center for Education and Careers, CA; **Phoebe Kang**, Brock University, ON (Canada); **Mary Kaufman**, Brewster Technical Center, FL; **Jeanne Kearsley**, City College San Francisco Chinatown, CA; **Sallyann Kovacs**, The Hayward Center for Education & Careers (Adult School), CA; **Jennifer Latzgo**, Lehigh Carbon Community College, PA; **Sandy Lawler**, East Side Adult Education, CA; **Xinhua Li**, City College of San Francisco, CA; **Renata Lima**, TALK International School of Languages, FL; **Luz M. Lopez**, Sweetwater Union High School District, CA; **Osmara Lopez**, Bronx Community College, NY; **Heather Lozano**, North Lake College, TX; **Marcia Luptak**, Elgin Community College, IL; **Betty Lynch**, Arlington Education and Employment Program (REEP), VA; **Matthew Lyter**, Tri-County OIC, PA; **Meera Madan**, REID Park Elementary School, NC; **Julia Maffei**, Texas State IEP, TX; **Ivanna Mann Thrower**, Charlotte Mecklenburg Schools, NC; **Anna Mariani**, The English Center (TLC Online), FL; **Michael R. Mason**, Loma Vista Adult Center, CA; **Terry Masters**, American Schools of Water for Ishmael, OH; **Debbie Matsumura**, CBET Program Moreland School District, CA; **Holley Mayville**, Charlotte Mecklenburg Schools, NC; **Margaret McCabe**, United Methodist Cooperative Ministries, FL; **David McCarthy**, Stony Brook University, NY; **Todd McDonald**, Hillsborough Adult Education, FL; **Nancy A. McKeand**, ESL Consultant, LA; **Rebecca L. McLain**, Gaston College, NC; **John M. Mendoza**, Redlands Adult School, CA; **Nancy Meredith**, Austin Community College, TX; **Marcia Merriman**, Community College of Baltimore County, MD; **Bet Messmer**, Santa Clara Adult Education Center, CA; **Holly Milkowart**, Johnson County Community College, KS; **Jose Montes**, The English Center M-DCPS, FL; **Elaine Moore**, Escondido Adult School, CA; **Lisa Munoz**, Metropolitan Education District, CA; **Mary Murphy-Clagett**, Sweetwater Union High School District, CA; **Jonetta Myles**, Rockdale County High School, GA; **Marwan Nabi**, Troy High School, CA; **Dale Nave**, San Marcos Academy, TX; **Dr. Christine L. Nelsen**, Salvation Army Community Center, FL; **Michael W. Newman**, Arlington Education and Employment Program (REEP), VA; **Virginia Nicolai**, Colorado Mountain College, CO; **Phoebe Nip**, East Side Adult Education, CA; **Rehana Nusrat**, Huntington Beach Adult School, CA; **Cindy Oakley-Paulik**, Embry-Riddle Aeronautical University, FL; **Judy O'Louglin**, CATESOL, CA; **Brigitte Oltmanns**, Triton College, IL; **Nora Onayemi**, Montgomery College, MD; **Lorena Orozco**, Catholic Charities, NM; **Allison Pickering**, Escondido Adult School, CA; **Odette Petrini**, Huron High School, MI; **Eileen Purcell**, Clatsop Community College, OR; **Teresa Reen**, East Side Adult Education, CA; **Jean Renoll**, Fairfax County Public Schools – ACE, VA; **Carmen Rivera-Diaz**, Calvary Church; **Fatiana Roganova**, The Hayward Center for Education & Careers (Adult School), CA; **Rosa Rojo**, Escondido Adult School, CA; **Lorraine Romero**, Houston Community College, TX; **Phoebe B. Rouse**, Louisiana State University, LA; **Dr. Susan Rouse**, Southern Wesleyan University, SC; **Blair Roy**, Chapman Education Center, CA; **Sharon Saylors**, The Hayward Center for Education & Careers (Adult School), CA; **Margret Schaefer**, Round Rock ISD, TX; **Arlene R. Schwartz**, Broward Community Schools, FL; **Geraldyne Blake Scott**, Truman College, IL; **Sharada Sekar**, Antioch High School Freshman Academy, TN; **Denise Selleck**, City College San Francisco Civic Center, CA; **Dr. Cheryl J. Serrano**, Lynn University, FL; **Janet Setzekorn**, United Methodist Cooperative Ministries, FL; **Terry Shearer**, EDUCALL Learning Services, TX; **Rob Sheppard**, Quincy Asian Resources, Inc., MA; **Dr. Ira M. Sheskin**, University of Miami, FL; **Glenda Sinks**, Community College of Denver, CO; **Elisabeth Sklar**, Township High School District 113, IL; **Jacqueline Sport**, LBWCC Luverne Center, AL; **Kathryn Spyksma**, The Hayward Center for Education & Careers (Adult School), CA; **Linda Steele**, Black Hawk College, IL; **Robert Stein**, BEGIN Managed Programs, NY; **Martin Steinman**, Canal Alliance, CA; **Ruth Sutton**, Township High School District 113, IL; **Alisa Takeuchi**, Chapman Education Center, CA; **Grace Tanaka**, Santa Ana College School of Continuing Education, CA; **Annalisa Te**, East Side Adult Education, CA; **Oscar Tellez**, Daley College, IL; **Fotini Terzi**, University of Texas at Austin, TX; **Geneva Tesh**, Houston Community College, TX; **Maiko Tomizawa**, D.D.S., NY; **Don Torluemke**, South Bay Adult School, CA; **Francisco Torres**, Olive-Harvey College, IL; **Shawn Tran**, East Side Adult Education, CA; **Serife Turkol**, Literary Council of Northern Virginia, VA; **Cristina Urena**, CC/Tech Center, FL; **Maliheh Vafai**, East Side Adult Education, CA; **Charlotte van Londen**, MCAEL, MD; **Tara Vasquez**, Robert Waters School, NJ; **Nina Velasco**, Naples Language Center, FL; **Colin Ward**, Lone Star College-North Harris, TX; **Theresa Warren**, East Side Adult Center, CA; **Lucie Gates Watel**, Truman College, IL; **Wendy Weil**, Arnold Middle School, TX; **Patricia Weist**, TALK International School of Languages, FL; **Dr. Carole Lynn Weisz**, Lehman College, NY; **Desiree Wesner**, Robert Waters School, NJ; **David Wexler**, Napa Valley Adult School, CA; **Kathy Wierseman**, Black Hawk College, IL; **Cynthia Wiseman**, Borough of Manhattan Community College, NY; **Nancy Whitmire**, University of Arkansas Community College at Batesville, AR; **Debbie Cullinane Wood**, Lincoln Education Center, CA; **Banu Yaylali**, Miami Dade College, FL; **Hongyan Zheng**, Milpitas Adult Education, Milpitas, CA; **Yelena Zimon**, Fremont Adult and Continuing Education, CA; **Arlene Zivitz**, ESOL Teacher, FL

Table of Contents 目錄

Contents 目錄

8. Transportation 交通

9. Job Search 求職

10. The Workplace 工作場所

11. Academic Study 學校學習

12. Recreation 娛樂

The Oxford Picture Dictionary Third Canadian Edition provides unparalleled support for vocabulary teaching and language development.

- Illustrations present over 4,000 English words and phrases within **meaningful, real-life contexts**.
- **New and expanded topics** including job search, career planning, and digital literacy prepare students to meet the requirements of their daily lives.
- Updated activities prepare students for **work, academic study, and citizenship**.
- **Oxford 3000 vocabulary** ensures students learn the most useful and important words.

Color coding and icons make it easy to navigate through *OPD*.

Vibrant illustrations and rich contexts improve vocabulary acquisition.

Subtopics present the words in easy-to-learn "chunks."

Revised practice activities help students develop academic and workforce skills.

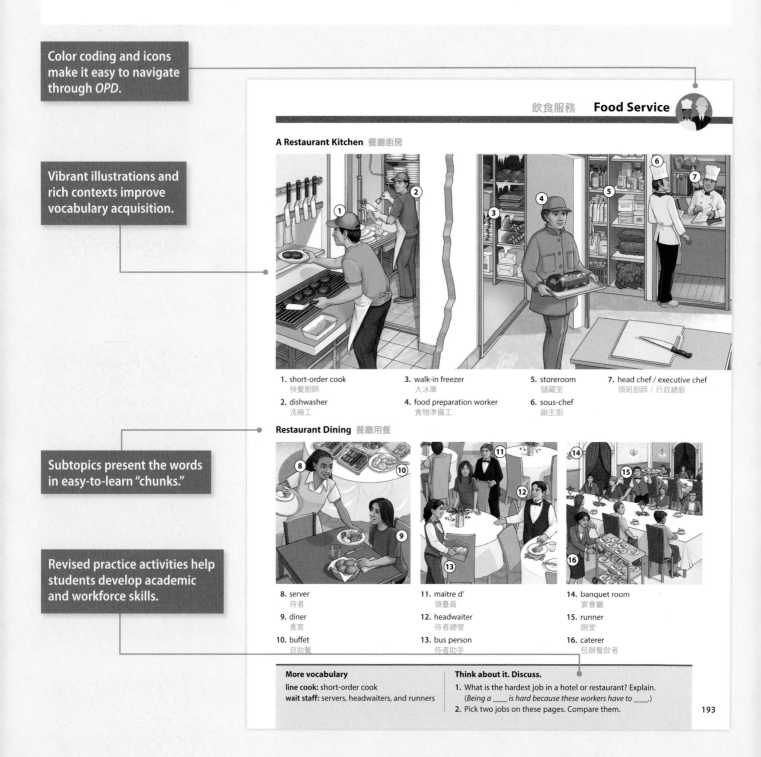

飲食服務 **Food Service**

A Restaurant Kitchen 餐廳廚房

1. short-order cook
   快餐廚師
2. dishwasher
   洗碗工
3. walk-in freezer
   大冰庫
4. food preparation worker
   食物準備工
5. storeroom
   儲藏室
6. sous-chef
   副主廚
7. head chef / executive chef
   領班廚師 / 行政總廚

Restaurant Dining 餐廳用餐

8. server
   侍者
9. diner
   食客
10. buffet
    自助餐
11. maitre d'
    領臺員
12. headwaiter
    侍者總管
13. bus person
    侍者助手
14. banquet room
    宴會廳
15. runner
    跑堂
16. caterer
    包辦餐飲者

More vocabulary
line cook: short-order cook
wait staff: servers, headwaiters, and runners

Think about it. Discuss.
1. What is the hardest job in a hotel or restaurant? Explain.
   (*Being a ____ is hard because these workers have to ____.*)
2. Pick two jobs on these pages. Compare them.

193

X

Intro pages open each unit with key vocabulary related to the unit theme. Clear, engaging artwork promotes questions, conversations, and writing practice for all levels.

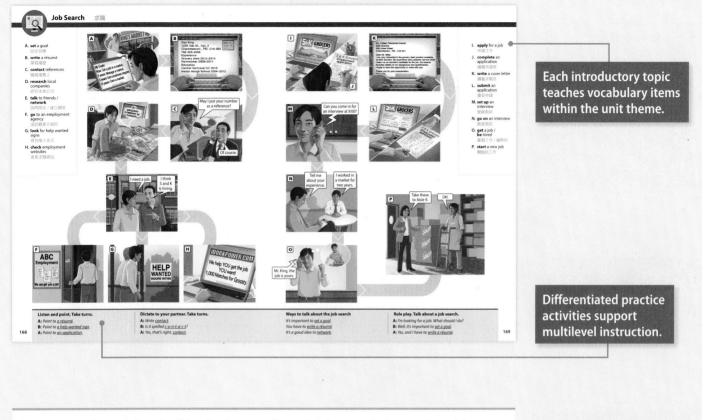

Each introductory topic teaches vocabulary items within the unit theme.

Differentiated practice activities support multilevel instruction.

Story pages close each unit with a lively scene for reviewing vocabulary and teaching additional language. Meanwhile, rich visual contexts recycle words from the unit.

Pre-reading questions build students' previewing and predicting skills.

End-of-unit readings promote literacy skills.

Post-reading questions support critical thinking and textual analysis skills.

The word list previews key vocabulary that students will encounter in the story.

Meeting and Greeting 見面與問候

A. **Say**, "Hello."
   説「您好。」

B. **Ask**, "How are you?"
   問「您好嗎？」

C. **Respond**, "Fine, thanks."
   答「很好，謝謝。」

D. **Introduce** yourself.
   自我介紹。

E. **Smile**.
   微笑。

F. **Hug**.
   擁抱。

G. **Wave**.
   招手。

Tell your partner what to do. Take turns.

1. *Say, "Hello."*
2. *Bow.*
3. *Smile.*
4. *Shake hands.*
5. *Wave.*
6. *Say, "Goodbye."*

Dictate to your partner. Take turns.

A: *Write <u>smile</u>.*
B: *Is it spelled <u>s-m-i-l-e</u>?*
A: *Yes, that's right.*

Ways to greet people

Good morning.
Good afternoon.
Good evening.

Ways to introduce yourself

I'm Tom.
My name is Tom.
Hello. I'm Tom Lee.

Pair practice. Make new conversations.

A: *Good morning. My name is Tom.*
B: *Nice to meet you, Tom. I'm Sara.*
A: *Nice to meet you, Sara.*

3

A. **Say** your name.
說出您的名字。

B. **Spell** your name.
拼出您的名字。

C. **Print** your name.
正楷書寫您的名字。

D. **Type** your name.
鍵入您的名字。

E. **Sign** your name.
簽名。

Filling Out a Form 填寫表格

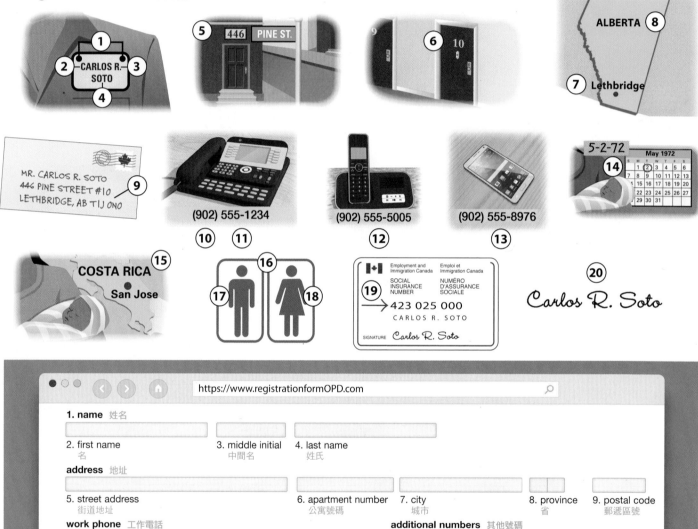

Pair practice. Make new conversations.

A: *My first name is Carlos.*
B: *Please spell Carlos for me.*
A: *C-a-r-l-o-s.*

Internet Research: popular names in BC

Type "popular baby names in BC" in a search engine.
Report: *According to my research, Emma is the number 1 female name.*

Campus 校園

Administrators 管理人員

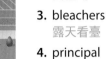

Around Campus 校園各處

More vocabulary

Students do not pay to attend a **public school**.

Students pay to attend a **private school**.

A church, mosque, or temple school is a **parochial school**.

Use contractions and talk about the pictures.

He **is** = He**'s**   She **is** = She**'s**

It **is** = It**'s**   They **are** = They**'re**

He's a teacher.   ***They're** students.*

1. whiteboard
   白板
2. screen
   投影幕
3. chalkboard
   黑板
4. teacher / instructor
   教師 / 講師
5. LCD projector
   液晶投影機
6. student
   學生
7. desk
   書桌
8. headphones
   耳機

A. Raise your hand.
舉手。

B. Talk to the teacher.
與老師談話。

C. Listen to a recording.
聽錄音。

D. Stand up.
站起來。

E. Write on the board.
寫在板上。

F. Sit down. / Take a seat.
坐下。

G. Open your book.
打開書本。

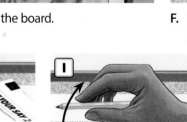

H. Close your book.
闔上書本。

I. Pick up the pencil.
拿起鉛筆。

J. Put down the pencil.
放下鉛筆。

A B C D E F G H I J K L M N O P Q R S T U V W X Y Z

9. clock
時鐘

10. bookcase
書架

11. chair
椅子

12. map
地圖

13. alphabet
字母表

14. bulletin board
佈告欄

15. computer
電腦

16. document camera
實物投影機

There are three ways

HAVE YOUR SAY 2
Listening and Speaking Skills and Practice
IRENE S. McKAY

17. dry-erase marker
白板筆

18. chalk
粉筆

19. eraser
黑板擦

20. pencil
鉛筆

21. (pencil) eraser
(鉛筆) 橡皮擦

22. pen
筆

23. pencil sharpener
削鉛筆刀

24. permanent marker
永久性記號筆

25. highlighter
螢光筆

26. textbook
教科書

27. workbook
練習本

28. 3-ring binder / notebook
三孔活頁夾 / 筆記本

29. binder paper
活頁紙

30. spiral notebook
螺線型筆記本

31. learner's dictionary
學生辭典

32. picture dictionary
圖解辭典

Grammar Point: *there is / there are*

*There **is** a map.*   *There **are** 15 students.*

Describe your classroom. Take turns.

A: *There's a clock.*   B: *There are 20 chairs.*

Survey your class. Record the responses.

1. Do you prefer pens or pencils?

2. Do you prefer talking or listening?

Report: *Most of us... Some of us...*

7

Learning New Words 學習生字

A. **Look up** the word.
查字典。

B. **Read** the definition.
讀定義。

C. **Translate** the word.
翻譯生字。

D. **Check** the pronunciation.
查看發音。

E. **Copy** the word.
抄寫生字。

F. **Draw** a picture.
畫圖。

Working with Your Classmates 與同學合作

G. **Discuss** a problem.
討論問題。

H. **Brainstorm** solutions / answers.
思考答案。

I. **Work** in a group.
團隊合作。

J. **Help** a classmate.
幫助同學。

Working with a Partner 與夥伴合作

K. **Ask** a question.
提出問題。

L. **Answer** a question.
回答問題。

M. **Share** a book.
共用書本。

N. **Dictate** a sentence.
句子聽寫。

Following Directions 遵循指示

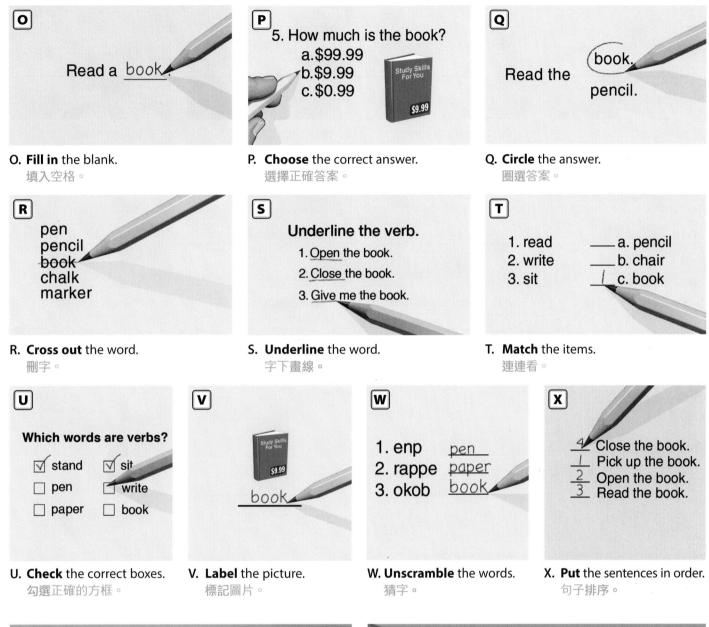

O. **Fill in** the blank.
填入空格。

P. **Choose** the correct answer.
選擇正確答案。

Q. **Circle** the answer.
圈選答案。

R. **Cross out** the word.
刪字。

S. **Underline** the word.
字下畫線。

T. **Match** the items.
連連看。

U. **Check** the correct boxes.
勾選正確的方框。

V. **Label** the picture.
標記圖片。

W. **Unscramble** the words.
猜字。

X. **Put** the sentences in order.
句子排序。

O. Read a _book_.

P. 5. How much is the book?
a. $99.99
b. $9.99
c. $0.99
Study Skills For You $9.99

Q. Read the ⟨book.⟩ pencil.

R. pen / pencil / ~~book~~ / chalk / marker

S. Underline the verb.
1. Open the book.
2. Close the book.
3. Give me the book.

T. 1. read — a. pencil
2. write — b. chair
3. sit — c. book

U. Which words are verbs?
☑ stand ☑ sit
☐ pen ☑ write
☐ paper ☐ book

V. Study Skills For You $9.99 / book

W. 1. enp _pen_
2. rappe _paper_
3. okob _book_

X. 4 Close the book.
1 Pick up the book.
2 Open the book.
3 Read the book.

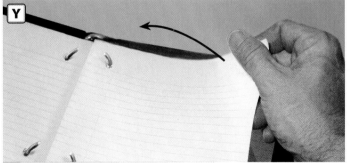

Y. **Take out** a piece of paper.
取出一頁紙。

Z. **Put away** your books.
收起書本。

Survey your class. Record the responses.

1. Do you prefer to study in a group or with a partner?
2. Do you prefer to translate or draw new words?
Report: *Most of us… Some of us…*

Identify Tom's problem. Brainstorm solutions.

Tom wants to study English with a group.
He wants to ask his classmates, "Do you want to study together?" but he's embarrassed.

Ways to Succeed 成功的途徑

A. Set goals.
設定目標。

B. Participate in class.
到教室上課。

C. Take notes.
記筆記。

D. Study at home.
在家自習。

E. Pass a test.
通過考試。

F. Ask for help. / **Request** help.
請求幫助。

G. Make progress.
取得進步。

H. Get good grades.
獲得好分數。

Taking a Test 參加考試

Numeric Grade	Standard Grade	Grade Point Average
90%-100%	A	4.0
80%-89%	B	3.0
70%-79%	C	2.0
60%-69%	D	1.0
Less than 60%	F (Fail)	0.0

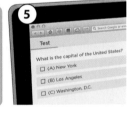

1. test booklet
考題冊

2. answer sheet
答題頁

3. score
分數

4. grades
分數等級

5. online test
線上考試

I. Clear off your desk.
清理書桌。

J. Work on your own.
自己作業。

K. Fill in the answer.
塗滿答案。

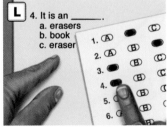

L. Check your work.
檢查結果。

M. Erase the mistake.
擦掉錯誤答案。

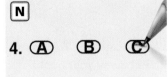

N. Correct the mistake.
更正錯誤。

O. Hand in your test.
交試卷。

P. Submit your test.
提交試卷。

A. **Walk** to class.
走著去教室。

B. **Run** to class.
跑著去教室。

C. **Enter** the room.
走進教室。

D. **Turn on** the lights.
開燈。

E. **Lift / Pick up** the books.
拿起書本。

F. **Carry** the books.
搬書本。

G. **Deliver** the books.
送書本。

H. **Take** a break.
休息。

I. **Eat**.
吃。

J. **Drink**.
喝。

K. **Buy** a snack.
買小吃。

L. **Have** a conversation.
會話。

M. **Go back** to class.
返回教室。

N. **Throw away** garbage.
扔垃圾。

O. **Leave** the room.
離開教室。

P. **Turn off** the lights.
關燈。

Grammar Point: present continuous

Use **be** + **verb** + **ing** (*What **are** they **doing**?*)
*He **is walking**. They **are talking**.*
Note: run—run**n**ing　leave—leav**ing** [**e**]

Look at the pictures. Describe what is happening.

A: *They are <u>entering the room</u>.*
B: *He is <u>walking</u>.*
C: *She's <u>eating</u>.*

11

A. **start** a conversation
開始會話

B. **make** small talk
簡短交談

C. **compliment** someone
稱讚他人

D. **thank** someone
感謝他人

E. **offer** something
提供某物

F. **refuse** an offer
拒絕他人的提供

G. **apologize**
道歉

H. **accept** an apology
接受道歉

I. **invite** someone
邀請他人

J. **accept** an invitation
接受邀請

K. **decline** an invitation
謝絕邀請

L. **agree**
同意

M. **disagree**
不同意

N. **explain** something
解釋某事

O. **check** your understanding
檢查您是否理解

More vocabulary

accept a compliment: to thank someone for a compliment

make a request: to ask for something

Pair practice. Follow the directions.

1. Start a conversation with your partner.
2. Make small talk with your partner.
3. Compliment each other.

Temperature 溫度

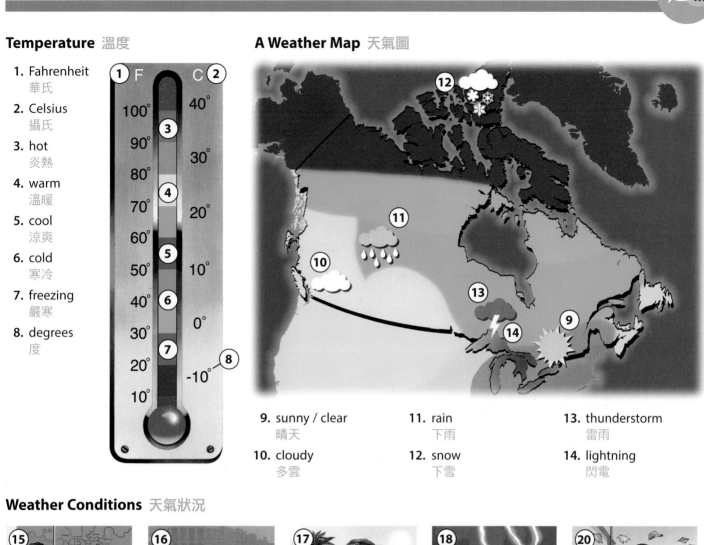

1. Fahrenheit
   華氏
2. Celsius
   攝氏
3. hot
   炎熱
4. warm
   溫暖
5. cool
   涼爽
6. cold
   寒冷
7. freezing
   嚴寒
8. degrees
   度

A Weather Map 天氣圖

9. sunny / clear
   晴天
10. cloudy
    多雲
11. rain
    下雨
12. snow
    下雪
13. thunderstorm
    雷雨
14. lightning
    閃電

Weather Conditions 天氣狀況

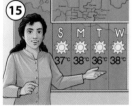

15. heat wave
    熱浪
16. smoggy
    有霧霾
17. humid
    潮濕
18. thunderstorm
    暴風雨
19. lightning
    閃電
20. windy
    風大
21. dust storm
    塵暴
22. foggy
    霧重
23. hail
    冰雹
24. icy
    結冰
25. snowstorm / blizzard
    暴風雪

Ways to talk about the weather

It's <u>sunny</u> and <u>hot</u> in <u>Toronto</u>.
It's <u>raining</u> in <u>Edmonton</u>.
<u>Winnipeg</u> is having <u>thunderstorms</u>.

Internet Research: weather

Type any city and "weather" in a search engine.
Report: It's <u>cloudy</u> in <u>Winnipeg</u>. It's <u>19 degrees</u>.

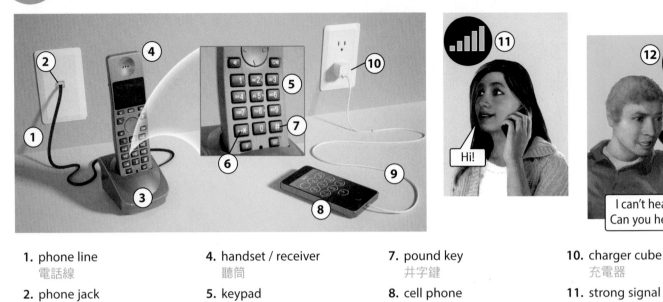

1. phone line
電話線

2. phone jack
電話插孔

3. base
基座

4. handset / receiver
聽筒

5. keypad
鍵盤

6. star key
星號鍵

7. pound key
井字鍵

8. cell phone
行動電話

9. charger cord
充電器電線

10. charger cube
充電器

11. strong signal
強訊號

12. weak signal
弱訊號

13. headset
頭戴收話器

14. Bluetooth headset
藍牙頭戴收話器

15. contact list
通訊錄

16. missed call
未接來電

17. voice mail
語音留言

18. text message
文字短訊

19. Internet phone call
網路電話

20. operator
接線生

21. directory assistance
查號服務

22. automated phone system
自動電話系統

23. phone card
電話卡

24. access number
接駁號碼

1531-5471-2923-889

25. smartphone
智慧手機

26. TDD*
TDD

Reading a Phone Bill 讀電話帳單

27. carrier
電話公司

28. area code
區號

29. phone number
電話號碼

30. billing period
計費週期

31. monthly charges
月費

32. additional charges
附加費

HORIZON

BILL SUMMARY
For 250-555-1357
From May 15, 2018 to June 14, 2018

5/15 - 6/14 charges	$40.00
Other charges	$5.34
Tax	$9.84
TOTAL CHARGES	**$55.18**

Types of Charges 收費種類

33. local call
本地電話

34. long-distance call
國內長途電話

35. international call
國際長途電話

36. data
數據

Making a Phone Call 打電話

A. **Dial** the phone number.
撥電話號碼。

B. **Press** "talk".
按「通話」鍵。

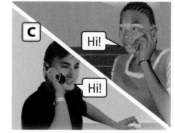

Hi!
Hi!

C. **Talk** on the phone.
電話交談。

D. **Hang up**. / **End** the call.
掛電話。/ 結束通話。

Making an Emergency Call 打緊急電話

E. **Dial** 911.
撥 911.

This is
Roy Chu.

F. **Give** your name.
告知您的姓名。

There's a fire on
5th at Oak.

G. **State** the emergency.
陳述緊急情況。

Please stay
on the line.

H. **Stay** on the line.
保持連接。

*telecommunication device for the deaf

Cardinal Numbers 基數

0	zero 零	20	twenty 二十
1	one 一	21	twenty-one 二十一
2	two 二	22	twenty-two 二十二
3	three 三	23	twenty-three 二十三
4	four 四	24	twenty-four 二十四
5	five 五	25	twenty-five 二十五
6	six 六	30	thirty 三十
7	seven 七	40	forty 四十
8	eight 八	50	fifty 五十
9	nine 九	60	sixty 六十
10	ten 十	70	seventy 七十
11	eleven 十一	80	eighty 八十
12	twelve 十二	90	ninety 九十
13	thirteen 十三	100	one hundred 一百
14	fourteen 十四	101	one hundred one 一百零一
15	fifteen 十五	1,000	one thousand 一千
16	sixteen 十六	10,000	ten thousand 一萬
17	seventeen 十七	100,000	one hundred thousand 十萬
18	eighteen 十八	1,000,000	one million 一百萬
19	nineteen 十九	1,000,000,000	one billion 十億

Ordinal Numbers 序數

1st	first 第一	16th	sixteenth 第十六
2nd	second 第二	17th	seventeenth 第十七
3rd	third 第三	18th	eighteenth 第十八
4th	fourth 第四	19th	nineteenth 第十九
5th	fifth 第五	20th	twentieth 第二十
6th	sixth 第六	21st	twenty-first 第二十一
7th	seventh 第七	30th	thirtieth 第三十
8th	eighth 第八	40th	fortieth 第四十
9th	ninth 第九	50th	fiftieth 第五十
10th	tenth 第十	60th	sixtieth 第六十
11th	eleventh 第十一	70th	seventieth 第七十
12th	twelfth 第十二	80th	eightieth 第八十
13th	thirteenth 第十三	90th	ninetieth 第九十
14th	fourteenth 第十四	100th	one hundredth 第一百
15th	fifteenth 第十五	1,000th	one thousandth 第一千

Roman Numerals 羅馬數字

I = 1	VII = 7	XXX = 30
II = 2	VIII = 8	XL = 40
III = 3	IX = 9	L = 50
IV = 4	X = 10	C = 100
V = 5	XV = 15	D = 500
VI = 6	XX = 20	M = 1,000

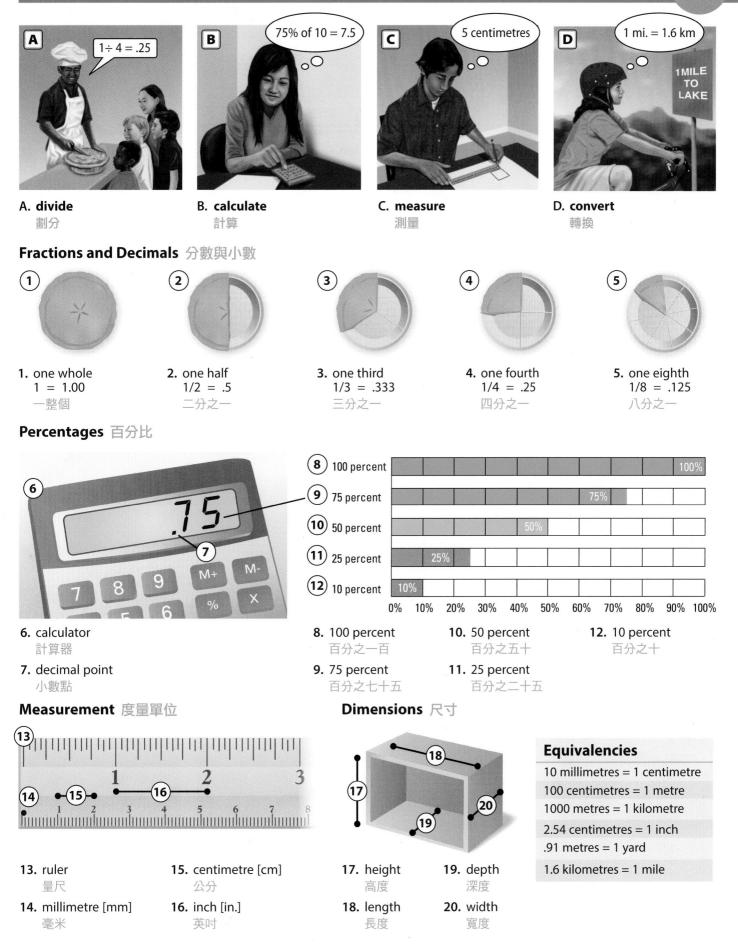

A 1 ÷ 4 = .25

B 75% of 10 = 7.5

C 5 centimetres

D 1 mi. = 1.6 km

1 MILE TO LAKE

A. divide
劃分

B. calculate
計算

C. measure
測量

D. convert
轉換

Fractions and Decimals 分數與小數

1. one whole
1 = 1.00
一整個

2. one half
1/2 = .5
二分之一

3. one third
1/3 = .333
三分之一

4. one fourth
1/4 = .25
四分之一

5. one eighth
1/8 = .125
八分之一

Percentages 百分比

8 100 percent — 100%

9 75 percent — 75%

10 50 percent — 50%

11 25 percent — 25%

12 10 percent — 10%

0% 10% 20% 30% 40% 50% 60% 70% 80% 90% 100%

6. calculator
計算器

7. decimal point
小數點

8. 100 percent
百分之一百

9. 75 percent
百分之七十五

10. 50 percent
百分之五十

11. 25 percent
百分之二十五

12. 10 percent
百分之十

Measurement 度量單位

13. ruler
量尺

14. millimetre [mm]
毫米

15. centimetre [cm]
公分

16. inch [in.]
英吋

Dimensions 尺寸

17. height
高度

18. length
長度

19. depth
深度

20. width
寬度

Equivalencies

10 millimetres = 1 centimetre

100 centimetres = 1 metre

1000 metres = 1 kilometre

2.54 centimetres = 1 inch

.91 metres = 1 yard

1.6 kilometres = 1 mile

Telling Time 述説時間

1. hour
小時

2. minutes
分鐘

3. seconds
秒鐘

4. a.m.
上午

5. p.m.
下午

6. 1:00
one o'clock
一時

7. 1:05
one-oh-five
five after one
一時五分

8. 1:10
one-ten
ten after one
一時十分

9. 1:15
one-fifteen
a quarter after one
一時十五分
一時一刻

10. 1:20
one-twenty
twenty after one
一時二十分

11. 1:30
one-thirty
half past one
一時三十分
一時半

12. 1:40
one-forty
twenty to two
一時四十分

13. 1:45
one-forty-five
a quarter to two
一時四十五分

Times of Day 時段

14. sunrise
清晨

15. morning
上午

16. noon
中午

17. afternoon
下午

18. sunset
傍晚

19. evening
晚上

20. night
夜間

21. midnight
午夜

Ways to talk about time

I wake up at 6:30 a.m.
I wake up at 6:30 in the morning.
I wake up at 6:30.

Pair practice. Make new conversations.

A: *What time do you wake up on weekdays?*
B: *At 6:30 a.m. How about you?*
A: *I wake up at 7:00.*

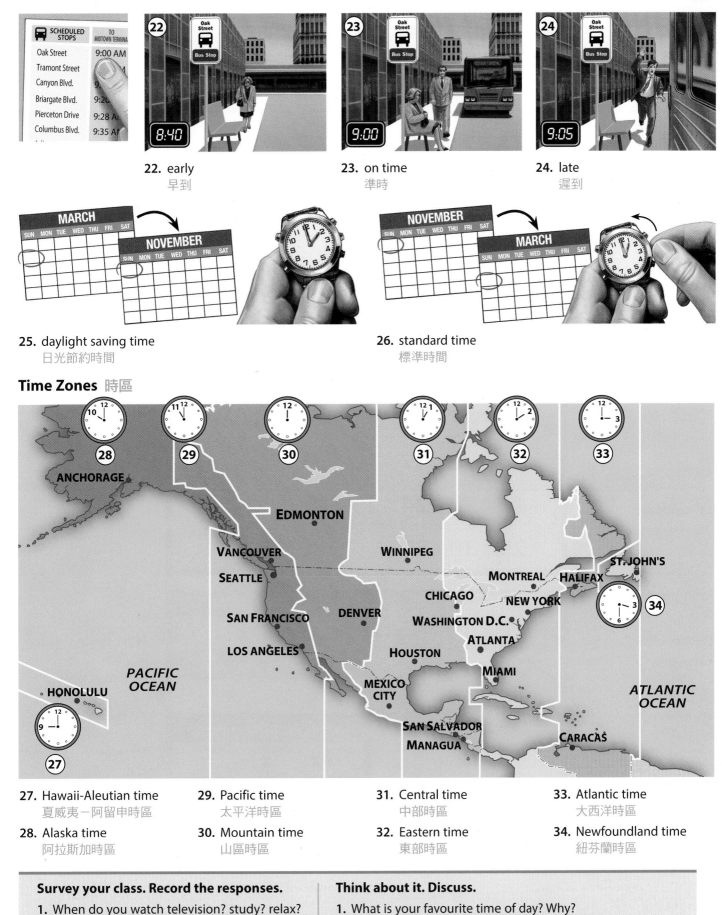

22. early
早到

23. on time
準時

24. late
遲到

25. daylight saving time
日光節約時間

26. standard time
標準時間

Time Zones 時區

27. Hawaii-Aleutian time
夏威夷–阿留申時區

28. Alaska time
阿拉斯加時區

29. Pacific time
太平洋時區

30. Mountain time
山區時區

31. Central time
中部時區

32. Eastern time
東部時區

33. Atlantic time
大西洋時區

34. Newfoundland time
紐芬蘭時區

Survey your class. Record the responses.

1. When do you watch television? study? relax?
2. Do you like to stay up after midnight?

Report: *Most of us… Some of us…*

Think about it. Discuss.

1. What is your favourite time of day? Why?
2. Do you think daylight saving time is a good idea?
3. What's good about staying up after midnight?

19

1. date
   日期
2. day
   日
3. month
   月
4. year
   年

5. today
   今天
6. tomorrow
   明天
7. yesterday
   昨天

Days of the Week
星期幾

8. Sunday
   星期日
9. Monday
   星期一
10. Tuesday
    星期二
11. Wednesday
    星期三
12. Thursday
    星期四
13. Friday
    星期五
14. Saturday
    星期六

15. week
    星期
16. weekdays
    工作日
17. weekend
    週末

MAY

SUN	MON	TUE	WED	THU	FRI	SAT
1	2	3	4	5	6	7
8	9	10	11	12	13	14
15	16	17	18	19	20	21
22	23	24	25	26	27	28
29	30	31				

Frequency
頻度

18. last week
    上星期
19. this week
    這星期
20. next week
    下星期

MAY

SUN	MON	TUE	WED	THU	FRI	SAT
1	2	3	4	5	6	7
8	9	10	11	12	13	14
15	16	17	18	19	20	21
22	23	24	25	26	27	28
29	30	31				

SUN	MON	TUE	WED	THU	FRI	SAT
X	X	X	X	X	X	X

SUN	MON	TUE	WED	THU	FRI	SAT
	X					

SUN	MON	TUE	WED	THU	FRI	SAT
	X		X			

SUN	MON	TUE	WED	THU	FRI	SAT
	X	X		X		

21. every day / daily
    每天
22. once a week
    一星期一次
23. twice a week
    一星期兩次
24. three times a week
    一星期三次

Ways to say the date

Today is <u>May 10th</u>. It's the <u>tenth</u>.
Yesterday was <u>May 9th</u>.
The party is on <u>May 21st</u>.

Pair practice. Make new conversations.

A: The <u>test</u> is on <u>Friday</u>, <u>June 14th</u>.
B: Did you say <u>Friday</u>, the <u>fourteenth</u>?
A: Yes, the <u>fourteenth</u>.

Months of the Year
月份

(25) < JAN >

SUN	MON	TUE	WED	THU	FRI	SAT
						1
2	3	4	5	6	7	8
9	10	11	12	13	14	15
16	17	18	19	20	21	22
23	24	25	26	27	28	29
30	31					

(26) < FEB >

SUN	MON	TUE	WED	THU	FRI	SAT
		1	2	3	4	5
6	7	8	9	10	11	12
13	14	15	16	17	18	19
20	21	22	23	24	25	26
27	28					

(27) < MAR >

SUN	MON	TUE	WED	THU	FRI	SAT
		1	2	3	4	5
6	7	8	9	10	11	12
13	14	15	16	17	18	19
20	21	22	23	24	25	26
27	28	29	30	31		

(28) < APR >

SUN	MON	TUE	WED	THU	FRI	SAT
					1	2
3	4	5	6	7	8	9
10	11	12	13	14	15	16
17	18	19	20	21	22	23
24	25	26	27	28	29	30

(29) < MAY >

SUN	MON	TUE	WED	THU	FRI	SAT
1	2	3	4	5	6	7
8	9	10	11	12	13	14
15	16	17	18	19	20	21
22	23	24	25	26	27	28
29	30	31				

(30) < JUN >

SUN	MON	TUE	WED	THU	FRI	SAT
			1	2	3	4
5	6	7	8	9	10	11
12	13	14	15	16	17	18
19	20	21	22	23	24	25
26	27	28	29	30		

(31) < JUL >

SUN	MON	TUE	WED	THU	FRI	SAT
					1	2
3	4	5	6	7	8	9
10	11	12	13	14	15	16
17	18	19	20	21	22	23
24	25	26	27	28	29	30
31						

(32) < AUG >

SUN	MON	TUE	WED	THU	FRI	SAT
	1	2	3	4	5	6
7	8	9	10	11	12	13
14	15	16	17	18	19	20
21	22	23	24	25	26	27
28	29	30	31			

(33) < SEP >

SUN	MON	TUE	WED	THU	FRI	SAT
				1	2	3
4	5	6	7	8	9	10
11	12	13	14	15	16	17
18	19	20	21	22	23	24
25	26	27	28	29	30	

(34) < OCT >

SUN	MON	TUE	WED	THU	FRI	SAT
						1
2	3	4	5	6	7	8
9	10	11	12	13	14	15
16	17	18	19	20	21	22
23	24	25	26	27	28	29
30	31					

(35) < NOV >

SUN	MON	TUE	WED	THU	FRI	SAT
		1	2	3	4	5
6	7	8	9	10	11	12
13	14	15	16	17	18	19
20	21	22	23	24	25	26
27	28	29	30			

(36) < DEC >

SUN	MON	TUE	WED	THU	FRI	SAT
				1	2	3
4	5	6	7	8	9	10
11	12	13	14	15	16	17
18	19	20	21	22	23	24
25	26	27	28	29	30	31

25. January
一月

26. February
二月

27. March
三月

28. April
四月

29. May
五月

30. June
六月

31. July
七月

32. August
八月

33. September
九月

34. October
十月

35. November
十一月

36. December
十二月

(37) **(38)**

(39) **(40)**

Seasons
季節

37. spring
春天

38. summer
夏天

39. fall / autumn
秋天

40. winter
冬天

Dictate to your partner. Take turns.

A: *Write Monday.*
B: *Is it spelled M-o-n-d-a-y?*
A: *Yes, that's right.*

Survey your class. Record the responses.

1. What is the busiest day of your week?
2. What is your favourite day?
Report: *Ten of us said Monday is our busiest day.*

1. birthday
生日

2. wedding
結婚

3. anniversary
週年紀念

4. appointment
預約

5. parent-teacher conference
家長會

6. vacation
度假

7. religious holiday
宗教節日

8. statutory holiday
法定節日

Statutory Holidays 法定節日

Happy New Year!

JAN 1

MARI APR

MAY

Queen Victoria

JULY 1

PROUD TO WORK

SEPT

OCT

NOV 11

DEC 25

DEC 26

SALE

9. New Year's Day
元旦

10. Good Friday
耶穌受難日

11. Victoria Day
維多利亞日

12. Canada Day
加拿大日

13. Labour Day
勞動節

14. Thanksgiving
感恩節

15. Remembrance Day
國殤紀念日

16. Christmas Day
聖誕節

17. Boxing Day
節禮日

Pair practice. Make new conversations.

A: When is your <u>birthday</u>?
B: It's on <u>January 31st</u>. How about yours?
A: It's on <u>December 22nd</u>.

Internet Research: independence day

Type "independence day, world" in the search bar.
Report: <u>Peru</u> celebrates its independence on <u>7/28</u>.

1. **little** hand
小手

2. **big** hand
大手

3. **fast** driver
開快車的司機

4. **slow** driver
開慢車的司機

5. **hard** chair
硬椅

6. **soft** chair
軟椅

7. **thick** book
厚書

8. **thin** book
薄書

9. **full** glass
滿杯

10. **empty** glass
空杯

11. **noisy** children /
loud children
吵鬧的孩童

12. **quiet** children
安靜的孩童

13. **heavy** box
重箱

14. **light** box
輕箱

15. **same** colour
相同的顏色

16. **different** colours
不同的顏色

17. **bad** news
壞消息

18. **good** news
好消息

There was an earthquake.
Everyone is OK!

19. **expensive** ring
昂貴的戒指

20. **cheap** ring
便宜的戒指

25¢

21. **beautiful** view
美麗的景緻

22. **ugly** view
難看的景緻

23. **easy** problem
簡單的問題

24. **difficult** problem /
hard problem
困難的問題

$1 + 1 = 2$
$x^2 - 22\frac{1}{2}x =$
$-8\frac{1}{3}x^2 - 11\frac{2}{3}$

Survey your class. Record the responses.

1. Are you a slow walker or a fast walker?
2. Do you prefer loud parties or quiet parties?
Report: _Five of us prefer quiet parties._

Use the new words.

Look at pages 154–155. Describe the things you see.

A: _The subway is full._
B: _The motorcycle is noisy._

Basic Colours 基本色

1. red
紅色

2. yellow
黃色

3. blue
藍色

4. orange
橙色

5. green
綠色

6. purple
紫色

7. pink
粉紅色

8. violet
紫蘿蘭色

9. turquoise
藍綠色

10. dark blue
深藍色

11. light blue
淡藍色

12. bright blue
蔚藍色

Neutral Colours 中性色

13. black
黑色

14. white
白色

15. grey
灰色

16. cream / ivory
乳白色

17. brown
棕色

18. beige / tan
黃褐色

Survey your class. Record the responses.

1. What colours are you wearing today?
2. What colours do you like? What colours do you dislike?

Report: *Most of us… Some of us…*

Use the new words. Look at pages 86–87.
Take turns naming the colours you see.

A: *His shirt is <u>blue</u>.*
B: *Her shoes are <u>white</u>.*

1. The yellow sweaters are **on the left**.
   黃色毛衣在左邊。

2. The purple sweaters are **in the middle**.
   紫色毛衣在中間。

3. The brown sweaters are **on the right**.
   褐色毛衣在右邊。

4. The red sweaters are **above** the blue sweaters.
   紅色毛衣在藍色毛衣的上邊。

5. The blue sweaters are **below** the red sweaters.
   藍色毛衣在紅色毛衣的下邊。

6. The turquoise sweater is **in** the box.
   藍綠色毛衣在盒子裡。

7. The white sweater is **in front of** the black sweater.
   白色毛衣在黑色毛衣的前面。

8. The black sweater is **behind** the white sweater.
   黑色毛衣在白色毛衣的後面。

9. The violet sweater is **next to** the grey sweater.
   紫色毛衣在灰色毛衣的旁邊。

10. The grey sweater is **under** the orange sweater.
    灰色毛衣在橘色毛衣的下面。

11. The orange sweater is **on** the grey sweater.
    橘色毛衣在灰色毛衣的上面。

12. The green sweater is **between** the pink sweaters.
    綠色毛衣在兩疊粉紅色毛衣的中間。

More vocabulary

near: in the same area
far from: not near

Role play. Make new conversations.

A: *Excuse me. Where are the <u>red</u> sweaters?*
B: *They're <u>on the left</u>, <u>above</u> the <u>blue</u> sweaters.*
A: *Thanks very much.*

Coins 硬幣

1. $.05 = 5¢
a nickel / 5 cents
五分

2. $.10 = 10¢
a dime / 10 cents
十分

3. $.25 = 25¢
a quarter / 25 cents
二角五分

4. $1.00
a loonie / a dollar
一元

5. $2.00
a toonie / two dollars
二元

Bills 紙幣

6. $5.00
five dollars
五元

7. $10.00
ten dollars
十元

8. $20.00
twenty dollars
二十元

9. $50.00
fifty dollars
五十元

10. $100.00
one hundred dollars
一百元

A. Get change.
換零錢。

B. Borrow money.
向人借錢。

C. Lend money.
借給人錢。

D. Pay back the money.
還錢。

Pair practice. Make new conversations.

A: *Do you have change for a dollar?*
B: *Sure. How about two quarters and five dimes?*
A: *Perfect!*

Identify Mark's problem. Brainstorm solutions.

Mark doesn't like to lend money. His boss, Lia, asks, "Can I borrow $20.00?" What can Mark say? What will Lia say?

26

Ways to Pay 付款方式

A. pay cash
付現金

B. use a credit card
使用信用卡

C. use a debit card
使用轉帳卡

D. write a (personal) cheque
開（個人）支票

E. use a gift card
使用禮物卡

F. cash a traveller's cheque
兌現旅行支票

Lamp Shop
1 lamp @	$12.50
1 lamp @	$12.50
Subtotal	$25.00
Tax	$2.06
You pay	$27.06

TOTAL $27.06

| 1. price tag 價格標籤 | 3. sale price 折扣價格 | 5. SKU number SKU 號碼 | 7. price / cost 價格 | 9. total 總計 |
| 2. regular price 正常價格 | 4. bar code 條碼 | 6. receipt 收據 | 8. sales tax 銷售稅 | 10. cash register 收銀機 |

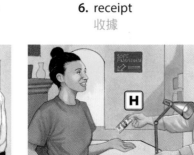

G. buy / pay for
購買 / 付錢

H. return
退貨

I. exchange
換貨

1. twins
   雙胞胎
2. sweater
   毛衣
3. matching
   配對
4. disappointed
   失望
5. navy blue
   海軍藍
6. happy
   高興

A. **shop**
   選購
B. **keep**
   保留

What do you see in the pictures?

1. Who is the woman shopping for?

2. Does she buy matching sweaters or different sweaters?

3. How does Anya feel about her green sweater? What does she do?

4. What does Manda do with her sweater?

📄 **Read the story.**

Same and Different

Mrs. Kumar likes to <u>shop</u> for her <u>twins</u>. Today she's looking at <u>sweaters</u>. There are many different colours on sale. Mrs. Kumar chooses two <u>matching</u> green sweaters.

The next day, Manda and Anya open their gifts. Manda likes the green sweater, but Anya is <u>disappointed</u>. Mrs. Kumar understands the problem. Anya wants to be different.

Manda <u>keeps</u> her sweater, but Anya goes to the store. She exchanges her green sweater for a <u>navy blue</u> sweater. It's an easy answer to Anya's problem. Now the twins can be warm, <u>happy</u>, and different.

Reread the story.

1. Underline the last sentence in each paragraph. Why are these sentences important?

2. Retell the story in your own words.

What do you think?

3. Imagine you are Anya. Would you keep the sweater or exchange it? Why?

Adults and Children 成年人與孩童

1. man
   男人
2. woman
   女人
3. women
   女人們
4. men
   男人們
5. senior citizen
   長者

Listen and point. Take turns.

A: *Point to <u>a woman</u>.*
B: *Point to <u>a senior citizen</u>.*
A: *Point to <u>an infant</u>.*

Dictate to your partner. Take turns.

A: *Write <u>woman</u>.*
B: *Is that spelled <u>w-o-m-a-n</u>?*
A: *Yes, that's right, <u>woman</u>.*

30

6. infant
初生嬰兒

7. baby
嬰兒

8. toddler
幼兒

9. 6-year-old boy
六歲男孩

10. 10-year-old girl
十歲女孩

11. teenager / teen
少年

Ways to talk about age

1 month–3 months old = **infant**

18 months–3 years old = **toddler**

3 years old–12 years old = **child**

13–19 years old = **teenager**

18+ years old = **adult**

65+ years old = **senior citizen**

Pair practice. Make new conversations.

A: *How old is <u>Sandra</u>?*

B: *<u>She's</u> <u>13</u> years old.*

A: *Wow, <u>she's a teenager</u> now!*

31

Describing People 描述人

Age 年齡

1. young
年輕

2. middle-aged
中年

3. elderly
老年

Height 身高

4. tall
高

5. average height
一般高度

6. short
矮

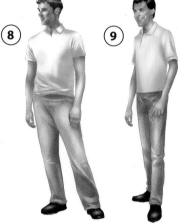

Weight 重量

7. heavy / fat
重 / 胖

8. average weight
一般體重

9. thin / slender
瘦 / 苗條

Disabilities 殘障

10. physically challenged
肢體殘障

11. visually impaired / blind
視力障礙 / 目盲

12. hearing-impaired / deaf
聽力障礙 / 耳聾

Appearance 外觀

13. attractive
好看

14. cute
可愛

15. pregnant
懷孕

16. mole
黑痣

17. pierced ear
耳環孔

18. tattoo
刺青

Ways to describe people

He's a <u>heavy</u>, <u>young</u> man.
She's a <u>pregnant</u> woman with <u>a mole</u>.
He's <u>sight-impaired</u>. (visually-impaired)

Use the new words.

Look at pages 44-45. Describe the people you see. Take turns.

A: *This <u>elderly</u> woman is <u>short</u> and a little <u>heavy</u>.*
B: *This <u>young</u> man is <u>physically challenged</u>.*

1. short hair
短頭髮

2. shoulder-length hair
及肩頭髮

3. long hair
長頭髮

4. part
分髮

5. mustache
小鬍子

6. beard
大鬍子

7. sideburns
側鬚

8. bangs
瀏海

9. straight hair
直髮

10. wavy hair
波浪髮

11. curly hair
捲髮

12. black hair
黑髮

13. red hair
紅髮

14. blond hair
金髮

15. brown hair
棕髮

16. sanitizing jar
消毒罐

17. scissors
剪刀

18. rollers
髮捲

19. comb
梳子

20. brush
髮刷

21. blow dryer
吹風機 / 風筒

22. cornrows
玉米壟辮子

23. grey hair
白頭髮

24. bald
禿頭

Style Hair 做髮型

A. cut hair
剪髮

B. perm hair
燙髮

C. add highlights
做挑染

D. colour hair / **dye** hair
染髮

Ways to talk about hair

Describe hair in this order: length, style, and then colour.
She has <u>long</u>, <u>straight</u>, <u>brown</u> hair.

Role play. Talk to a stylist.

A: *I need a new hairstyle.*
B: *How about <u>short</u> and <u>straight</u>?*
A: *Great. Do you think I should <u>dye</u> it?*

1. grandmother
   祖母
2. grandfather
   祖父
3. mother
   母親
4. father
   父親
5. sister
   姊妹
6. brother
   兄弟
7. aunt
   姨媽 / 姑媽
8. uncle
   姨丈 / 姑丈
9. cousin
   堂表兄弟姊妹

Tim Lee's Family

GRANDPARENTS

Immediate Family

① Min ② Lu

PARENTS

③ Rose ④ Ken ⑦ Lynn ⑧ Dan

Tim ⑤ Lily ⑥ Alex CHILDREN ⑨ Emily

10. mother-in-law
    婆婆 / 丈母
11. father-in-law
    公公 / 丈人
12. wife
    太太
13. husband
    先生
14. daughter
    女兒
15. son
    兒子
16. sister-in-law
    兄嫂 / 弟婦
17. brother-in-law
    大伯 / 小叔
18. niece
    姪女
19. nephew
    姪子

Ana Garcia's Family

Extended Family

⑩ Eva ⑪ Sam

⑫ Ana ⑬ Tito ⑯ Marta ⑰ Carlos

⑭ Sara ⑮ Felix ⑱ Alice ⑲ Eddie

More vocabulary

Tim is Min and Lu's **grandson**.
Lily and Emily are Min and Lu's **granddaughters**.
Alex is Min's youngest **grandchild**.

Ana is Eva and Sam's **daughter-in-law**.
Carlos is Eva and Sam's **son-in-law**.
Note: Ana's married. = Ana **is** married.
Ana's **husband** = the man married to Ana

20. married couple
    已婚夫婦
21. divorced couple
    離婚夫婦
22. single mother
    單親母親
23. single father
    單親父親

Carol, Bruce, and Lisa

Lisa, Age 4

Lisa Green's Family

Lisa, Age 7

Rick | Carol | Bruce | Sue

Lisa, Today

Mary | David | Kim | Bill

24. remarried
    再婚
25. stepfather
    繼父
26. stepmother
    繼母
27. half sister
    同母異父姊妹 /
    同父異母姊妹
28. half brother
    同母異父兄弟 /
    同父異母兄弟
29. stepsister
    繼姊妹
30. stepbrother
    繼兄弟

More vocabulary

Bruce is Carol's **former husband** or **ex-husband**.
Carol is Bruce's **former wife** or **ex-wife**.
Lisa is the **stepdaughter** of both Rick and Sue.

Use the new words.

Ask and answer questions about Lisa's family.

A: *Who is Lisa's half sister*?
B: *Mary is. Who is Lisa's stepsister*?

35

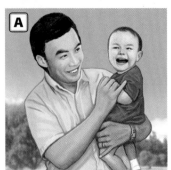

A. hold
抱

B. nurse
哺乳

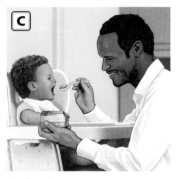

C. feed
餵食

D. rock
搖

E. undress
脫衣

F. bathe
洗澡

G. change a diaper
換尿布

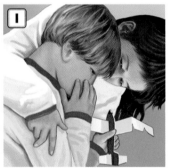

H. dress
穿衣

I. comfort
安慰

Good job!

J. praise
讚揚

No!

K. discipline
管教

L. buckle up
繫上安全帶

M. play with
一起玩耍

N. read to
講故事

O. sing a lullaby
唱搖籃曲

P. kiss goodnight
晚安之吻

Look at the pictures.
Describe what is happening.

A: She's <u>changing her baby's diaper</u>.
B: He's <u>kissing his son goodnight</u>.

Talk about your experience.

*I am great at <u>play**ing** with toddlers</u>.*
*I have a lot of experience <u>chang**ing** diapers</u>.*
I know how to <u>hold an infant</u>.

36

1. bottle
奶瓶

2. nipple
奶嘴

3. formula
配方奶粉

4. baby food
嬰兒食品

5. bib
圍兜

6. high chair
兒童高座椅

7. diaper pail
尿布桶

8. cloth diaper
布尿布

9. safety pins
安全別針

10. disposable diaper
紙尿布

11. diaper bag
尿布袋

12. wipes
溼巾

13. baby lotion
嬰兒潤膚乳液

14. baby powder
嬰兒爽身粉

15. potty seat
孩童坐便器

16. training pants
訓練尿布褲

17. baby carrier
嬰兒提籃

18. stroller
幼兒手推車

19. carriage
嬰兒車

20. car safety seat
汽車安全座椅

21. booster car seat
汽車增高坐墊

22. rocking chair
搖椅

23. nursery rhymes
兒歌

24. teddy bear
泰迪熊

25. pacifier
安撫奶嘴

26. teething ring
磨牙圈

27. rattle
響環

28. night light
夜燈

Dictate to your partner. Take turns.

A: *Write pacifier.*
B: *Was that pacifier, p-a-c-i-f-i-e-r?*
A: *Yes, that's right.*

Think about it. Discuss.

1. How can parents discipline toddlers? teens?
2. What are some things you can say to praise a child?
3. Why are nursery rhymes important for young children?

37

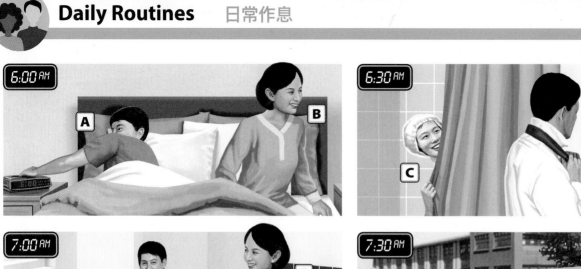

A. wake up
睡醒

B. get up
起床

C. take a shower
淋浴

D. get dressed
穿衣服

E. eat breakfast / **have** breakfast
吃早餐

F. make lunch
準備午餐

G. take the children to school / **drop off** the kids
送孩子到學校 / 放下孩子

H. take the bus to school
搭車到學校

I. drive to work / **go** to work
開車上班 / 去上班

J. be in class
在上課

K. work
工作

L. go to the grocery store
去雜貨店購物

M. pick up the kids
接孩子

N. leave work
下班

Grammar Point: third-person singular

For *he* and *she*, add **-s** or **-es** to the verb:
He eats breakfast.   *He watches TV.*
She makes lunch.   *She goes to the store.*

For two-part verbs, put the **-s** on the first part: wake**s** up, drop**s** off.
Be and *have* are different (irregular).
He is in bed at 5 a.m. He has breakfast at 7 a.m.

O. **clean** the house
清理房子

P. **exercise**
運動

Q. **cook** dinner / **make** dinner
做晚飯

R. **come** home / **get** home
回家

S. **have** dinner / **eat** dinner
吃晚飯

T. **do** homework
作家庭作業

U. **relax**
放輕鬆

V. **read** the paper
看報

W. **check** email
查看電子郵件

X. **watch** TV
看電視

Y. **go** to bed
上床

Z. **go** to sleep
睡覺

Pair practice. Make new conversations.

A: *When does he <u>go to work</u>?*
B: *He <u>goes to work</u> at <u>8:00 a.m.</u> When does she <u>make dinner</u>?*
A: *She <u>makes dinner</u> at <u>6:00 p.m.</u>*

Internet Research: child care

Type "society and community time use" in a search engine.
Report: *According to the survey, in 2010, <u>women</u> cared for young children more than <u>6 hours</u>.*

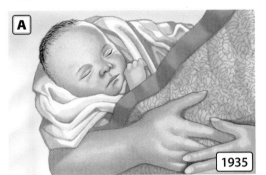

A. be born
出生
1935

B. start school
入學
1940

DEPARTMENT OF IMMIGRATION

C. immigrate
移民
1950

D. graduate
畢業
1953

E. learn to drive
學開車
1953

F. get a job
就業
1954

G. become a citizen
入籍公民
1954

H. fall in love
戀愛
1955

REGISTRO CIVIL
Acta de Nacimiento
MARTÍN PEREZ DE LÉON　B0983456
01-05-1935
Registro Civil
Acta de Nacimiento

1. birth certificate
出生證明

Government of Canada　Gouvernement du Canada　PERMANENT RESIDENT CARD　CARTE DE RÉSIDENT PERMANENT
PEREZ
MARTIN
0018-5978 21 JUN/JUIN 2008
Martin Perez
Canada

2. permanent resident card
永久居民卡

SIR JOHN A. MACDONALD SECONDARY SCHOOL
MARTIN PEREZ
Rachid Hababi
Josephine C. Klee
Loretta Sommers

3. diploma
文憑

DRIVER'S LICENCE
DL: 9999999
Class: 5****
PEREZ, MARTIN
65
Issued: June 5, 2009
Expiry: June 5, 2014
1234-5678-90
Martin Perez

4. driver's licence
駕照

Employment and Immigration Canada　Emploi et Immigration Canada
SOCIAL INSURANCE NUMBER　NUMÉRO D'ASSURANCE SOCIALE
476 012 000
MARTIN PEREZ
SIGNATURE　Martin Perez

5. social insurance number card
社會保險號卡

Certificate of Canadian Citizenship　Certificat de Citoyenneté Canadienne
MARTIN PEREZ

6. citizenship certificate
公民證書

Grammar Point: past tense

start ⎫
learn ⎬ + ed
travel ⎭

immigrate ⎫
graduate ⎬ + d
retire ⎭
die

These verbs are different (irregular):

be – was　　　go – went　　　buy – bought
get – got　　　have – had
become – became　fall – fell

I. go to college
上大學

J. get engaged
訂婚

CARLETON UNIVERSITY

Martin Perez

Bachelor of Arts
High Honours in English

7. university degree
大學文憑

K. get married
結婚

L. have a baby
生育兒女

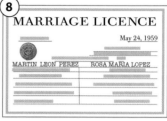

MARRIAGE LICENCE

May 24, 1959

MARTIN LEON PEREZ   ROSA MARIA LOPEZ

8. marriage licence
結婚證書

M. buy a home
購屋

N. become a grandparent
成為祖父母

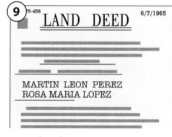

F5-456　　　6/7/1965

LAND   DEED

MARTIN LEON PEREZ
ROSA MARIA LOPEZ

9. deed
地契

O. retire
退休

P. travel
旅行

CANADA

10. passport
護照

Q. volunteer
做義工

R. die
死亡

CERTIFICATE OF DEATH

MARTIN LEON PEREZ
December 12th, 2008

11. death certificate
死亡證書

More vocabulary

When a husband dies, his wife becomes a **widow**.
When a wife dies, her husband becomes a **widower**.
Someone who is not living is **dead** or **deceased**.

Survey your class. Record the responses.

1. When did you start school? immigrate? learn to drive?
2. Do you want to become a citizen? travel? retire?
Report: *Most of us… Some of us…*

1. hot
   熱

2. thirsty
   渴

3. sleepy
   睏

4. cold
   冷

5. hungry
   餓

6. full / satisfied
   飽

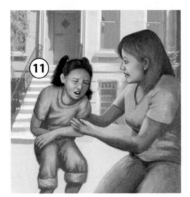

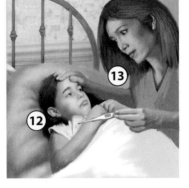

7. disgusted
   作嘔

8. calm
   平靜

9. uncomfortable
   不舒服

10. nervous
    緊張

11. in pain
    痛苦

12. sick
    生病

13. worried
    擔憂

14. well
    感覺舒服

15. relieved
    舒解

16. hurt
    傷心

17. lonely
    寂寞

18. in love
    戀愛中

Pair practice. Make new conversations.

A: *How are you doing?*
B: *I'm <u>hungry</u>. How about you?*
A: *I'm <u>hungry</u> and <u>thirsty</u>, too!*

Use the new words.
Look at pages 40–41. Describe what each person is feeling.

A: *Martin is <u>excited</u>.*
B: *Martin's mother is <u>proud</u>.*

19. sad
    悲傷
20. homesick
    想家
21. proud
    驕傲

22. excited
    興奮
23. scared / afraid
    害怕
24. embarrassed
    難堪

25. bored
    無聊
26. confused
    困惑
27. frustrated
    沮喪

28. upset
    不高興
29. angry
    生氣

30. surprised
    驚訝
31. happy
    高興
32. tired
    疲倦

In image 26: 14 (tan 63°)　$T = V_0 / g$　79.00 − .40 (79.00)

In image 27: $-1/2\, gt^2 + V_0\, t + h$　$\sin^2 t + \cos^2 t + 1$　$\tan(\pi \cdot t) = -\tan t$

Identify Kenge's problem. Brainstorm solutions.

Kenge wants to learn English quickly, but it's difficult.
He makes a lot of mistakes and gets frustrated.
And he's homesick, too. What can he do?

More vocabulary

exhausted: very tired　　**overjoyed:** very happy
furious: very angry　　**starving:** very hungry
humiliated: very embarrassed　　**terrified:** very scared

A Family Reunion 家庭聚會

LU FAMILY REUNION

1. banner
横幅

2. baseball game
棒球比賽

3. opinion
觀點

4. balloons
汽球

5. glad
高興

6. relatives
親戚

A. **laugh**
歡笑

B. **misbehave**
淘氣

I think large families are best.

What do you see in the picture?

1. How many relatives are there at this reunion?

2. How many children are there? Which children are misbehaving?

3. What are people doing at this reunion?

Read the story.

A Family Reunion

Ben Lu has a lot of <u>relatives</u> and they're all at his house. Today is the Lu family reunion.

There is a lot of good food. There are also <u>balloons</u> and a <u>banner</u>. And this year there are four new babies!

People are having a good time at the reunion. Ben's grandfather and his aunt are talking about the <u>baseball game</u>. His cousins <u>are laughing</u>. His mother-in-law is giving her <u>opinion</u>. And many of the children <u>are misbehaving</u>.

Ben looks at his family and smiles. He loves his relatives, but he's <u>glad</u> the reunion is once a year.

Reread the story.

1. Find this sentence in the story: "He loves his relatives, but he's glad the reunion is once a year." Explain what this sentence means.

2. Retell the story in your own words.

What do you think?

3. You are at Ben's party. You see a child misbehave. No other guests see him. What do you do? What do you say?

45

The Home　住房

1. yard
   庭院

2. roof
   屋頂

3. bedroom
   睡房

4. door
   門

5. bathroom
   浴室

6. kitchen
   廚房

7. floor
   地板

8. dining area
   用餐區

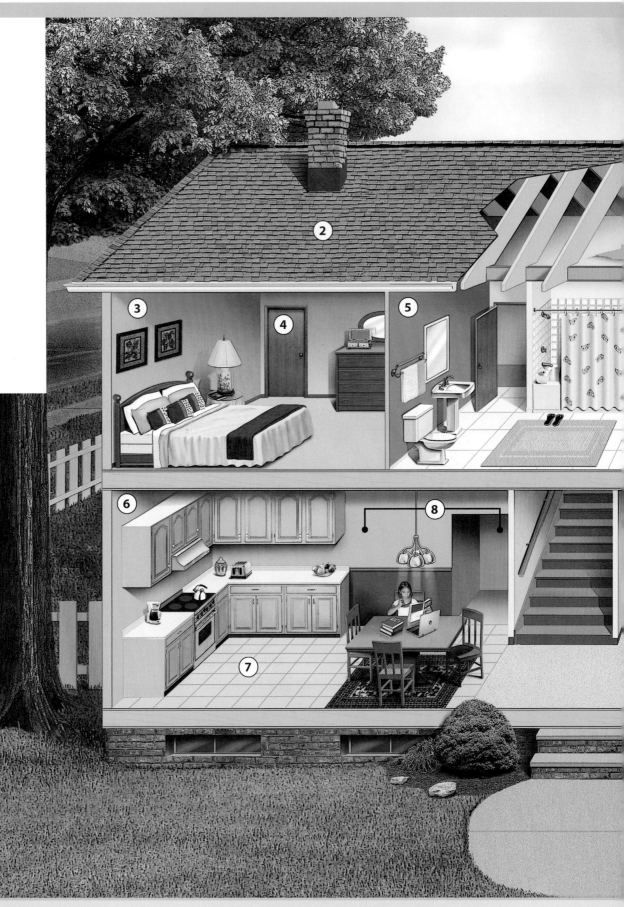

Listen and point. Take turns.

A: *Point to the kitchen.*
B: *Point to the living room.*
A: *Point to the basement.*

Dictate to your partner. Take turns.

A: *Write kitchen.*
B: *Was that k-i-t-c-h-e-n?*
A: *Yes, that's right, kitchen.*

9. attic
   閣樓

10. kids' bedroom
    孩子的睡房

11. baby's room /
    nursery
    嬰兒房

12. window
    窗口

13. living room
    起居室

14. basement
    地下室

15. garage
    車房

Ways to give locations

*I'm **at** home.*
*I'm **in** the kitchen.*
*I'm **on** the roof.*

*It's **in** the laundry room.*
*It's **on** the floor.*

Pair practice. Ask and answer questions.

A: *Where's the <u>man</u>?*
B: *<u>He's</u> in the <u>attic</u>. Where's the <u>mother</u>?*
A: *<u>She's</u> in the <u>living room</u>.*

Finding a Home 找房子

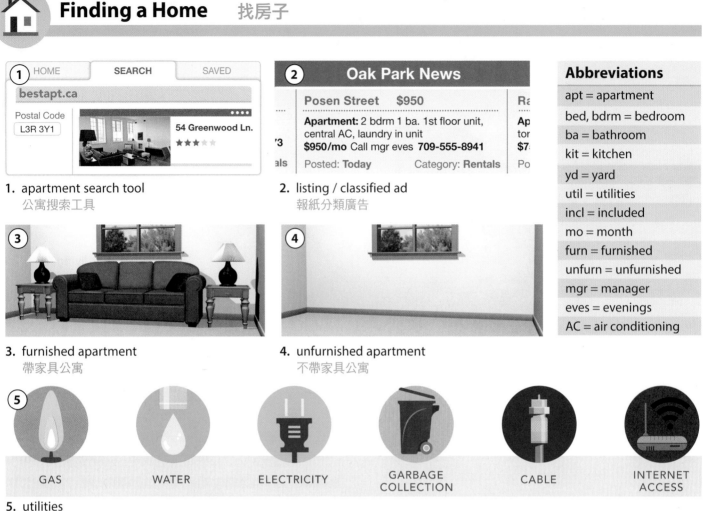

1. apartment search tool
公寓搜索工具

2. listing / classified ad
報紙分類廣告

Oak Park News

Posen Street $950

Apartment: 2 bdrm 1 ba. 1st floor unit, central AC, laundry in unit
$950/mo Call mgr eves **709-555-8941**

Posted: **Today**   Category: **Rentals**

Abbreviations

apt = apartment
bed, bdrm = bedroom
ba = bathroom
kit = kitchen
yd = yard
util = utilities
incl = included
mo = month
furn = furnished
unfurn = unfurnished
mgr = manager
eves = evenings
AC = air conditioning

3. furnished apartment
帶家具公寓

4. unfurnished apartment
不帶家具公寓

GAS   WATER   ELECTRICITY   GARBAGE COLLECTION   CABLE   INTERNET ACCESS

5. utilities
公用事業

Renting an Apartment 租公寓

A. Call the manager.
打電話給公寓經理。

Are utilities included?

No, they aren't.

B. Ask about the features.
詢問房屋情況。

Rental Application
Name: Khalidah Ali
Telephone number: 709-555-8407

C. Submit an application.
提交申請。

D. Sign the rental agreement.
在租賃協定上簽名。

E. Pay the first and last month's rent.
付首月和末月房租。

F. Move in.
遷入新居。

More vocabulary

lease: a monthly or yearly rental agreement
redecorate: to change the paint and furniture in a home
move out: to pack and leave a home

Survey your class. Record the responses.

1. What features do you look for in a home?
2. How did you find your current home?
Report: *Most of us… Some of us…*

Buying a House 買房子

G. Meet with a realtor.
會見房地產經紀人。

H. Look at houses.
看房子。

I. Make an offer.
出價。

Congratulations!

APPROVED

J. Get a loan.
申請貸款。

K. Take ownership.
獲得房屋所有權。

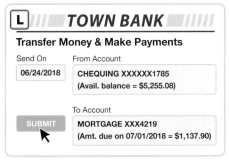

TOWN BANK

Transfer Money & Make Payments

Send On
06/24/2018

From Account
CHEQUING XXXXXX1785
(Avail. balance = $5,255.08)

SUBMIT

To Account
MORTGAGE XXX4219
(Amt. due on 07/01/2018 = $1,137.90)

L. Make a mortgage payment.
償付房屋抵押貸款。

Moving In 遷入新居

M. Pack.
裝箱。

N. Unpack.
拆箱。

We have a new address.

PHONE
ELECTRICITY
GAS
CABLE

GAS

O. Put the utilities in your name.
用您的名義接通公用事業。

P. Paint.
油漆。

Q. Arrange the furniture.
擺放家具。

Welcome!

R. Meet the neighbours.
結識鄰居。

Ways to ask about a home's features

Are <u>utilities</u> included?
Is <u>the kitchen</u> large and sunny?
Are <u>the neighbours</u> quiet?

Role play. Talk to an apartment manager.

A: *Hi. I'm calling about <u>the apartment</u>.*
B: *OK. It's <u>unfurnished</u> and rent is $<u>1000</u> a month.*
A: *Are <u>utilities included</u>?*

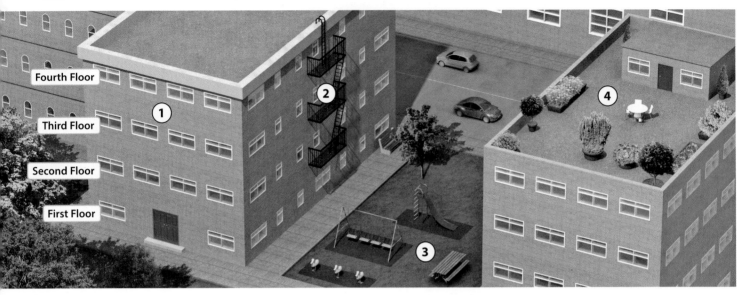

Fourth Floor

Third Floor

Second Floor

First Floor

1. apartment building 公寓樓	**2.** fire escape 太平梯	**3.** playground 運動遊樂場	**4.** roof garden 屋頂花園

Entrance 入口

5. intercom / speaker
對講機

6. tenant
房客

7. vacancy sign
出租牌示

8. manager / superintendent
經理 / 管理員

Lobby 大堂

9. elevator
電梯

10. stairs / stairway
樓梯

11. mailboxes
信箱

Basement 地下室

LAUNDRY ROOM

RECREATION ROOM

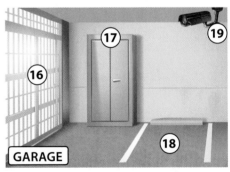

GARAGE

12. washer 洗衣機	**14.** big-screen TV 大螢幕電視
13. dryer 乾衣機	**15.** pool table 撞球 / 桌球

16. security gate 安全門 / 保安閘	**18.** parking space 停車位
17. storage locker 儲藏箱	**19.** security camera 保全攝影機

Grammar Point: Is there…? / Are there…?

Is there a rec room?   **Are there** stairs?
Yes, there is.   Yes, there are.
No, there isn't.   No, there aren't.

Look at the pictures.
Describe the apartment building.

A: There's *a pool table* in *the recreation room*.
B: There **are** *parking spaces* in *the garage*.

APARTMENT COMPLEX

20. balcony 陽台	**22.** swimming pool 游泳池	**24.** alley 小巷
21. courtyard 庭院	**23.** garbage bin 垃圾箱	

Hallway 走廊

25. emergency exit
緊急出口

26. garbage chute
垃圾滑運槽

Rental Office 出租辦公室

27. landlord
房東

28. lease / rental agreement
租賃協定

29. prospective tenant
未來的房客

An Apartment Entrance 公寓入口

It's Joe.

Come up.

30. smoke detector 煙霧警報器	**32.** buzzer 對講機	**34.** door chain 門鍊
31. key 鑰匙	**33.** peephole 窺孔	**35.** deadbolt lock 門栓鎖

More vocabulary

upstairs: the floor(s) above you
downstairs: the floor(s) below you
fire exit: another name for emergency exit

Role play. Talk to a landlord.

A: *Is there <u>a swimming pool</u> in this <u>complex</u>?*
B: *Yes, there is. It's near the <u>courtyard</u>.*
A: *Is there…?*

1. the city / an urban area
城市 / 市區

2. the suburbs
郊區

3. a small town / a village
小鎮 / 鄉村

4. the country / a rural area
鄉野地區

5. condominium / condo
公寓式住宅 / 共管大廈

6. townhouse
連幢屋

7. mobile home
活動房屋

8. college / university residence
學院宿舍 / 大學宿舍

9. farm
農場

10. ranch
牧場

11. seniors housing / seniors residence
老人住宅 / 老人住所

12. nursing home
養老院

13. shelter
收容所

More vocabulary

co-op: an apartment building owned by residents
duplex: a house divided into two homes
two-story house: a house with two floors

Think about it. Discuss.

1. Compare life in a city and a small town.
2. Compare life in a city and the country.

Front Yard and House 前院與房屋

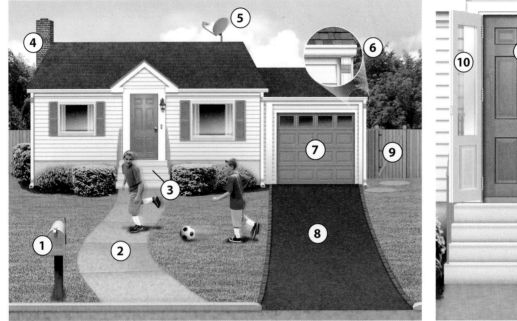

Front Porch 前門廊

1. mailbox
   信箱
2. front walk
   前門走道
3. steps
   階梯

4. chimney
   煙囪
5. satellite dish
   衛星天線
6. gutter
   屋頂邊溝

7. garage door
   車房門
8. driveway
   車道
9. gate
   院門

10. storm door
    風雨門
11. front door
    前門
12. doorknob
    門把

13. porch light
    門廊燈
14. doorbell
    門鈴
15. screen door
    紗門

Backyard 後院

16. patio
    庭院台
17. barbeque
    煎烤架
18. sliding glass door
    滑動玻璃門

19. patio furniture
    庭院家具
20. flower bed
    花床
21. hose
    水管

22. sprinkler
    灑水器
23. hammock
    吊床
24. garbage can
    垃圾桶

25. compost pile
    堆肥
26. lawn
    草坪
27. vegetable garden
    菜園

A. **take** a nap
   睡午覺
B. **garden**
   侍弄花草

1. **cabinet**
   廚櫃

2. **shelf**
   廚架

3. **paper towels**
   大紙巾

4. **sink**
   水槽 / 洗碗盆

5. **dish rack**
   碗盤架 / 碗碟架

6. **coffee maker**
   咖啡機

7. **garbage disposal**
   廢物處理機

8. **dishwasher**
   洗碗機

9. **refrigerator**
   冰箱

10. **freezer**
    凍庫

11. **toaster**
    烤麵包機

12. **blender**
    攪碎機

13. **microwave**
    微波爐

14. **electric can opener**
    電開罐器

15. **toaster oven**
    烤麵包機兼烤箱

16. **pot**
    鍋子

17. **kettle**
    水壺

18. **stove**
    爐子

19. **burner**
    爐頭

20. **oven**
    烤箱

21. **oven drawer**
    烤箱抽屜

22. **counter**
    料理臺

23. **drawer**
    抽屜

24. **pan**
    平底鍋

25. **electric mixer**
    電攪拌器

26. **food processor**
    食物處理器

27. **cutting board**
    切菜板

28. **mixing bowl**
    攪拌大碗

Ways to talk about location using *on* and *in*

Use *on* for the counter, shelf, burner, stove, and cutting board. *It's on the counter.* Use *in* for the dishwasher, oven, sink, and drawer. *Put it in the sink.*

Pair practice. Make new conversations.

A: *Please move the <u>blender</u>.*
B: *Sure. Do you want it <u>in the cabinet</u>?*
A: *No, put it <u>on the counter</u>.*

1

2

3

4

5

6

7

1. dish / plate 盤 / 碟	7. coffee mug 咖啡杯	13. salt and pepper shakers 鹽與胡椒瓶	19. fan 電風扇
2. bowl 碗	8. dining room chair 餐椅	14. sugar bowl 糖罐	20. platter 餐盤
3. fork 叉	9. dining room table 餐桌	15. creamer 奶脂罐	21. serving bowl 大餐碗
4. knife 刀	10. napkin / serviette 餐巾	16. teapot 茶壺	22. hutch 餐具櫃
5. spoon 匙	11. placemat 餐具墊	17. tray 托盤	23. vase 花瓶
6. teacup 茶杯	12. tablecloth 桌布	18. light fixture 電燈裝置	24. buffet 碗櫥

Ways to make requests at the table

May I have the sugar bowl?
Would you pass the creamer, please?
Could I have a coffee mug?

Role play. Request items at the Table.

A: *What do you need?*
B: *Could I have a coffee mug?*
A: *Certainly. And would you…?*

55

1. **loveseat**
雙人沙發座

2. **throw cushion**
抱枕

3. **basket**
籃子

4. **houseplant**
室內植物

5. **entertainment centre**
娛樂中心

6. **TV (television)**
電視機

7. **digital video recorder (DVR)**
數位錄影機

8. **stereo system**
音響系統

9. **painting**
圖畫

10. **wall**
牆壁

11. **mantel**
壁爐罩

12. **fire screen**
爐火簾

13. **fireplace**
壁爐

14. **end table**
小茶几

15. **floor lamp**
立燈

16. **drapes / curtains**
窗簾

17. **window**
窗戶

18. **sofa / couch**
沙發

19. **coffee table**
大茶几

20. **candle**
蠟燭

21. **candle holder**
蠟燭架

22. **armchair / easy chair**
扶手椅 / 安樂椅

23. **ottoman / footrest**
軟墊凳 / 腳凳

24. **carpet**
地毯

More vocabulary

light bulb: the light inside a lamp
magazine rack: a piece of furniture for magazines
sofa cushions: the cushions that are part of the sofa

Internet Research: furniture prices

Type any furniture item and the word "price" in a search engine.
Report: *I found a sofa for $300.00.*

1. hamper 髒衣籃	8. faucet 水龍頭	15. towel rack 毛巾架	22. medicine cabinet 藥櫃
2. bathtub 浴缸	9. hot water 熱水	16. bath towel 浴巾	23. toothbrush 牙刷
3. soap dish 香皂盒	10. cold water 冷水	17. hand towel 擦手巾	24. toothbrush holder 牙刷座台
4. soap 香皂	11. grab bar 扶手桿	18. mirror 鏡子	25. sink 水槽 / 洗面盆
5. rubber mat 橡膠墊	12. tile 瓷磚	19. toilet paper 衛生紙	26. wastebasket 垃圾桶
6. washcloth 擦洗巾	13. showerhead 淋浴頭	20. toilet brush 馬桶刷	27. scale 磅秤
7. drain 排水口	14. shower curtain 淋浴簾	21. toilet 馬桶	28. bath mat 浴墊

More vocabulary

stall shower: a shower without a bathtub
half bath: a bathroom with no shower or tub
linen closet: a closet for towels and sheets

Survey your class. Record the responses.

1. Is your toothbrush on the sink or in the medicine cabinet?
2. Do you have a bathtub or a shower?
Report: *Most of us… Some of us…*

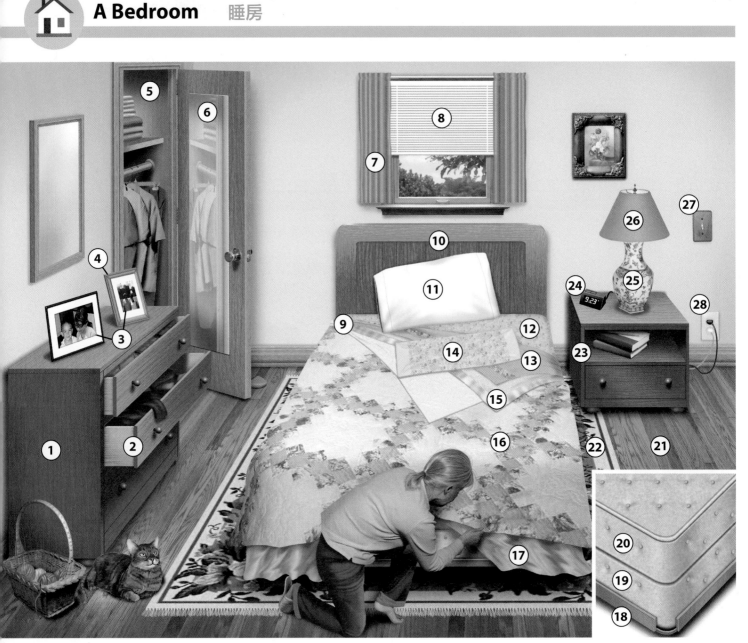

1. dresser / bureau 衣櫃 / 梳妝檯	8. mini-blinds 百葉窗	15. blanket 毯子	22. rug 小地毯
2. drawer 抽屜	9. bed 床	16. quilt 被子	23. night table / nightstand 床頭桌
3. photos 相片	10. headboard 床頭板	17. dust ruffle 床墊裙罩	24. alarm clock 鬧鐘
4. picture frame 相框	11. pillow 枕頭	18. bed frame 床架	25. lamp 檯燈
5. closet 壁櫃	12. fitted sheet 床罩	19. box spring 彈簧床墊	26. lampshade 燈罩
6. full-length mirror 長鏡	13. flat sheet 床單	20. mattress 床墊	27. light switch 電燈開關
7. curtains 窗簾	14. pillowcase 枕頭套	21. wood floor 木地板	28. outlet 插座

Look at the pictures.
Describe the bedroom.

A: *There's a lamp on the nightstand*.
B: *There's a mirror in the closet*.

Survey your class. Record the responses.

1. Do you prefer a hard or a soft mattress?
2. How many pillows do you like on your bed?
Report: *All of us… A few of us…*

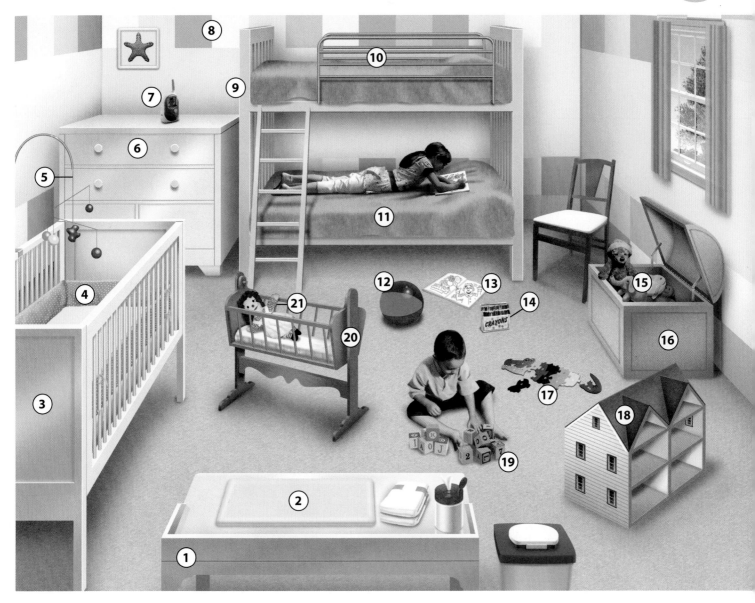

Furniture and Accessories 家具及配件

1. changing table
尿布更換台

2. changing pad
尿布更換墊

3. crib
嬰兒床

4. bumper pad
嬰兒床圍墊

5. mobile
旋吊玩飾

6. chest of drawers
抽屜櫃

7. baby monitor
嬰兒監視器

8. wallpaper
壁紙

9. bunk beds
雙層床

10. safety rail
安全扶手

11. bedspread
床罩

Toys and Games 玩具與遊戲

12. ball
球

13. colouring book
著色簿

14. crayons
粉蠟筆

15. stuffed animals
填塞玩具

16. toy chest
玩具箱

17. puzzle
拼圖

18. dollhouse
娃娃屋

19. blocks
積木

20. cradle
搖籃

21. doll
娃娃

Pair practice. Make new conversations.

A: *Where's the changing pad?*

B: *It's on the changing table.*

Think about it. Discuss.

1. Which toys help children learn? How?
2. Which toys are good for older and younger children?
3. What safety features does this room need? Why?

59

A. **dust** the furniture
拭去家具上的灰塵

B. **recycle** the newspapers
回收報紙

C. **clean** the oven
清理烤箱

D. **mop** the floor
拖地板

E. **polish** the furniture
擦光家具

F. **make** the bed
鋪床

G. **put away** the toys
放好玩具

H. **vacuum** the carpet
吸地毯

I. **wash** the windows
擦洗窗戶

J. **sweep** the floor
掃地

K. **scrub** the sink
擦洗水槽 / 擦洗洗面盆

L. **empty** the garbage
倒垃圾

M. **wash** the dishes
洗碗盤 / 洗碗碟

N. **dry** the dishes
拭乾碗盤 / 拭乾碗碟

O. **wipe** the counter
擦拭料理臺

P. **change** the sheets
換床單

Q. **take out / put out**
the garbage
倒垃圾

Pair practice. Make new conversations.

A: *Let's clean this place. First, I'll* <u>sweep the floor</u>.
B: *I'll* <u>mop the floor</u> *when you finish.*
A: *OK. After that we can…*

Think about it. Discuss.

1. Rank housework tasks from difficult to easy.
2. Categorize housework tasks by age: children, teens, adults.

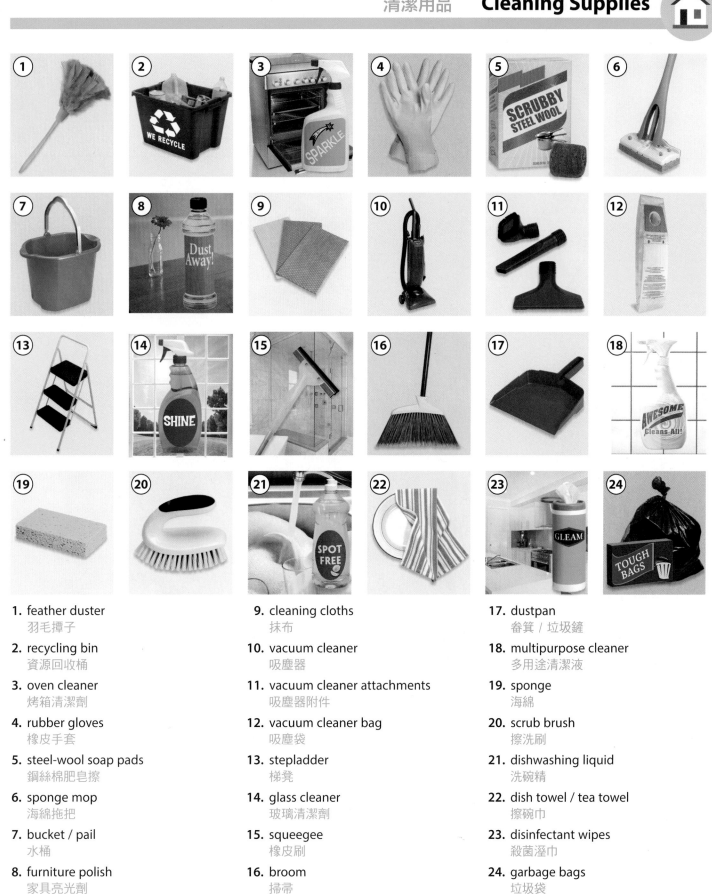

1. feather duster
   羽毛撢子

2. recycling bin
   資源回收桶

3. oven cleaner
   烤箱清潔劑

4. rubber gloves
   橡皮手套

5. steel-wool soap pads
   鋼絲棉肥皂擦

6. sponge mop
   海綿拖把

7. bucket / pail
   水桶

8. furniture polish
   家具亮光劑

9. cleaning cloths
   抹布

10. vacuum cleaner
    吸塵器

11. vacuum cleaner attachments
    吸塵器附件

12. vacuum cleaner bag
    吸塵袋

13. stepladder
    梯凳

14. glass cleaner
    玻璃清潔劑

15. squeegee
    橡皮刷

16. broom
    掃帚

17. dustpan
    畚箕 / 垃圾鏟

18. multipurpose cleaner
    多用途清潔液

19. sponge
    海綿

20. scrub brush
    擦洗刷

21. dishwashing liquid
    洗碗精

22. dish towel / tea towel
    擦碗巾

23. disinfectant wipes
    殺菌溼巾

24. garbage bags
    垃圾袋

Ways to ask for something

Please hand me the squeegee.
Can you get me the broom?
I need the sponge mop.

Pair practice. Make new conversations.

A: *Please hand me the sponge mop.*
B: *Here you go. Do you need the bucket?*
A: *Yes, please. Can you get me the rubber gloves, too?*

61

1. The water heater is **not working**.
   熱水爐壞了。

2. The power is **out**.
   停電了。

3. The roof is **leaking**.
   屋頂漏水。

4. The tile is **cracked**.
   瓷磚破了。

5. The window is **broken**.
   窗戶破了。

6. The lock is **broken**.
   鎖壞了。

7. The steps are **broken**.
   階梯壞了。

8. roofer
   屋頂工人

9. electrician
   電工

10. repairperson
    修理工

11. locksmith
    鎖匠

12. carpenter
    木匠

13. fuse box
    保險絲盒

14. gas meter
    瓦斯表

More vocabulary

fix: to repair something that is broken
pests: termites, fleas, rats, etc.
exterminate: to kill household pests

Pair practice. Make new conversations.

A: *The <u>faucet is leaking</u>.*
B: *I think I can fix it.*
A: *I think we should call <u>a plumber</u>.*

15. The furnace is **broken**.
暖風爐壞了。

16. The pipes are **frozen**.
水管凍結。

17. The faucet is **dripping**.
水龍頭漏水。

18. The sink is **overflowing**.
水槽堵塞。

19. The toilet is **stopped up / plugged**.
馬桶阻塞。

20. plumber
水管工

21. exterminator
滅蟲人員

22. termites
白蟻

23. ants
螞蟻

24. bedbugs
臭蟲

25. fleas
跳蚤

26. cockroaches / roaches
蟑螂

27. rats
大老鼠

28. mice*
小老鼠

***Note:** one mouse, two mice

Ways to ask about repairs

How much will it cost?
When can you begin?
How long will it take?

Role play. Talk to a repairperson.

A: *Can you <u>fix the roof</u>?*
B: *Yes, but it will take <u>two weeks</u>.*
A: *How much will it cost?*

The Tenant Meeting 房客開會

1. roommates
   室友
2. party
   派對
3. music
   音樂
4. DJ
   音樂播放師
5. noise
   噪音
6. irritated
   生氣
7. rules
   規定
8. mess
   雜亂
9. invitation
   邀請
A. **dance**
   跳舞

What do you see in the pictures?

1. What happened in apartment 2B? How many people were there?

2. How did the neighbour feel? Why?

3. What rules did they write at the tenant meeting?

4. What did the roommates do after the tenant meeting?

Read the story.

The Tenant Meeting

Sally Lopez and Tina Green are <u>roommates</u>. They live in apartment 2B. One night they had a big <u>party</u> with <u>music</u> and a <u>DJ</u>. There was a <u>mess</u> in the hallway. Their neighbours were very unhappy. Mr. Clark in 2A was very <u>irritated</u>. He hates <u>noise</u>!

The next day there was a tenant meeting. Everyone wanted <u>rules</u> about parties and loud music. The girls were very embarrassed.

After the meeting, the girls cleaned the mess in the hallway. Then they gave each neighbour an <u>invitation</u> to a new party. Everyone had a good time at the rec room party. Now the tenants have two new rules and a new place to <u>dance</u>.

Reread the story.

1. Find the word "irritated" in Paragraph 1. What does it mean in this story?

2. Retell the story in your own words.

What do you think?

3. Imagine you are the neighbour in 2A. What do you say to Tina and Sally?

4. What are the most important rules in an apartment building? Why?

Back from the Market 從市場回來

1. fish
   魚
2. meat
   肉
3. chicken
   雞
4. cheese
   乳酪
5. milk
   牛奶
6. butter
   牛油
7. eggs
   雞蛋
8. vegetables
   蔬菜

Listen and point. Take turns.

A: *Point to the <u>vegetables</u>.*
B: *Point to the <u>bread</u>.*
A: *Point to the <u>fruit</u>.*

Dictate to your partner. Take turns.

A: *Write <u>vegetables</u>.*
B: *Please spell <u>vegetables</u> for me.*
A: *<u>V-e-g-e-t-a-b-l-e-s</u>.*

9. fruit
   水果
10. rice
    米
11. bread
    麵包
12. pasta
    義大利麵
13. grocery bag /
    shopping bag
    購物袋
14. shopping list
    購物清單
15. coupons
    折扣券

Ways to talk about food.

Do we need <u>eggs</u>?
Do we have any <u>pasta</u>?
We have some <u>vegetables</u>, but we need <u>fruit</u>.

Role play. Talk about your shopping list.

A: *Do we need <u>eggs</u>?*
B: *No, we have some.*
A: *Do we have any…?*

67

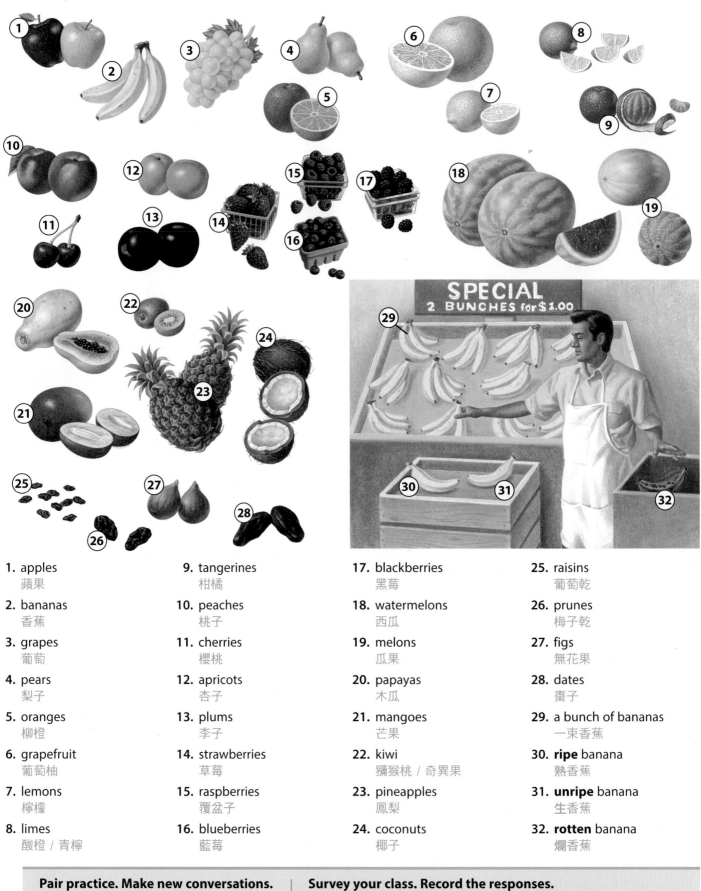

1. apples
   蘋果

2. bananas
   香蕉

3. grapes
   葡萄

4. pears
   梨子

5. oranges
   柳橙

6. grapefruit
   葡萄柚

7. lemons
   檸檬

8. limes
   酸橙 / 青檸

9. tangerines
   柑橘

10. peaches
    桃子

11. cherries
    櫻桃

12. apricots
    杏子

13. plums
    李子

14. strawberries
    草莓

15. raspberries
    覆盆子

16. blueberries
    藍莓

17. blackberries
    黑莓

18. watermelons
    西瓜

19. melons
    瓜果

20. papayas
    木瓜

21. mangoes
    芒果

22. kiwi
    獼猴桃 / 奇異果

23. pineapples
    鳳梨

24. coconuts
    椰子

25. raisins
    葡萄乾

26. prunes
    梅子乾

27. figs
    無花果

28. dates
    棗子

29. a bunch of bananas
    一束香蕉

30. **ripe** banana
    熟香蕉

31. **unripe** banana
    生香蕉

32. **rotten** banana
    爛香蕉

Pair practice. Make new conversations.

A: *What's your favourite fruit?*
B: *I like* <u>apples</u>. *Do you?*
A: *I prefer* <u>bananas</u>.

Survey your class. Record the responses.

1. What kinds of fruit are common in your native country?
2. What kinds of fruit are uncommon?
Report: *According to* <u>Luis</u>, <u>papayas</u> *are* <u>common</u> *in* <u>Peru</u>.

1. lettuce 生菜	9. celery 芹菜	17. potatoes 馬鈴薯	25. zucchini 夏南瓜 / 翠玉瓜
2. cabbage 甘藍菜 / 椰菜	10. cucumbers 黃瓜	18. sweet potatoes 蕃薯	26. asparagus 蘆筍
3. carrots 胡蘿蔔	11. spinach 菠菜	19. onions 洋蔥	27. mushrooms 香菇 / 磨菇
4. radishes 蘿蔔	12. corn 玉蜀黍	20. green onions / scallions 青蔥	28. parsley 荷蘭芹
5. beets 甜菜	13. broccoli 綠花椰菜 / 西蘭花	21. peas 豌豆	29. chili peppers 辣椒
6. tomatoes 番茄	14. cauliflower 白花椰菜 / 椰菜花	22. artichokes 朝鮮薊	30. garlic 大蒜
7. bell peppers 甜椒	15. bok choy 白菜	23. eggplants 茄子	31. a **bag of** lettuce 一袋生菜
8. string beans 菜豆	16. turnips 大頭菜	24. squash 西葫蘆	32. a **head of** lettuce 一顆生菜

Pair practice. Make new conversations.

A: *Do you eat <u>broccoli</u>?*
B: *Yes. I like most vegetables, but not <u>peppers</u>.*
A: *Really? Well, I don't like <u>cauliflower</u>.*

Survey your class. Record the responses.

1. Which vegetables do you prefer to eat raw?
2. Which vegetables do you prefer to eat cooked?
Report: ____ *of us prefer <u>raw carrots</u>.* ____ *of us prefer <u>cooked carrots</u>.*

69

Meat and Poultry 肉類和家禽類

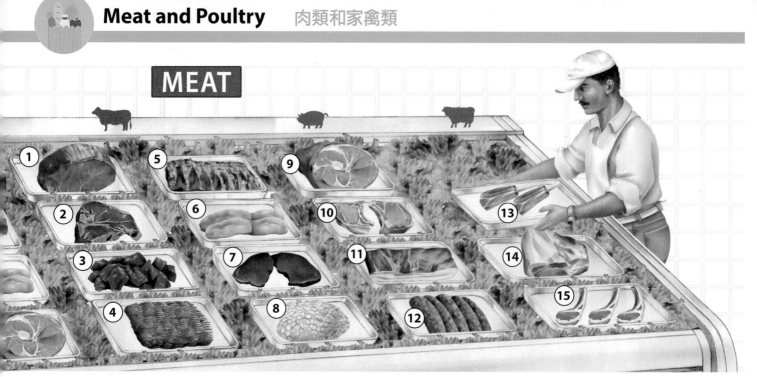

MEAT

Beef 牛肉

1. roast
   烤焙用牛肉
2. steak
   牛排
3. stewing beef
   燉煮用牛肉
4. ground beef
   絞牛肉

5. beef ribs
   牛排骨
6. veal cutlets
   小牛肉片
7. liver
   牛肝
8. tripe
   牛肚

Pork 豬肉

9. ham
   火腿
10. pork chops
    豬排
11. bacon
    醃豬肉 / 煙肉
12. sausage
    香腸

Lamb 羊肉

13. lamb shanks
    羊小腿
14. leg of lamb
    羊腿
15. lamb chops
    羊排

POULTRY

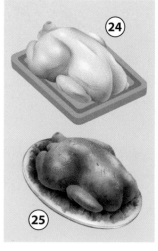

Poultry 家禽類

16. chicken
    雞
17. turkey
    火雞

18. duck
    鴨
19. breasts
    雞胸肉

20. wings
    雞翅膀
21. legs
    雞腿

22. thighs
    雞大腿
23. drumsticks
    雞小腿

24. **raw** turkey
    生火雞
25. **cooked** turkey
    熟火雞

More vocabulary

boneless: meat and poultry without bones
skinless: poultry without skin
vegetarian: a person who doesn't eat meat

Ways to ask about meat prices

*How much **is** that <u>roast</u>?*
*How much **are** those <u>cutlets</u>?*
*How much **is** the <u>ground beef</u>?*

Fish 魚類

1. trout
鱒魚

2. catfish
鯰魚

3. whole salmon
整隻鮭魚

4. salmon steak
鮭魚排

5. swordfish
旗魚

6. halibut steak
比目魚排

7. tuna
鮪魚

8. cod
鱈魚

Shellfish 貝類

9. crab
螃蟹

10. lobster
龍蝦

11. shrimp
蝦

12. scallops
扇貝

13. mussels
貽貝

14. oysters
牡蠣

15. clams
蛤

16. fresh fish
新鮮魚

17. frozen fish
冷凍魚

18. white bread
白麵包

19. wheat bread
全麥麵包

20. rye bread
裸麥麵包

21. roast beef
烤牛肉

22. corned beef
醃牛肉

23. pastrami
醃薰牛肉

24. salami
義大利香腸

25. smoked turkey
薰火雞

26. American cheese
美國乳酪

27. Swiss cheese
瑞士乳酪

28. cheddar cheese
黃色硬乾酪

29. mozzarella cheese
義大利白乾酪

Ways to order at the counter

I'd like some <u>roast beef</u>.
I'll have <u>a halibut steak</u> and some <u>shrimp</u>.
Could I get some <u>Swiss cheese</u>?

Pair practice. Make new conversations.

A: *What can I get for you?*
B: *I'd like some <u>roast beef</u>. How about a pound?*
A: *A pound of <u>roast beef</u> coming up!*

71

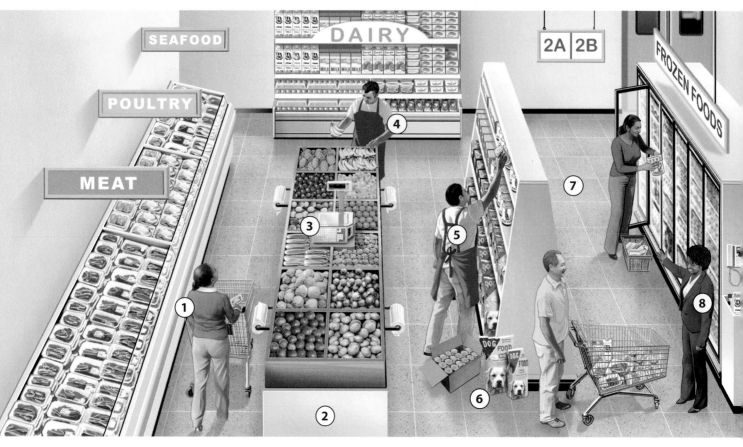

1. customer
   顧客
2. produce section
   蔬果
3. scale
   磅秤
4. grocery clerk
   雜貨店職員
5. stocker
   上貨員
6. pet food
   寵物食品
7. aisle
   走道
8. manager
   經理

Canned Foods
罐頭食物

17. beans
    豆子
18. soup
    湯
19. tuna
    鮪魚

Dairy
奶製品

20. margarine
    植物奶油 / 植物牛油
21. sour cream
    優酪乳油
22. yogurt
    酸乳酪

Grocery Products
雜貨產品

23. aluminum foil
    鋁箔紙
24. plastic wrap
    保鮮膜
25. plastic storage bags
    塑膠儲藏袋

Frozen Foods
冷凍食物

26. ice cream
    冰淇淋
27. frozen vegetables
    冷凍蔬菜
28. frozen dinner
    冷凍晚餐

Ways to ask for information in a grocery store

Excuse me, where are <u>the carrots</u>?
Can you please tell me where to find <u>the dog food</u>?
Do you have any <u>lamb chops</u> today?

Pair practice. Make new conversations.

A: *<u>Can you please tell me where to find the dog food</u>?*
B: *Sure. It's in <u>Aisle 1B</u>. Do you need anything else?*
A: *Yes, where are <u>the carrots</u>?*

9. shopping basket 購物籃	**11.** line 排隊	**13.** checkout 結帳櫃台	**15.** bagger 裝袋員
10. self-checkout 自助付款	**12.** cart 手推車	**14.** cashier 收銀員	**16.** cash register 收銀機

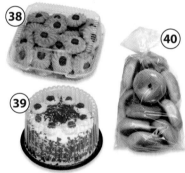

Baking Products
烘烤用品

Beverages
飲料

Snack Foods
點心小吃

Baked Goods
烘烤食品

29. flour 麵粉	**32.** apple juice 蘋果汁	**35.** potato chips 洋芋片 / 薯片	**38.** cookies 餅乾
30. sugar 糖	**33.** coffee 咖啡	**36.** nuts 堅果	**39.** cake 蛋糕
31. oil 食用油	**34.** soft drink / pop 軟飲料 / 汽水	**37.** chocolate bar 巧克力條	**40.** bagels 硬麵包圈

Survey your class. Record the responses.

1. What is your favourite grocery store?
2. Do you prefer to shop alone or with someone?
Report: *Most of us… Some of us…*

Think about it. Discuss.

1. Compare small grocery stores and large supermarkets.
2. Categorize the foods on this page as healthy or unhealthy. Explain your answers.

Containers and Packaging 容器和包裝

1. bottles
瓶子

2. jars
廣口瓶

3. cans
罐頭

4. cartons
紙盒

5. containers
容器

6. boxes
盒子

7. bags
袋子

8. packages
包

9. six-packs
六瓶罐包裝

10. loaves
整條麵包

11. rolls
紙捲

12. tubes
軟筒

13. a bottle of water
一瓶水

14. a jar of jam
一瓶果醬

15. a can of beans
一罐豆子

16. a carton of eggs
一盒雞蛋

17. a container of cottage cheese
一包乳酪

18. a box of cereal
一盒麥片

19. a bag of flour
一袋麵粉

20. a package of cookies
一包餅乾

21. a six-pack of pop
六罐裝汽水

22. a loaf of bread
一條麵包

23. a roll of paper towels
一捲紙巾

24. a tube of toothpaste
一條牙膏

Grammar Point: count and noncount

Some foods can be counted: *an apple, two apples.*
Some foods can't be counted: *some rice, some water.*
For noncount foods, count containers: *two bags of rice.*

Pair practice. Make new conversations.

A: *How many <u>boxes of cereal</u> do we need?*
B: *We need <u>two boxes</u>.*

A. **Measure** the ingredients.
量秤原料。

B. **Weigh** the food.
秤食品重量。

1 cup = 237 millilitres

C. **Convert** the measurements.
換算單位。

Liquid Measures 液體度量單位

① 1 fl. oz.

② 1 c.

③ 500 mL

④ 1 L

⑤ 4 L

1. a fluid ounce of milk
一盎斯牛奶
2. a cup of oil
一杯油

3. 500 millilitres (mL) of frozen yogurt
五百毫升冷凍優酪乳
4. a litre of milk
一公升牛奶

5. a 4-litre jug or a gallon of water
四公升或一加侖瓶裝水

Dry Measures 固體度量單位

⑥ 5 mL

⑦ 15 mL

⑧ 60 mL

⑨ 118 mL

⑩ 237 mL

6. 5 mL or a teaspoon (tsp.) of salt
五毫升或一茶匙鹽
7. 15 mL or a tablespoon (tbsp.) of sugar
十五毫升或一湯匙糖

8. 60 mL / 1/4 cup (c.) of brown sugar
六十毫升或四分之一杯紅糖
9. 118 mL or a half cup of raisins
118毫升或半杯葡萄乾

10. 237 mL or a cup of flour
237毫升或一杯麵粉

Weight 重量

⑪ .500 KG

⑫ 1 KG

11. 500 grams of cheese
五百克乳酪

12. a kilogram of roast beef
一公斤烤牛肉

Equivalencies	
3 tsp. = 1 tbsp.	5 ml = 1 tsp.
2 tbsp. = 1 fl. oz.	15 mL = 1 tbsp.
8 fl. oz. = 1 c.	

Volume
1 fl. oz. = 30 ml
1 c. = 237 ml
1 pt. = .47 L
1 L = 1000 mL
1 gal. = 3.79 L

Weight
1 oz. = 28.35 grams (g)
1 lb. = 453.6 g
2.205 lbs. = 1 kilogram (kg)
1 lb. = 16 oz.
1 kg = 1000 g

Food Preparation and Safety 食物烹飪方式與安全

Food Safety 食物安全

A. **clean**
   清潔

B. **separate**
   分開處理

C. **cook**
   煮熟

D. **chill**
   冷藏

A Clean counters! **20 SECONDS** Wash your hands!

B Use separate cutting boards for vegetables and meat!

C Cook to the right temperature!

D Refrigerate leftovers quickly!

Ways to Serve Meat and Poultry 肉類和家禽類的烹飪方式

1. fried chicken
   炸雞

2. barbecued / grilled ribs
   烤排骨

3. broiled steak
   烘烤牛排

4. roasted turkey
   烤焙火雞

5. boiled ham
   煮火腿

6. stir-fried beef
   炒牛肉

Ways to Serve Eggs 雞蛋的烹飪方式

7. scrambled eggs
   炒蛋

8. hard-boiled eggs
   煮雞蛋

9. poached eggs
   水波蛋

10. eggs sunny-side up
    單面煎荷包蛋

11. eggs over easy
    兩面煎荷包蛋

12. omelette
    蛋捲 / 奄列

More vocabulary

bacteria: very small living things that often cause disease
surface: a counter, a table, or the outside part of something
disinfect: to remove bacteria from a surface

Pair practice. Make new conversations.

A: *How do you like your eggs?*
B: *I like them _scrambled_. And you?*
A: *I like them _hard-boiled_.*

Cheesy Tofu Vegetable Casserole 烘焙乳酪豆腐蔬菜

A. **Preheat** the oven.
預熱烤箱。

B. **Grease** a baking pan.
在烤盤上塗油。

C. **Slice** the tofu.
將豆腐切片。

D. **Steam** the broccoli.
蒸綠花椰菜。

E. **Sauté** the mushrooms.
炒蘑菇。

F. **Spoon** sauce on top.
澆湯。

G. **Grate** the cheese.
乳酪銼成細條。

H. **Bake** at 350° F or 200° C.
烘烤於華氏350度或攝氏200度。

Easy Chicken Soup 簡易雞湯

I. **Cut up** the chicken.
雞肉切塊。

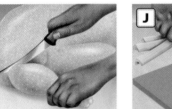

J. **Dice** the celery.
芹菜切段。

K. **Peel** the carrots.
胡蘿蔔削皮。

L. **Chop** the onions.
洋蔥切碎。

M. **Boil** the chicken.
煮雞肉。

N. **Add** the vegetables.
加入蔬菜。

O. **Stir**.
攪拌。

P. **Simmer**.
慢火煮。

Quick and Easy Cake 簡易蛋糕

Q. **Break** 2 eggs into a microwave-safe bowl.
在可用於微波爐的碗內打兩個雞蛋。

R. **Mix** the ingredients.
混合所有配料。

S. **Beat** the mixture.
攪打均勻。

T. **Microwave** for 5 minutes.
微波五分鐘。

1. can opener 開罐器	9. wooden spoon 木勺	17. colander 濾鍋	25. saucepan / cooking pot 鍋
2. grater 銼絲器	10. casserole dish 焙盤	18. kitchen timer 炊煮計時器	26. cake pan 蛋糕盤
3. steamer 蒸鍋	11. garlic press 大蒜碾碎器	19. spatula 刮刀	27. cookie sheet 餅乾盤
4. storage container 存放容器	12. carving knife 切刀	20. egg beater 打蛋器	28. pie pan 派餅盤
5. frying pan 煎鍋	13. roasting pan 烘烤盤	21. whisk 攪拌器	29. pot holders 防燙墊
6. pot 湯鍋	14. roasting rack 烘烤架	22. strainer 濾網	30. rolling pin 麵棍
7. ladle 長柄勺子	15. vegetable peeler 蔬菜削皮刀	23. tongs 夾鉗	31. mixing bowl 攪拌大碗
8. double boiler 雙層鍋	16. paring knife 削皮刀	24. lid 鍋蓋	

Pair practice. Make new conversations.

A: *Please hand me the whisk.*

B: *Here's the whisk. Do you need anything else?*

A: *Yes, pass me the casserole dish.*

Use the new words.

Look at page 77. Name the kitchen utensils you see.

A: *This is a grater.*

B: *This is a mixing bowl.*

1. hamburger 漢堡	**7.** nachos 墨西哥黍片	**13.** ice-cream cone 蛋筒冰淇淋	**19.** plastic utensils 塑膠餐具
2. french fries 炸薯條	**8.** taco 墨西哥塔可餅	**14.** milkshake 奶昔	**20.** sugar substitute 代糖
3. cheeseburger 乳酪漢堡	**9.** burrito 墨西哥捲餅	**15.** doughnut / donut 甜甜圈	**21.** ketchup 番茄醬
4. onion rings 炸洋蔥圈	**10.** pizza 披薩	**16.** muffin 鬆餅	**22.** mustard 芥末
5. chicken sandwich 雞肉三明治	**11.** pop 汽水	**17.** counter person 櫃台售貨員	**23.** mayonnaise 美奶滋
6. hot dog 熱狗	**12.** iced tea 冰茶	**18.** straw 吸管	**24.** salad bar 沙拉吧

Grammar Point: yes/no questions (do)

Do you like hamburgers? Yes, I do.
Do you like nachos? No, I don't.
Practise asking about the food on the page.

Think about it. Discuss.

1. Which fast foods are healthier than others? How do you know?
2. Compare the benefits of a fast-food lunch and a lunch from home.

A Coffee Shop Menu　咖啡店菜單

1. bacon
   醃豬肉 / 煙肉
2. sausage
   香腸
3. hash browns
   脆薯餅
4. toast
   烤麵包
5. English muffin
   英式鬆餅
6. biscuits
   比司吉
7. pancakes
   鬆餅
8. waffles
   蛋奶烘餅
9. hot cereal
   熱燕麥
10. grilled cheese sandwich
    炙烤乳酪三明治
11. pickle
    酸黃瓜
12. club sandwich
    總匯三明治
13. spinach salad
    菠菜沙拉
14. chef's salad
    主廚沙拉
15. house salad /
    garden salad
    本樓沙拉 / 時蔬沙拉
16. soup
    湯
17. rolls
    小麵包
18. coleslaw
    碎菜沙拉
19. potato salad
    馬鈴薯沙拉
20. pasta salad
    義麵沙拉
21. fruit salad
    水果沙拉

Menu

Breakfast Special
Served 6 a.m. to 11 a.m.

Two egg omelette with one side

Lunch
Served 11 a.m. to 2 p.m • All sandwiches come with soup or salad.

Side salads

Dressings
Thousand Island　Ranch　Italian　Blue Cheese

Survey your class. Record the responses.

1. Do you prefer soup or salad?
2. Which do you prefer, tea or coffee?

Report: *Five* of us prefer *tea*. *Most* of us prefer *soup*.

Pair practice. Make new conversations.

A: *What's your favourite side salad?*
B: *I like coleslaw. How about you?*
A: *I like potato salad.*

Dinner

Desserts

Beverages

22. roast chicken
烤雞

23. mashed potatoes
馬鈴薯泥

24. steak
牛排

25. baked potato
烤馬鈴薯

26. spaghetti
義大利麵

27. meatballs
肉丸

28. garlic bread
大蒜麵包

29. grilled fish
烤魚

30. rice
米飯

31. meatloaf
肉糜糕

32. steamed vegetables
蒸蔬菜

33. layer cake
夾心蛋糕

34. cheesecake
乳酪蛋糕

35. pie
派餅

36. mixed berries
混合莓果

37. coffee
咖啡

38. decaf coffee
無咖啡因咖啡

39. tea
茶

40. herbal tea
草茶

41. cream
乳脂

42. low-fat milk
低脂牛奶

Ways to order from a menu

I'd like <u>a grilled cheese sandwich</u>.
I'll have <u>a bowl of tomato soup</u>.
Could I get <u>the chef's salad</u> with <u>ranch dressing</u>?

Role play. Order a dinner from the menu.

A: *Are you ready to order?*
B: *I think so. I'll have <u>the roast chicken</u>.*
A: *Would you also like…?*

81

1. **dining room**
   餐室

2. **hostess**
   帶位

3. **high chair**
   兒童高座椅

4. **booth**
   車廂位

5. **to-go box**
   外賣盒

6. **patron / diner**
   用餐客人

7. **menu**
   菜單

8. **server / waiter**
   侍者 / 男侍者

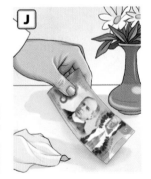

A. **set** the table
   擺放餐具

B. **seat** the customer
   帶客入座

C. **pour** the water
   倒水

D. **order** from the menu
   點菜

E. **take** the order
   記下點菜

F. **serve** the meal
   上菜

G. **clear / bus** the dishes
   清理碗盤 / 清理碗碟

H. **carry** the tray
   端托盤

I. **pay** the bill
   付帳

J. **leave** a tip
   給小費

More vocabulary

eat out: to go to a restaurant to eat

get takeout: to buy food at a restaurant and take it home to eat

Look at the pictures.

Describe what is happening.

A: *She's seating the customer*.
B: *He's taking the order*.

9. server / waitress
侍者 / 女侍者

10. dessert tray
甜點盤

11. bread basket
麵包籃

12. busser
侍者助手

13. dish room
碗盤室

14. dishwasher
洗碗工

15. kitchen
廚房

16. chef
廚師

17. place setting
放置碗碟

18. dinner plate
主食盤 / 餐碟

19. bread-and-butter plate
麵包牛油盤

20. salad plate
沙拉盤

21. soup bowl
湯碗

22. water glass
水杯

23. wine glass
酒杯

24. cup
茶杯

25. saucer
茶碟

26. napkin
餐巾

27. salad fork
沙拉叉

28. dinner fork
餐叉

29. steak knife
牛排刀

30. knife
餐刀

31. teaspoon
茶匙

32. soup spoon
湯匙

Pair practice. Make new conversations.

A: *Excuse me, this spoon is dirty.*
B: *I'm so sorry. I'll get you a clean spoon right away.*
A: *Thanks.*

Role play. A new busser needs help.

A: *Do the salad forks go on the left?*
B: *Yes. They go next to the dinner forks.*
A: *What about the…?*

83

The Farmers' Market 農夫市場

1. live music
   現場演唱

2. organic
   有機食物

3. lemonade
   檸檬水

4. sour
   酸

5. samples
   品嚐樣品

6. avocados
   酪梨 / 牛油果

7. vendors
   商販

8. sweets
   甜食

9. herbs
   香草

A. **count**
   數數

HOT FOOD

Cara's Bakery

7

8

CHIVES   DILL

PARSLEY

9

What do you see in the picture?

1. How many vendors are at the market today?
2. Which vegetables are organic?
3. What are the children eating?
4. What is the woman counting? Why?

Read the story.

The Farmers' Market

On Saturdays, the Novaks go to the farmers' market. They like to visit the vendors. Alex Novak always goes to the hot food stand for lunch. His children love to eat the fruit samples. Alex's father usually buys some sweets and lemonade. The lemonade is very sour.

Nina Novak likes to buy organic herbs and vegetables. Today, she is buying avocados. The market worker counts eight avocados. She gives Nina one more for free.

There are other things to do at the market. The Novaks like to listen to the live music. Sometimes they meet friends there. The farmers' market is a great place for families on a Saturday afternoon.

Reread the story.

1. Read the first sentence of the story. How often do the Novaks go to the farmers' market? How do you know?
2. The story says, "The farmers' market is a great place for families." Find examples in the story that support this statement.

What do you think?

3. What's good, bad, or interesting about shopping at a farmers' market?
4. Imagine you are at the farmers' market. What will you buy?

Everyday Clothes 日常穿衣

1. shirt
   襯衫

2. jeans
   牛仔褲

3. dress
   洋裝 / 長裙

4. T-shirt
   T 恤

5. baseball cap
   棒球帽

6. socks
   襪子

7. running shoes
   跑鞋

A. **tie**
   繫鞋帶

BEST OF JAZZ CONCERT

TICKETS

BEST OF JAZZ

Listen and point. Take turns.

A: Point to <u>the dress</u>.
B: Point to <u>the T-shirt</u>.
A: Point to <u>the baseball cap</u>.

Dictate to your partner. Take turns.

A: Write <u>dress</u>.
B: Is that spelled <u>d-r-e-s-s</u>?
A: Yes, that's right.

ONE NIGHT ONLY

DOORS OPEN AT 8:00

8. blouse
女上衣

9. handbag / purse
手提袋

10. skirt
裙子 / 短裙

11. suit
西裝

12. slacks / pants
長褲

13. shoes
鞋

14. sweater
毛衣

B. **put on**
穿衣

Ways to compliment clothes

That's a pretty <u>dress</u>!
Those are great <u>shoes</u>!
I really like your <u>baseball cap</u>!

Role play. Compliment a friend.

A: <u>*That's a pretty dress! Green is a great colour on you.*</u>
B: *Thanks! I really like your…*

87

Casual, Work, and Formal Clothes 休閒、工作和正式服裝

Casual Clothes 休閒服裝

1. cap
   帽子

2. cardigan sweater
   羊毛衫

3. pullover sweater
   套頭毛衣

4. sport shirt
   運動衫

5. maternity dress
   孕婦裝

6. overalls
   工人裝

7. knit top
   毛織上衣

8. capris
   七分褲

9. sandals
   拖鞋

Work Clothes 工作服裝

10. uniform
    制服

11. business suit
    禮服西裝

12. tie
    領帶

13. briefcase
    公事包

More vocabulary

in fashion / in style: clothes that are popular now
outfit: clothes that look nice together
three-piece suit: matching jacket, vest, and slacks

Describe the people. Take turns.

A: *She's wearing a maternity dress.*
B: *He's wearing a uniform.*

Formal Clothes 正式服裝

14. sports jacket / sports coat
休閒外套

15. vest
背心

16. bow tie
領結

17. tuxedo
燕尾服

18. evening gown
晚禮服

19. clutch bag
手拿包

20. cocktail dress
雞尾酒裝

21. high heels
高跟鞋

Exercise Wear 運動服裝

22. sweatshirt / hoodie
長袖運動衫 / 連帽外套

23. sweatpants / track pants
運動褲

24. tank top
無袖短衫

25. shorts
短褲

Survey your class. Record the responses.

1. Do you prefer to wear formal or casual clothes?
2. Do you prefer to exercise in shorts or sweatpants?
Report: _25% of the class prefers to…_

Think about it. Discuss.

1. Look at pages 170–173. Which jobs require uniforms?
2. What's good and what's bad about wearing a uniform?
3. Describe a popular style. Do you like it? Why or why not?

89

1. hat 帽子	**5.** winter scarf 厚圍巾
2. (over)coat 外套	**6.** gloves 手套
3. headband 頭帶	**7.** headwrap 頭巾
4. leather jacket 皮夾克 / 皮褸	**8.** jacket 夾克 / 短褸

9. parka 風雪大衣	**13.** earmuffs 耳套
10. mittens 連指手套	**14.** down vest 羽絨背心
11. ski hat 滑雪帽	**15.** ski mask 滑雪面罩
12. leggings 緊身褲	**16.** down jacket 羽絨夾克 / 羽絨褸

17. umbrella 雨傘	**20.** rain boots 雨靴
18. raincoat 雨衣	**21.** trench coat 風雨衣
19. poncho 雨披	

22. swimming trunks 游泳褲	**25.** cover-up 衣罩
23. straw hat 草帽	**26.** swimsuit / bathing suit 泳裝
24. windbreaker 防風上衣	**27.** sunglasses 太陽眼鏡

Grammar Point: *should*

*It's raining. You **should** take an umbrella.*
*It's snowing. You **should** put on a scarf.*
*It's sunny. You **should** wear a straw hat.*

Pair practice. Make new conversations.

A: *It's <u>snowing</u>. You should put on <u>a scarf</u>.*
B: *Don't worry. I'm wearing my <u>parka</u>.*
A: *Good, and don't forget your <u>mittens</u>!*

Unisex Underwear
中性內衣

1. undershirt
   內衣

2. thermal undershirt
   保暖內衣

3. long underwear
   長袖內衣

Men's Underwear
男用內衣

4. boxer shorts
   拳擊短褲

5. briefs
   緊身內褲

6. athletic supporter / jockstrap
   護襠

Unisex Socks
中性襪子

7. ankle socks
   運動踝襪

8. crew socks
   半統襪

9. dress socks
   西裝襪

Women's Socks
女襪

10. low-cut socks
    短襪

11. ankle socks
    運動踝襪

12. knee-highs
    長筒襪

Women's Underwear 女用內衣

13. (bikini) panties
    （比基尼）
    三角褲

14. briefs / underpants
    內褲

15. body shaper / girdle
    緊身褲 /
    收腹塑型內衣

16. tights
    緊身褲

17. footless tights
    無襪緊身褲

18. pantyhose
    褲襪

19. bra
    胸罩

20. camisole
    內穿背心

21. shapewear slip
    塑身襯裙

22. half slip
    襯裙

Sleepwear 睡服

23. pajamas
    睡衣

24. nightgown
    長袍

25. slippers
    拖鞋

26. blanket sleeper
    棉被衣

27. nightshirt
    貼身睡衣

28. robe
    睡袍

More vocabulary

lingerie: underwear or sleepwear for women

loungewear: very casual clothing for relaxing around the home

Survey your class. Record the responses.

1. What colour socks do you prefer?
2. What type of socks do you prefer?

Report: *Joe prefers white crew socks.*

91

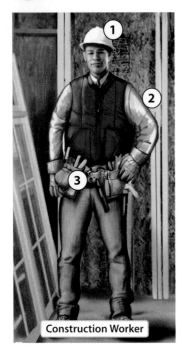

Construction Worker

Road Worker

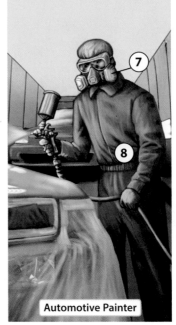

Automotive Painter

Food Processor

1. hard hat
安全頭盔

2. work shirt
工作衫

3. tool belt
工具腰帶

4. (high visibility) safety vest
(反光) 安全背心

5. work pants
工作褲

6. steel toe boots
鋼頭靴

7. ventilation mask
通風面罩

8. coveralls
連身工作服

9. bump cap
防衝撞安全帽

10. safety glasses
安全眼鏡

11. apron
圍裙

Manager   **Salesperson**

Farmworker

Ranch Hand

12. blazer
西裝外套

13. tie
領帶

14. polo shirt
馬球衫

15. name tag
名牌

16. bandana
頭巾

17. work gloves
工作手套

18. cowboy hat
牛仔帽

19. jeans
牛仔褲

Use the new words.
Look at pages 170–173. Name the workplace clothing you see.

A: *Look at #37. She's wearing a hard hat.*
B: *Look at #47. He's wearing a lab coat.*

Pair practice. Make sentences.
Dictate them to your classmates.

A. *Farm workers wear jeans to work.*
B. *A manager often wears a tie to work.*

Security Guard

Emergency Worker

Counterperson

Chef

Line Cook

20. security shirt
保安制服衫

21. badge
徽章

22. security pants
保安制服褲

23. helmet
頭盔

24. jumpsuit
連身衣

25. hairnet
髮網

26. smock
罩衫

27. disposable gloves
一次用手套

28. chef's hat
廚師帽

29. chef's jacket
廚師夾克

30. waist apron
腰圍裙

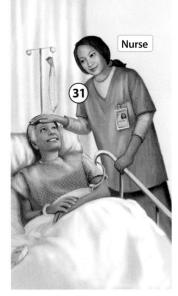

Nurse

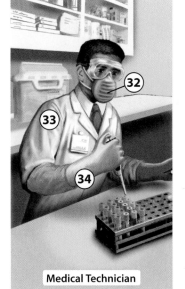

Medical Technician

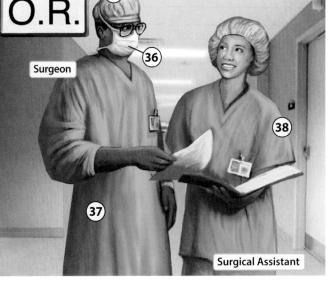

O.R.

Surgeon

Surgical Assistant

31. scrubs
護士服

32. face mask
口罩

33. lab coat
化驗室外衣

34. medical gloves
醫用手套

35. surgical scrub cap
手術帽

36. surgical mask
手術口罩

37. surgical gown
手術袍

38. surgical scrubs
手術服

Identify Anya's problem. Brainstorm solutions.

Anya works at a sandwich counter. Her bus ride to work is an hour. She has to wear a hairnet at work, but today she forgot it at home. What can she do?

Think about it. Discuss.

1. What other jobs require helmets? disposable gloves?
2. Is it better to have a uniform or wear your own clothes at work? Why?

A. purchase / buy
購買

B. wait in line
排隊等候

1. suspenders
吊帶

2. purses / handbags
皮包 / 手袋

3. salesclerk
銷售員

4. customer
顧客

5. display case
展示櫃

6. belts
皮帶

13. wallet
皮夾

14. change purse / coin purse
零錢包

15. cell phone case
行動電話套

16. (wrist)watch
手表

17. shoulder bag
肩背皮包

18. backpack
背包

19. tote bag
手提袋

20. belt buckle
皮帶環扣

21. sole
鞋底

22. heel
鞋跟

23. toe
鞋頭

24. shoelaces
鞋帶

More vocabulary

athletic shoes: tennis shoes, running shoes, etc.

gift / present: something you give to (or receive from) friends or family for a special occasion

Grammar Point: object pronouns

My **sister** loves jewellery. I'll buy **her** a necklace.

My **dad** likes belts. I'll buy **him** a belt buckle.

My **friends** love scarves. I'll buy **them** scarves.

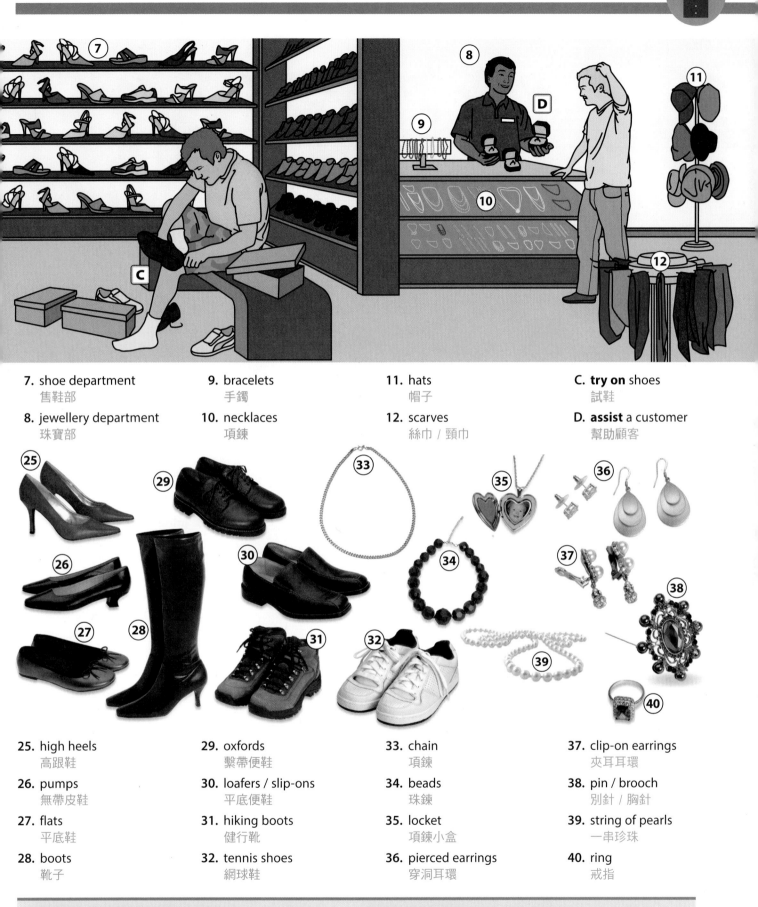

7. shoe department
售鞋部

8. jewellery department
珠寶部

9. bracelets
手鐲

10. necklaces
項鍊

11. hats
帽子

12. scarves
絲巾 / 頸巾

C. **try on** shoes
試鞋

D. **assist** a customer
幫助顧客

25. high heels
高跟鞋

26. pumps
無帶皮鞋

27. flats
平底鞋

28. boots
靴子

29. oxfords
繫帶便鞋

30. loafers / slip-ons
平底便鞋

31. hiking boots
健行靴

32. tennis shoes
網球鞋

33. chain
項鍊

34. beads
珠鍊

35. locket
項鍊小盒

36. pierced earrings
穿洞耳環

37. clip-on earrings
夾耳耳環

38. pin / brooch
別針 / 胸針

39. string of pearls
一串珍珠

40. ring
戒指

Ways to talk about accessories

I need <u>a hat</u> to wear with <u>this scarf</u>.
I'd like a pair of <u>earrings</u> to match <u>this necklace</u>.
Do you have <u>a belt</u> that would go with my <u>shoes</u>?

Role play. Talk to a salesperson.

A: Do you have <u>boots</u> that would go with <u>this skirt</u>?
B: Let me see. How about <u>these brown ones</u>?
A: Perfect. I also need…

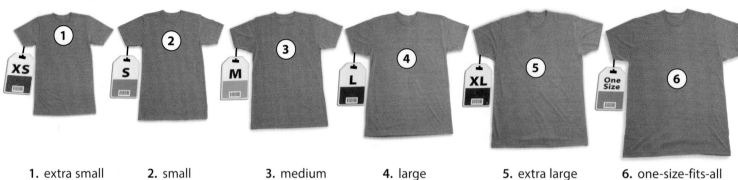

Describing Clothes 描述衣服

Sizes 尺寸

1. extra small
   特小號
2. small
   小號
3. medium
   中號
4. large
   大號
5. extra large
   特大號
6. one-size-fits-all
   超大號

Styles 款式

7. **crewneck** sweater
   短領毛衣
8. **V-neck** sweater
   尖領毛衣
9. **turtleneck** sweater
   高領毛衣
10. **scoop neck** sweater
    圓領毛衣

11. **sleeveless** shirt / tank top
    無袖襯衫 / 背心
12. **short-sleeved** shirt
    短袖襯衫
13. **3/4-sleeved** shirt
    七分袖襯衫
14. **long-sleeved** shirt
    長袖襯衫

15. **miniskirt**
    迷你裙
16. **short** skirt
    短裙
17. **mid-length** / **calf-length** skirt
    中長裙 / 中短裙
18. **long** skirt
    長裙 / 長短裙

Patterns 樣式

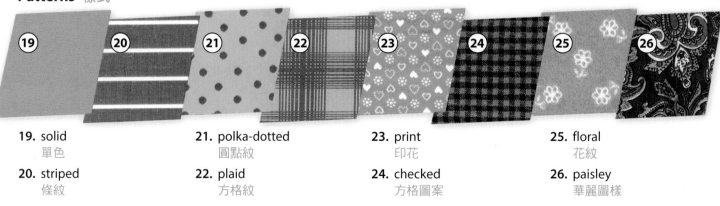

19. solid
    單色
20. striped
    條紋

21. polka-dotted
    圓點紋
22. plaid
    方格紋

23. print
    印花
24. checked
    方格圖案

25. floral
    花紋
26. paisley
    華麗圖樣

Survey your class. Record the responses.

1. What type of sweater do you prefer?
2. What patterns do you prefer?
Report: _Three_ out of _ten_ prefer ____.

Role play. Talk to a salesperson.

A: _Excuse me. I'm looking for this <u>V-neck sweater</u> in <u>large</u>._
B: _Here's a <u>large</u>. It's on sale for $<u>19.99</u>._
A: _Wonderful! I'll take it. I'm also looking for…_

Comparing Clothing 比較衣服

27. heavy jacket
厚夾克 / 厚褸

28. light jacket
輕便夾克 / 薄褸

29. tight pants
緊身長褲

30. loose / baggy pants
寬鬆褲

31. low heels
低跟鞋

32. high heels
高跟鞋

33. plain blouse
素面上衣

34. fancy blouse
時髦上衣

35. narrow tie
窄領帶

36. wide tie
寬領帶

Clothing Problems 衣服的問題

37. It's **too small**.
太小。

38. It's **too big**.
太大。

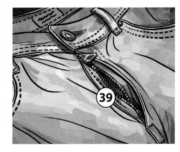

39. The zipper is **broken**.
拉鍊壞了。

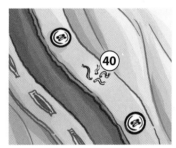

40. A button is **missing**.
鈕扣缺失。

41. It's **ripped / torn**.
衣服破了。

42. It's **stained**.
有汙跡。

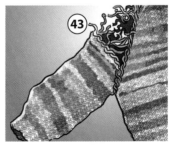

43. It's **unraveling**.
脫線。

44. It's **too expensive**.
太貴。

More vocabulary

complaint: a statement that something is not right
customer service: the place customers go with their complaints
refund: money you get back when you return an item to the store

Role play. Return an item to a salesperson.

A: *Welcome to Shopmart. How may I help you?*
B: *This sweater is new, but it's unraveling.*
A: *I'm sorry. Would you like a refund?*

Making Clothes 做衣服

Types of Material 布料種類

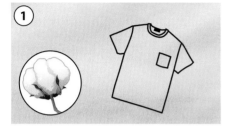

1. cotton
棉花

2. linen
亞麻

3. wool
羊毛

4. cashmere
山羊毛

5. silk
絲綢

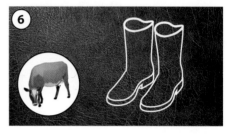

6. leather
皮革

A Garment Factory 車衣廠

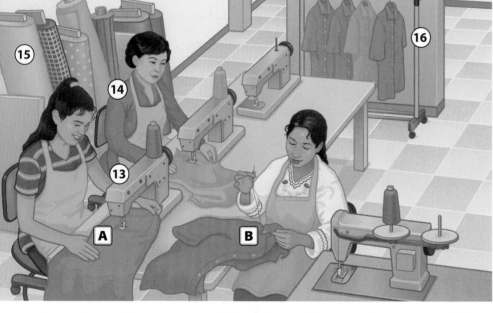

Parts of a Sewing Machine
縫紉機零件

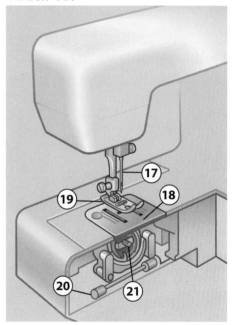

A. sew by machine 機器縫製	**14.** sewing machine operator 縫紉機操作員	**17.** needle 針	**20.** feed dog / feed bar 進給齒
B. sew by hand 手工縫製	**15.** bolt of fabric 布料卷	**18.** needle plate 針板	**21.** bobbin 線架
13. sewing machine 縫紉機	**16.** rack 衣架	**19.** presser foot 壓腳	

More vocabulary

fashion designer: a person who draws original clothes
natural materials: cloth made from things that grow in nature
synthetic materials: cloth made by people, such as nylon

Use the new words.

Look at pages 86–87. Name the materials you see.

A: *Look at her pants. They're denim.*
B: *Look at his shoes. They're leather.*

Types of Material 布料種類

7. denim
斜紋布 / 牛仔布

8. suede
仿麂皮

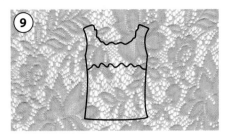

9. lace
花邊布

10. velvet
鵝絨布

11. corduroy
燈心絨

12. nylon
尼龍

A Fabric Store 布料店

Closures 鎖釦件

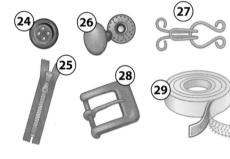

Trim 鑲邊

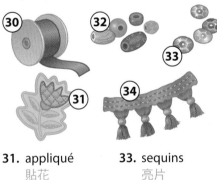

22. pattern 樣式	**25.** zipper 拉鍊	**28.** buckle 環扣
23. thread 線	**26.** snap 按扣	**29.** hook and loop fastener 鉤環固定件
24. button 鈕扣	**27.** hook and eye 掛扣	**30.** ribbon 條帶

31. appliqué 貼花	**33.** sequins 亮片
32. beads 珠鍊	**34.** fringe 飾邊

Survey your class. Record the responses.

1. Can you sew?
2. What's your favourite type of material to wear?

Report: _Five_ of us can't sew. _Most_ of us like to wear _denim_.

Think about it. Discuss.

1. Which jobs require sewing skills?
2. You're going to make a shirt. What do you do first?
3. Which is better, hand sewn or machine sewn? Why?

An Alterations Shop 裁縫店

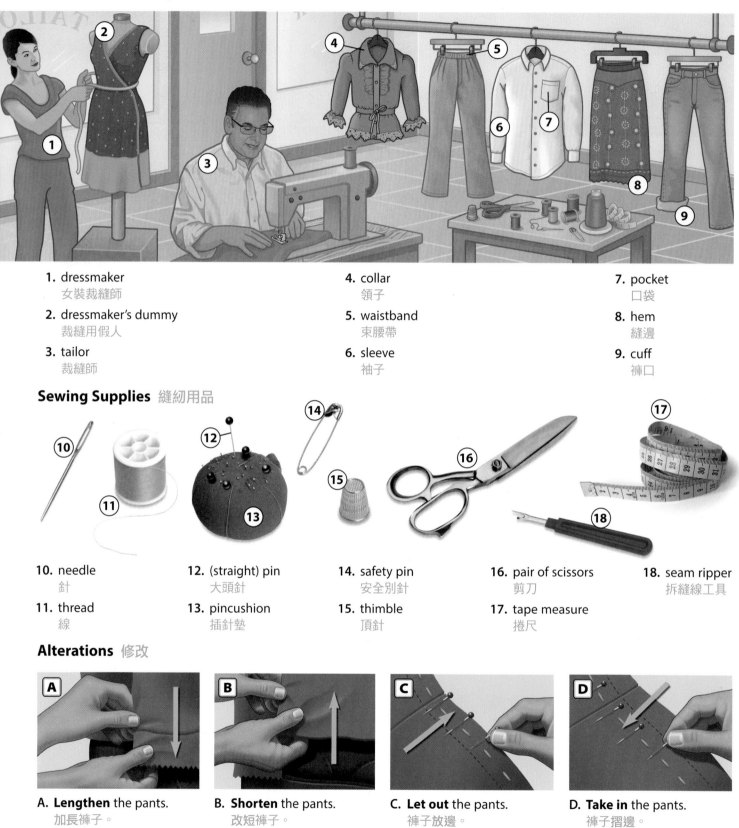

1. dressmaker
   女裝裁縫師
2. dressmaker's dummy
   裁縫用假人
3. tailor
   裁縫師

4. collar
   領子
5. waistband
   束腰帶
6. sleeve
   袖子

7. pocket
   口袋
8. hem
   縫邊
9. cuff
   褲口

Sewing Supplies 縫紉用品

10. needle
    針
11. thread
    線

12. (straight) pin
    大頭針
13. pincushion
    插針墊

14. safety pin
    安全別針
15. thimble
    頂針

16. pair of scissors
    剪刀
17. tape measure
    捲尺

18. seam ripper
    拆縫線工具

Alterations 修改

A. **Lengthen** the pants.
加長褲子。

B. **Shorten** the pants.
改短褲子。

C. **Let out** the pants.
褲子放邊。

D. **Take in** the pants.
褲子摺邊。

Pair practice. Make new conversations.

A: *Would you hand me the thread?*
B: *OK. What are you going to do?*
A: *I'm going to take in these pants.*

Survey your class. Record the responses.

1. How many pockets do you have?
2. How many pairs of scissors do you have at home?
Report: *Most of us have two ____.*

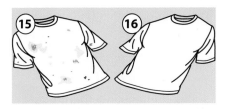
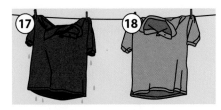
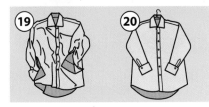

1. laundry
髒衣服

2. laundry basket
髒衣籃

3. washer
洗衣機

4. dryer
乾衣機

5. dryer sheets
烘乾紙

6. fabric softener
衣服鬆軟劑

7. bleach
漂白液

8. laundry detergent
洗衣粉

9. clothesline
掛衣繩

10. clothespin
衣夾

11. hanger
衣架

12. spray starch
噴衣漿

13. iron
熨斗

14. ironing board
燙衣板

15. **dirty** T-shirt
髒T恤

16. **clean** T-shirt
乾淨T恤

17. **wet** shirt
溼襯衫

18. **dry** shirt
乾襯衫

19. **wrinkled** shirt
有縐褶的襯衫

20. **ironed** shirt
燙平的襯衫

A. **Sort** the laundry.
髒衣分類。

B. **Add** the detergent.
放入洗衣粉。

C. **Load** the washer.
把衣服放入洗衣機內。

D. **Clean** the lint trap.
清理棉絨網。

E. **Unload / empty** the dryer.
把衣服從乾衣機內拿出來。

F. **Fold** the laundry.
疊衣服。

G. **Iron** the clothes.
燙熨衣服。

H. **Hang up** the clothes.
掛衣服。

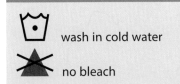 wash in cold water

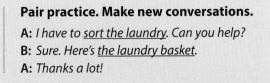 line dry

no bleach

dry clean only, do not wash

Pair practice. Make new conversations.

A: *I have to sort the laundry. Can you help?*
B: *Sure. Here's the laundry basket.*
A: *Thanks a lot!*

1. flyer
   廣告
2. used clothing
   舊衣服
3. sticker
   貼紙
4. folding card table
   摺疊方桌
5. folding chair
   摺疊椅
6. clock radio
   時鐘收音機
7. VCR
   卡式錄影機
8. CD / cassette player
   CD / 磁帶播放機
A. **bargain**
   講價
B. **browse**
   瀏覽

What do you see in the pictures?

1. What kinds of used clothing do you see?
2. What information is on the flyer?
3. Why are the stickers different colours?
4. How much is the clock radio? the VCR?

📄 Read the story.

A Garage Sale

Last Sunday, I had a garage sale. At 5:00 a.m., I put up <u>flyers</u> in my neighbourhood. Next, I put price <u>stickers</u> on my <u>used clothing</u>, my <u>VCR</u>, my <u>CD / cassette player</u>, and some other old things. At 7:00 a.m., I opened my <u>folding card table</u> and <u>folding chair</u>. Then I waited.

At 7:05 a.m., my first customer arrived. She asked, "How much is the sweatshirt?"

"Two dollars," I said.

She said, "It's stained. I can give you seventy-five cents." We <u>bargained</u> for a minute and she paid $1.00.

All day people came to <u>browse</u>, bargain, and buy. At 7:00 p.m., I had $85.00.

Now I know two things: garage sales are hard work, and nobody wants to buy an old <u>clock radio</u>!

Reread the story.

1. Look at the conversation. Circle the punctuation you see. What do you notice?

What do you think?

2. Do you like to buy things at garage sales? Why or why not?
3. Imagine you want the VCR. How will you bargain for it?

The Body 身體

1. head
   頭
2. hair
   頭髮
3. neck
   頸
4. chest
   胸
5. back
   背
6. nose
   鼻
7. mouth
   嘴
8. foot
   足

Listen and point. Take turns.

A: *Point to <u>the chest</u>.*
B: *Point to <u>the neck</u>.*
A: *Point to <u>the mouth</u>.*

Dictate to your partner. Take turns.

A: *Write <u>hair</u>.*
B: *Did you say <u>hair</u>?*
A: *That's right, <u>h-a-i-r</u>.*

9. leg
腿

10. toe
腳趾

11. eye
眼睛

12. ear
耳

13. shoulder
肩

14. arm
臂

15. hand
手

16. finger
手指

Grammar Point: imperatives

Please **touch** *your right foot.*
Put *your hands on your knees.*
Don't put *your hands on your shoulders.*

Pair practice. Take turns giving commands.

A: *Raise* your *arms*.
B: *Touch* your *feet*.
A: *Put* your *hand* on your *shoulder*.

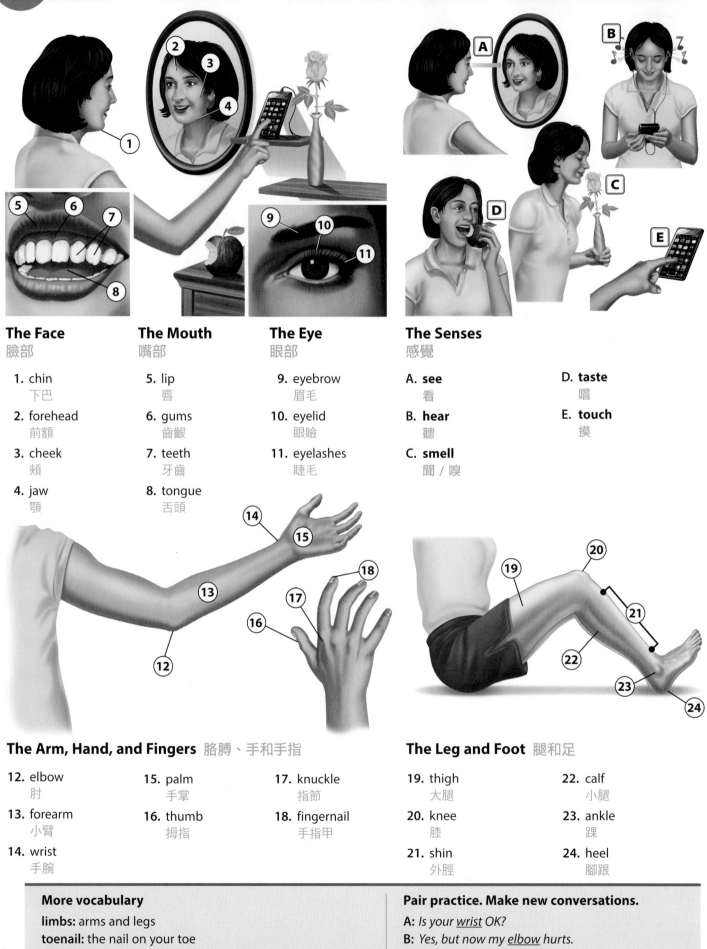

Inside and Outside the Body 身體內外

The Face
臉部

1. chin
   下巴
2. forehead
   前額
3. cheek
   頰
4. jaw
   顎

The Mouth
嘴部

5. lip
   唇
6. gums
   齒齦
7. teeth
   牙齒
8. tongue
   舌頭

The Eye
眼部

9. eyebrow
   眉毛
10. eyelid
    眼瞼
11. eyelashes
    睫毛

The Senses
感覺

A. see
   看
B. hear
   聽
C. smell
   聞 / 嗅
D. taste
   嚐
E. touch
   摸

The Arm, Hand, and Fingers 胳膊、手和手指

12. elbow
    肘
13. forearm
    小臂
14. wrist
    手腕
15. palm
    手掌
16. thumb
    拇指
17. knuckle
    指節
18. fingernail
    手指甲

The Leg and Foot 腿和足

19. thigh
    大腿
20. knee
    膝
21. shin
    外脛
22. calf
    小腿
23. ankle
    踝
24. heel
    腳跟

More vocabulary

limbs: arms and legs

toenail: the nail on your toe

torso: the part of the body from the shoulders to the pelvis

Pair practice. Make new conversations.

A: Is your wrist OK?

B: Yes, but now my elbow hurts.

A: I'm sorry to hear that.

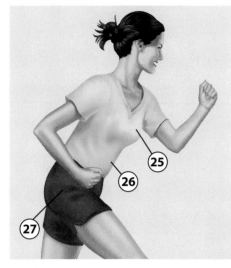

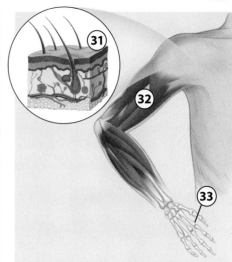

25. breast
乳房

26. abdomen
腹部

27. hip
髖部

28. shoulder blade
肩胛骨

29. lower back
腰

30. buttocks
臀

31. skin
皮膚

32. muscle
肌肉

33. bone
骨

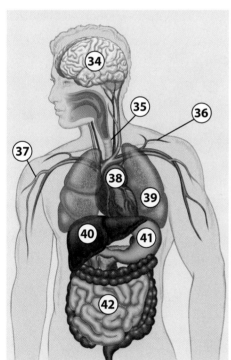

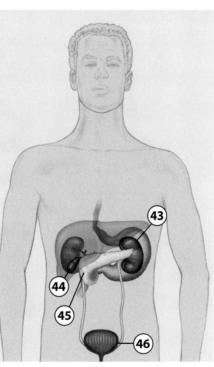

THE SKELETON

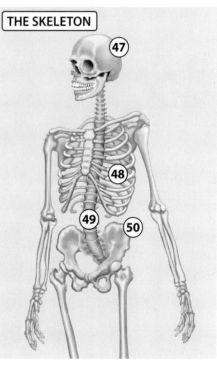

34. brain
腦

35. throat
喉嚨

36. artery
動脈

37. vein
靜脈

38. heart
心

39. lung
肺

40. liver
肝

41. stomach
胃

42. intestines
腸

43. kidney
腎

44. gallbladder
膽囊

45. pancreas
胰

46. bladder
膀胱

47. skull
顱骨

48. rib cage
肋骨

49. spinal column
脊椎

50. pelvis
骨盤

107

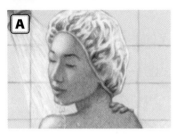

A. take a shower / **shower**
洗淋浴

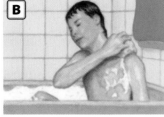

B. take a bath / **bathe**
洗盆浴

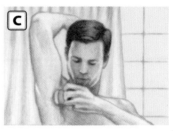

C. use deodorant
使用身體清香劑

D. put on sunscreen
擦防曬油

1. shower cap
   浴帽

2. shower gel
   沐浴凝膠

3. soap
   香皂

4. bath powder
   沐浴粉

5. deodorant / antiperspirant
   身體清香劑

6. perfume / cologne
   香水 / 古龍水

7. sunscreen
   防曬油

8. sunblock
   防曬霜

9. body lotion / moisturizer
   潤膚劑

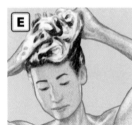

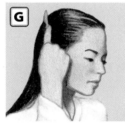
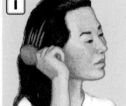

E. wash…hair
洗…頭髮

F. rinse…hair
沖洗…頭髮

G. comb…hair
梳…頭髮

H. dry…hair
吹乾…頭髮

I. brush…hair
刷…頭髮

10. shampoo
    洗髮精

11. conditioner
    潤髮乳

12. hairspray
    髮膠 / 定型噴霧

13. comb
    梳子

14. brush
    髮刷

15. pick
    挑梳

16. hair gel
    髮膠 / 啫喱

17. curling iron
    捲髮器

18. blow dryer
    吹風機 / 風筒

19. hair clip
    髮夾

20. barrette
    髮夾

21. bobby pins
    小髮夾

More vocabulary

hypoallergenic: a product that is better for people with allergies

unscented: a product without perfume or scent

Think about it. Discuss.

1. Which personal hygiene products are most important to use before a job interview? Why?

2. What is the right age to start wearing makeup? Why?

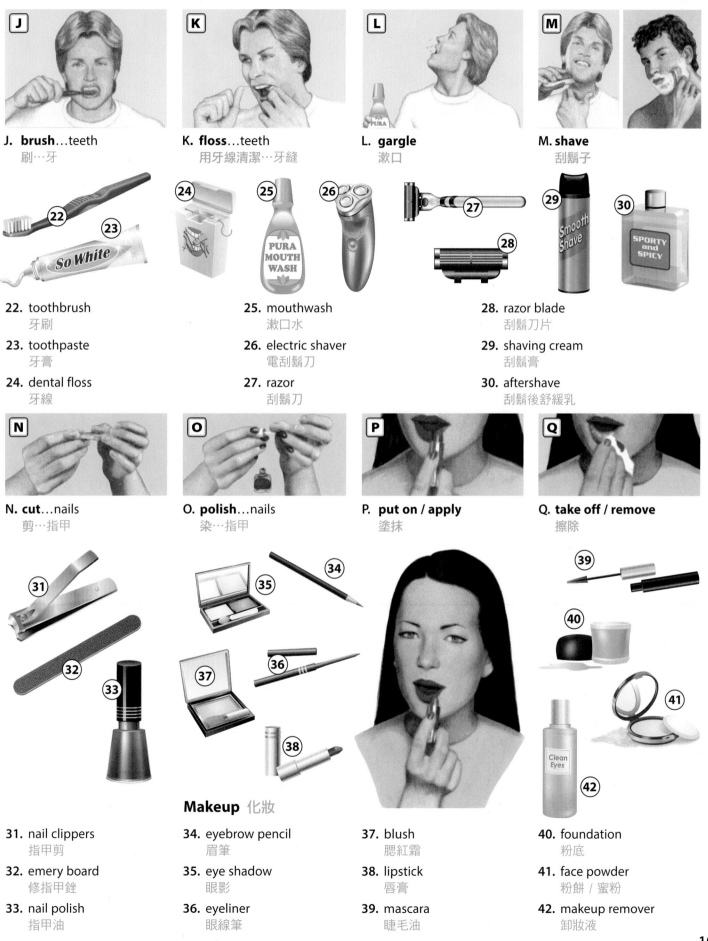

J. brush…teeth
刷…牙

K. floss…teeth
用牙線清潔…牙縫

L. gargle
漱口

M. shave
刮鬍子

22. toothbrush
牙刷

23. toothpaste
牙膏

24. dental floss
牙線

25. mouthwash
漱口水

26. electric shaver
電刮鬍刀

27. razor
刮鬍刀

28. razor blade
刮鬍刀片

29. shaving cream
刮鬍膏

30. aftershave
刮鬍後舒緩乳

N. cut…nails
剪…指甲

O. polish…nails
染…指甲

P. put on / apply
塗抹

Q. take off / remove
擦除

Makeup 化妝

31. nail clippers
指甲剪

32. emery board
修指甲銼

33. nail polish
指甲油

34. eyebrow pencil
眉筆

35. eye shadow
眼影

36. eyeliner
眼線筆

37. blush
腮紅霜

38. lipstick
唇膏

39. mascara
睫毛油

40. foundation
粉底

41. face powder
粉餅 / 蜜粉

42. makeup remover
卸妝液

109

 1
 2
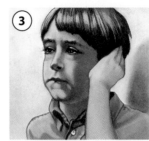 3
 A

 4
 5
 6
 B

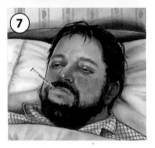 7
 8
 9
C

1. headache
頭痛

2. toothache
牙痛

3. earache
耳痛

4. stomach ache
胃痛

5. backache
背痛

6. sore throat
喉嚨痛

7. fever / temperature
發燒

8. chills
發冷

9. cough
咳嗽

A. feel dizzy
感覺暈眩

B. feel nauseous
感覺噁心

C. throw up / vomit
嘔吐

 10
 11
 12
13

 14
 15
 16
 17

10. insect bite
蚊蟲咬傷

11. bruise
瘀傷

12. cut
割傷

13. sunburn
曬傷

14. sprained ankle
腳踝扭傷

15. bleeding nose
流鼻血

16. swollen finger
手指紅腫

17. blister
水泡

18

WORKPLACE ACCIDENT NOTES

Name: _Thiu An_
Job Title: _Packer_
Date of accident: _Monday, 9/18/17_
Location of accident:
warehouse, Aisle 3
Description of accident:
3 boxes fell on me
Was safety equipment used?
☑ yes   ☐ no
Were you injured? _yes, sprained wrist_
and some bruises
....
PLEASE FILL OUT A COMPLETE ACCIDENT
FORM AS SOON AS POSSIBLE.

18. accident report
事故報告

Look at the pictures.
Describe the symptoms and injuries.

A: *He has a backache.*
B: *She has a toothache.*

Think about it. Discuss.
1. What do you recommend for a stomach ache?
2. What is the best way to stop a bleeding nose?
3. Who should stay home from work with a cold? Why?

In the Waiting Room 在候診室

Health Form

Name: *Andre Zolmar*
Date of birth: *July 8, 1983*
Current symptoms: *stomach ache*

Health History:

Childhood Diseases:
☑ chicken pox
☑ diphtheria
☑ rubella
☑ measles
☐ mumps
☐ other

Description of
symptoms:

Patient: Zolmar, Andre
Appt. Time: 2:00 PM

Patient:
Appt.Time: 2:30 PM
Patient:
Appt.Time: 3:00 PM

1. appointment
預約

2. receptionist
接待員

3. health card
保健卡

4. health history form
病歷表

In the Examining Room 在診斷室

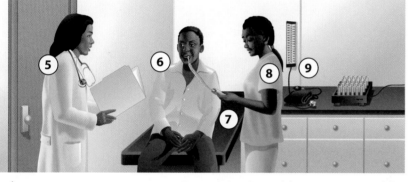

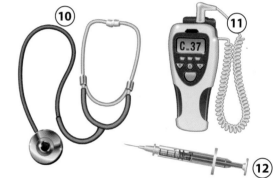

5. doctor
醫生

6. patient
病人

7. examination table
檢查床

8. nurse
護士

9. blood pressure gauge
血壓計

10. stethoscope
聽診器

11. thermometer
溫度計

12. syringe
注射器

Medical Procedures 醫療程序

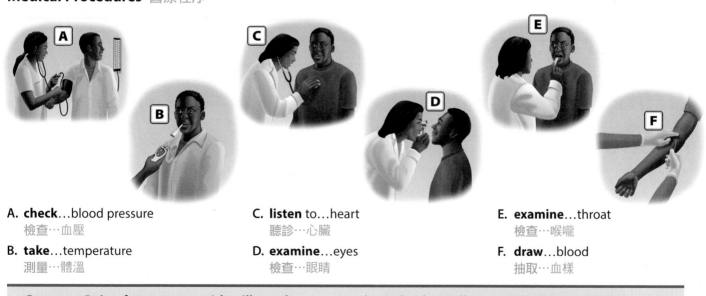

A. check…blood pressure
檢查…血壓

B. take…temperature
測量…體溫

C. listen to…heart
聽診…心臟

D. examine…eyes
檢查…眼睛

E. examine…throat
檢查…喉嚨

F. draw…blood
抽取…血樣

Grammar Point: future tense with *will* + verb

To describe a future action, use *will* + verb.
The contraction of *will* is *-'ll*.
She ***will draw*** your blood. = She***'ll draw*** your blood.

Role play. Talk to a medical receptionist.

A: *Will the nurse <u>examine my eyes</u>?*
B: *No, but she'll <u>draw your blood</u>.*
A: *What will the doctor do?*

111

Patient

First name | Last name | Reason for visit

_____ | _____ | _____

Common Illnesses 常見疾病

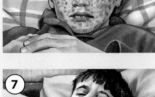

1. cold
   感冒

2. flu
   流行感冒

3. ear infection
   中耳炎

4. strep throat
   鏈球菌性喉炎

Medical History
Childhood and Infectious Diseases 童年疾病及傳染病

Vaccination date
免疫接種日期

5. measles   _____
   痲疹

6. chicken pox   _____
   水痘

7. mumps   _____
   腮腺炎

8. shingles   _____
   帶狀皰疹

9. hepatitis   _____
   肝炎

10. pneumonia   _____
    肺炎

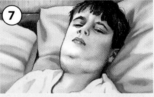 

11. allergies
    過敏

animals | shellfish | peanuts | drugs
動物 | 有殼水生動物 | 花生 | 藥物

I am allergic to:

_____

_____

_____

Survey your class. Record the responses.

1. Are you allergic to cats?
2. Are you allergic to shellfish?

Report: _Five of us are allergic to ____._

Identify Omar's problem. Brainstorm solutions.

Omar filled out only half of the medical history form at the clinic. Many words on the form were new to him, and two questions were very personal. The nurse was upset.

Allergic Reactions 過敏反應

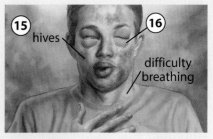

hives

difficulty breathing

12. sneezing
打噴嚏

13. nasal congestion
鼻塞

14. rash
疹子

15. anaphylaxis
急性過敏

16. swelling
腫脹

Medical Conditions 醫療狀況

	Patient		Family History			Patient		Family History
	Yes	No				Yes	No	
17. cancer 癌症	☐	☐	_____	**23.** TB / tuberculosis 肺結核		☐	☐	_____
18. asthma 氣喘	☐	☐	_____	**24.** high blood pressure / hypertension 高血壓		☐	☐	_____
19. dementia 癡呆	☐	☐	_____	**25.** intestinal parasites 腸內寄生蟲		☐	☐	_____
20. arthritis 關節炎	☐	☐	_____	**26.** diabetes 糖尿病		☐	☐	_____
21. HIV / AIDS 愛滋病	☐	☐	_____	**27.** kidney disease 腎病		☐	☐	_____
22. malaria 瘧疾	☐	☐	_____	**28.** heart disease 心臟病		☐	☐	_____

More vocabulary

AIDS (acquired immune deficiency syndrome): a medical condition that results from contracting the HIV virus
Alzheimer's disease: a disease that causes dementia

coronary disease: heart disease
infectious disease: a disease that is spread through air or water
influenza: flu

A Pharmacy 藥房

DROP-OFF

PICK-UP

Smallgreen Pharmacy
1818 Oak Ave
Moose Jaw, SK S6H 4K9   Dr. L. Luther   PHONE **555-5522**

NO **00859023–57988**   DATE 03/07/18

Alki Elmi
345 First Street, Moose Jaw, SK S6H 7Z1

TAKE ONE TABLET BY
MOUTH 2 TIMES A DAY
AS NEEDED FOR PAIN.

NAPROXEN 500 MG

REFILLS: 2

Discard after 03/07/20

May cause drowsiness.

Family Physician Medical Group Inc.
1515 Elm Court Suite 100, Moose Jaw, SK S6H 2M0
TEL: (800) 555-3999
CAL LIC. #54POI5U170   183098WUFCSDJE

PATIENT NAME: Bruce Kent
DOB: 02/28/78
DATE: 03/07/18

℞

Diclofenac 50 MG Refill: 0

Laura Lane, MD

1. **pharmacist**
   藥劑師

2. **prescription**
   處方

3. **prescription medication**
   處方藥

4. **prescription label**
   處方標籤

5. **prescription number**
   處方號

6. **dosage**
   劑量

7. **expiration date**
   有效日期

8. **warning label**
   警告標記

Medical Warnings 醫學警告

A. **Take** with food or milk.
與食物或牛奶一起服用。

B. **Take** one hour before eating.
飯前一小時服用。

C. **Finish** all medication.
服完所有藥物。

D. **Do not take** with dairy products.
不要與奶製品一起服用。

E. **Do not drive or operate** heavy machinery.
不要開車或操作重型機械。

F. **Do not drink** alcohol.
不要飲酒。

More vocabulary

prescribe medication: to write a prescription
fill prescriptions: to prepare medications for patients
pick up a prescription: to get prescription medication

Role play. Talk to the pharmacist.

A: *Hi. I need to pick up a prescription for <u>Jones</u>.*
B: *Here's your medication, <u>Mr. Jones</u>. Take these <u>once a day with milk or food</u>.*

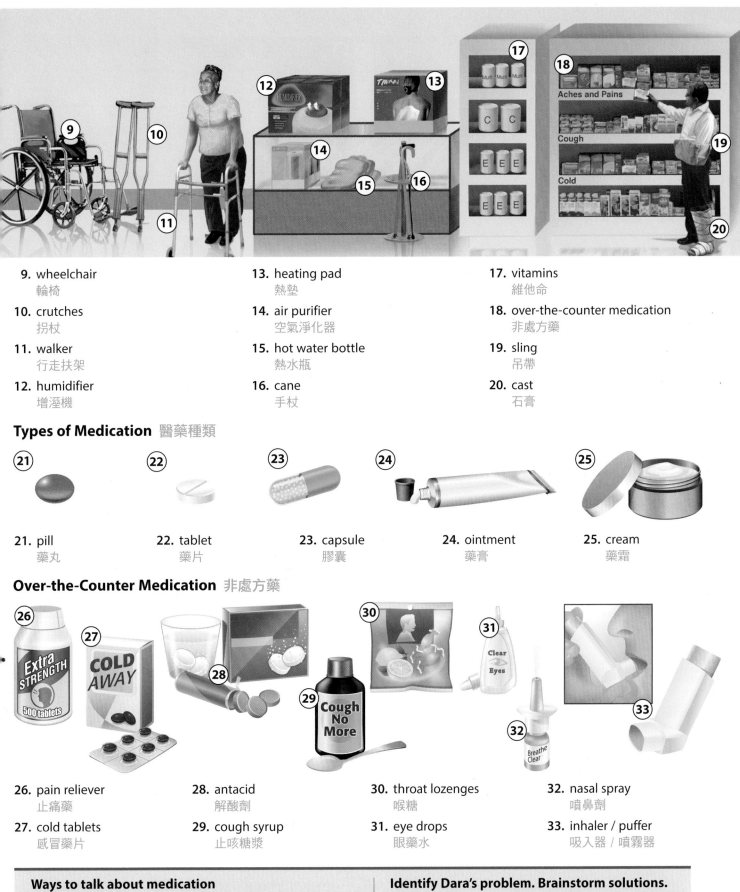

9. wheelchair
輪椅

10. crutches
拐杖

11. walker
行走扶架

12. humidifier
增溼機

13. heating pad
熱墊

14. air purifier
空氣淨化器

15. hot water bottle
熱水瓶

16. cane
手杖

17. vitamins
維他命

18. over-the-counter medication
非處方藥

19. sling
吊帶

20. cast
石膏

Types of Medication 醫藥種類

21. pill
藥丸

22. tablet
藥片

23. capsule
膠囊

24. ointment
藥膏

25. cream
藥霜

Over-the-Counter Medication 非處方藥

26. pain reliever
止痛藥

27. cold tablets
感冒藥片

28. antacid
解酸劑

29. cough syrup
止咳糖漿

30. throat lozenges
喉糖

31. eye drops
眼藥水

32. nasal spray
噴鼻劑

33. inhaler / puffer
吸入器 / 噴霧器

Ways to talk about medication

Use *take* for pills, tablets, capsules, and cough syrup.
Use *apply* for ointments and creams.
Use *use* for drops, nasal sprays, and inhalers.

Identify Dara's problem. Brainstorm solutions.

Dara's father is 85 and lives alone. She lives nearby.
Her dad has many prescriptions. He often forgets to
take his medication or takes the wrong pills.

115

Ways to Get Well 恢復健康的方式

A. Seek medical attention.
看醫生。

B. Get bed rest.
臥床休息。

C. Drink fluids.
飲用液體。

D. Take medicine.
吃藥。

Ways to Stay Well 保持健康的方式

E. Stay fit.
保持健康的體魄。

F. Eat a healthy diet.
吃健康飲食。

G. Don't smoke.
不吸菸。

Ms. Jones, you must stop smoking!

H. Have regular checkups.
定期檢查身體。

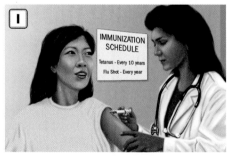

I. Get immunized.
打免疫針。

J. Follow medical advice.
遵循醫生囑咐。

More vocabulary

injection: medicine in a syringe that is put into the body
immunization / vaccination: an injection that stops serious diseases

Survey your class. Record the responses.

1. How do you stay fit?
2. Which two foods are a part of your healthy diet?
Report: *I surveyed ten people who said they ____.*

Types of Health Problems 健康問題的種類

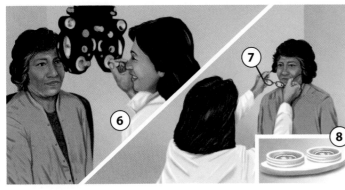
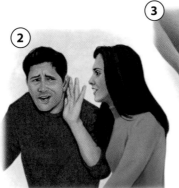

1. vision problems
視力問題

2. hearing loss
聽覺衰退

3. pain
疼痛

4. stress
緊張

5. depression
抑鬱

Help with Health Problems 幫助解決健康問題

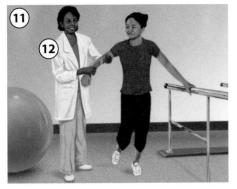

6. optometrist
驗光師

8. contact lenses
隱形眼鏡

9. audiologist
聽覺檢查師

10. hearing aid
助聽器

7. glasses
眼鏡

11. physiotherapy
理療

12. physiotherapist
理療師

13. talk therapy
談話治療

14. therapist
治療師

15. support group
互助小組

Ways to ask about health problems

Are you in pain?
Are you having vision problems?
Are you experiencing depression?

Pair practice. Make new conversations.

A: *Do you know a good optometrist?*
B: *Why? Are you having vision problems?*
A: *Yes, I might need glasses.*

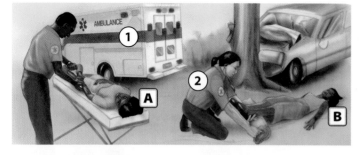
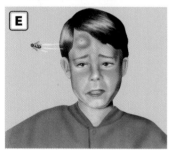

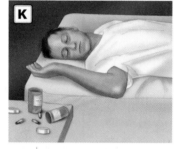

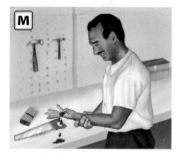

1. ambulance
   救護車

2. paramedic
   急救護理員

A. **be** unconscious
   失去知覺

B. **be** in shock
   休克

C. **be** injured / **be** hurt
   受傷

D. **have** a heart attack
   心臟病發作

E. **have** an allergic reaction
   發生過敏反應

F. **get** an electric shock
   觸電

G. **get** frostbite
   凍傷

H. **burn** (your)self
   灼傷（你）自己

I. **drown**
   溺水

J. **swallow** poison
   吞食有毒物質

K. **overdose** on drugs
   服藥過量

L. **choke**
   噎塞

M. **bleed**
   流血

N. **be unable to breathe**
   無法呼吸

O. **fall**
   跌倒

P. **break** a bone
   骨折

Grammar Point: past tense

For past tense, add -*d* or -*ed*.
burn**ed**, drown**ed**, swallow**ed**,
overdose**d**, choke**d**

These verbs are different (irregular):

be – was, were	get – got	break – broke
be unable – can't, couldn't	bleed – bled	
have – had	fall – fell	

First Aid 急救

1. first aid kit
急救箱

2. first aid manual
急救手冊

3. medical emergency bracelet
急救手環帶

4. AED / automated external defibrillator
自動體外電擊去顫器

Inside the Kit 急救箱內物品

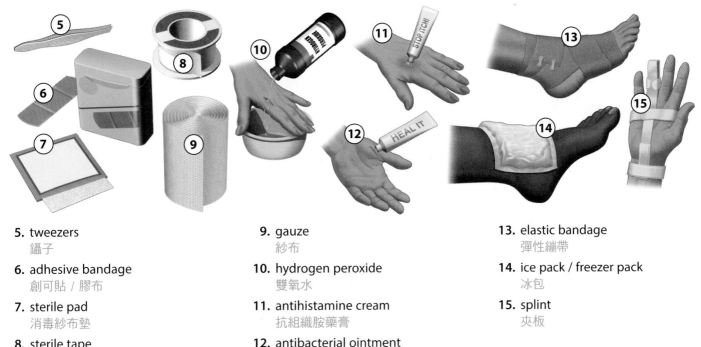

5. tweezers
鑷子

6. adhesive bandage
創可貼 / 膠布

7. sterile pad
消毒紗布墊

8. sterile tape
消毒膠布

9. gauze
紗布

10. hydrogen peroxide
雙氧水

11. antihistamine cream
抗組織胺藥膏

12. antibacterial ointment
消毒藥膏

13. elastic bandage
彈性繃帶

14. ice pack / freezer pack
冰包

15. splint
夾板

First Aid Procedures 急救程序

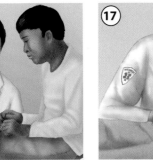

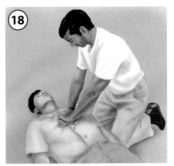

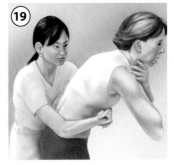

16. stitches
縫針

17. rescue breathing
人工呼吸

18. CPR (cardiopulmonary resuscitation)
心肺復甦

19. Heimlich manoeuvre
哈姆立克急救法

Pair practice. Make new conversations.

A: *What do we need in the first aid kit?*
B: *We need tweezers and gauze.*
A: *I think we need sterile tape, too.*

Internet Research: first aid class

Type "first aid," "class," and your postal code in a search engine. Look for a class near you.
Report: *I found a first aid class at ____.*

Dentistry 牙科

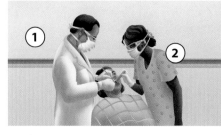

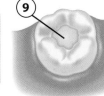

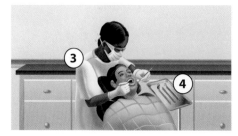

Orthodontics 齒列矯正

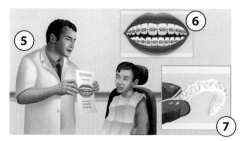

1. dentist
牙醫師

2. dental assistant
牙醫助理

3. dental hygienist
口腔衛生師

4. dental instruments
牙科器械

5. orthodontist
矯牙醫師

6. braces
牙套

7. retainer
維持器 / 固定器

Dental Problems 牙科問題

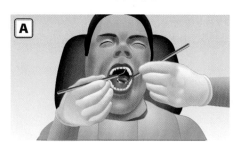

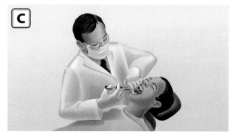

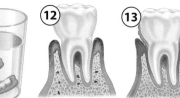

8. cavity / decay
蛀牙

9. filling
補牙粉

10. crown
牙冠

11. dentures
假牙

12. gum disease
牙周病

13. plaque
牙菌斑

An Office Visit 看牙醫

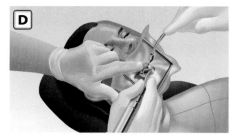

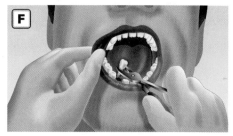

A. clean the teeth
清潔牙齒

B. take X-rays
拍攝X光片

C. numb the mouth
口腔麻醉

D. drill a tooth
鑽牙

E. fill a cavity
補牙

F. pull a tooth
拔牙

Role play. Talk to a dentist.

A: *I think I have a cavity.*
B: *Let me take a look. Yes. I will need to drill that tooth.*
A: *Oh! How much will that cost?*

Identify Leo's problem. Brainstorm solutions.

Leo has a bad toothache. His wife says, "Call the dentist." Leo doesn't want to call. He takes pain medication. The toothache doesn't stop.

Universal Health Care 全民醫療保健

1. doctor's office
   醫生診所

2. physician
   醫師

3. walk-in clinic
   無預約診所

4. hospital emergency room
   醫院急診室

5. injury
   受傷

6. operation
   手術

Primary Care 基本醫療保健

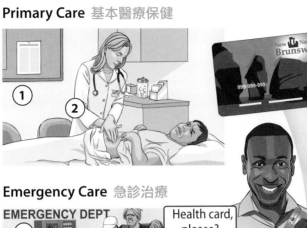

After-Hours Care 下班後治療

WALK-IN CLINIC

Emergency Care 急診治療

EMERGENCY DEPT

Health card, please?

Hospital Care 醫院治療

Other Health Needs 其他保健需求

Dental Care 牙科保健

Prescription Medications 處方藥物

Vision Care 眼科保健

Paramedical Services 輔助醫療服務

7. physiotherapy
   理療

8. chiropractic treatment
   脊骨按摩治療

9. massage therapy
   按摩治療

Paying for Other Health Needs 為其他保健需求付費

AMBULANCE STATION 12

You're hired!

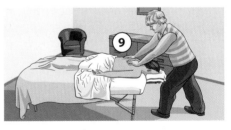

GreatNorth Health Insurance Company

10. out-of-pocket
    自付

11. employee benefits
    員工福利

12. private insurance
    私人保險

Medical Specialists 專科醫師

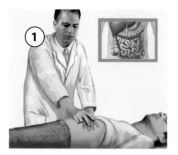

1. internist
內科醫師

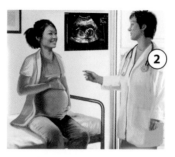

2. obstetrician
產科醫師

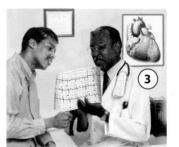

3. cardiologist
心臟科醫師

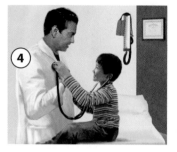

4. pediatrician
小兒科醫師

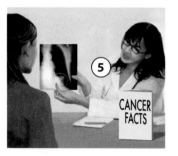

5. oncologist
腫瘤科醫師

CANCER FACTS

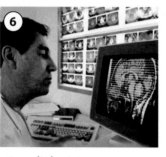

6. radiologist
放射科醫師

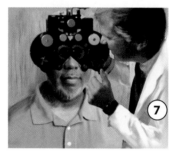

7. ophthalmologist
眼科醫師

8. psychiatrist
心理醫師

Nursing Staff 護理人員

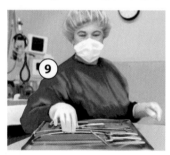

9. surgical nurse
外科護士

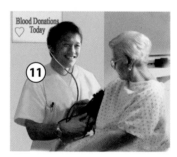

10. registered nurse (RN)
註冊護士

Blood Donations Today

11. registered practical nurse (RPN)
註冊執業護士

12. nursing assistant
助理護士

Hospital Staff 醫院職員

IN

13. administrator
管理人員

ADMISSIONS

14. admissions clerk
前台職員

15. dietician
營養師

16. orderly
勤雜工

More vocabulary

Gynecologists examine and treat women.
Nurse practitioners can give medical exams.
Nurse midwives deliver babies.

Chiropractors move the spine to improve health.
Orthopedists treat bone and joint problems.
Dermatologists treat skin conditions.
Urologists treat bladder and kidney problems.

A Hospital Room 醫院病房

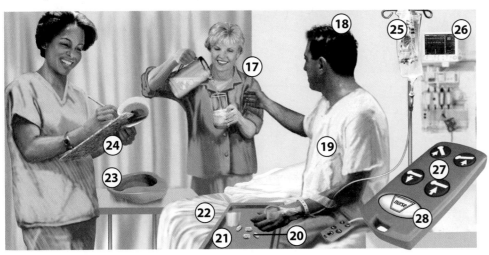

Lab 化驗室

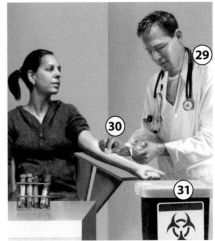

17. volunteer
    義工

18. patient
    病人

19. hospital gown
    病人袍

20. medication
    醫藥

21. over-bed table
    床桌

22. hospital bed
    病床

23. bedpan
    便盆

24. medical chart
    病歷表

25. IV (intravenous drip)
    靜脈滴注

26. vital signs monitor
    病人生理狀況監視器

27. bed control
    病床控制

28. call button
    呼叫鈕

29. phlebotomist
    抽血師

30. blood work / blood test
    驗血

31. medical waste disposal
    醫療用品垃圾桶

Emergency Room Entrance
急診室入口

Operating Room 手術室

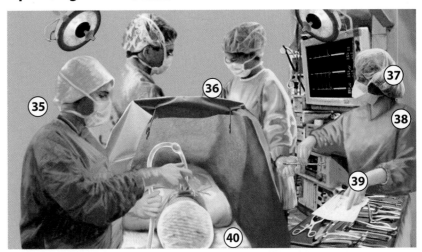

32. paramedic
    急救護理人員

33. stretcher / gurney
    擔架車

34. ambulance
    救護車

35. anesthesiologist
    麻醉師

36. surgeon
    外科醫生

37. surgical cap
    手術帽

38. surgical gown
    手術袍

39. surgical gloves
    手術手套

40. operating table
    手術台

Dictate to your partner. Take turns.

A: *Write this sentence: She's a volunteer.*
B: *She's a what?*
A: *Volunteer. That's v-o-l-u-n-t-e-e-r.*

Role play. Ask about a doctor.

A: *I need to find a good surgeon.*
B: *Dr. Jones is a great surgeon. You should call him.*
A: *I will! Please give me his number.*

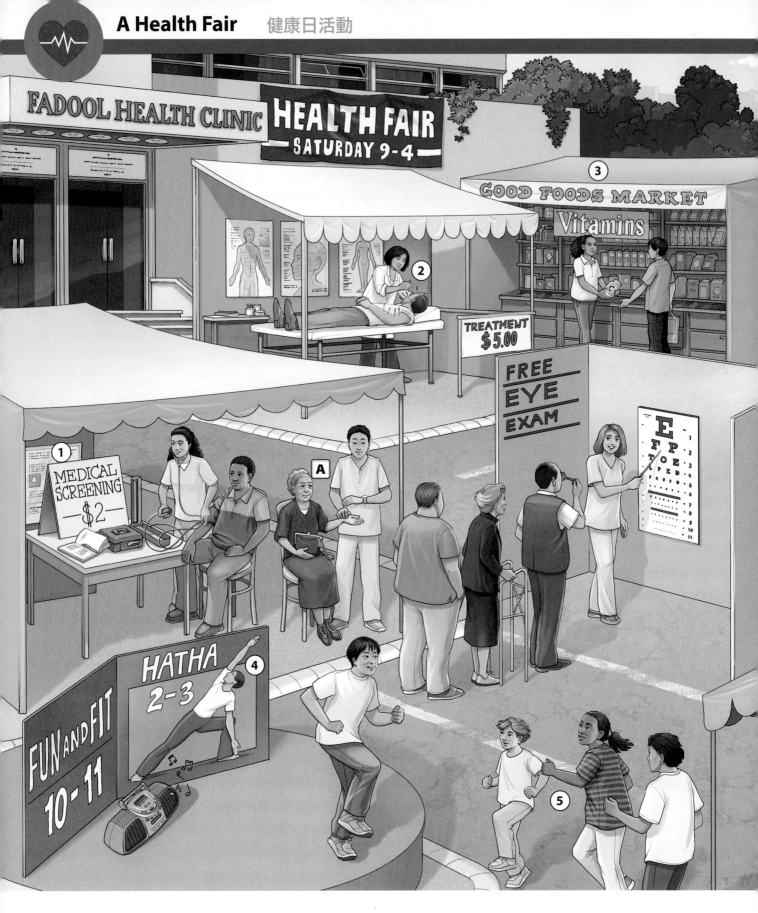

1. medical exam
   醫療檢查

2. acupuncture
   針灸

3. booth
   攤位

4. yoga
   瑜珈

5. aerobic exercise
   體操運動

6. demonstration
   示範

7. sugar-free
   無糖

8. nutrition label
   營養標籤

A. **check**…pulse
   檢查…心率

B. **give** a lecture
   講課

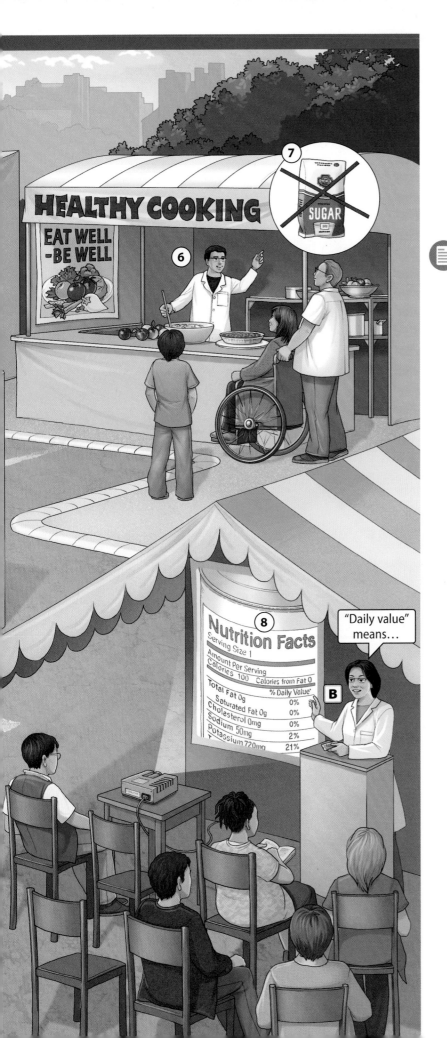

What do you see in the picture?

1. Where is this health fair?
2. What kinds of exams and treatments can you get at this fair?
3. What kinds of lectures and demonstrations can you attend here?
4. How much money should you bring? Why?

Read the article.

A Health Fair

Once a month the Fadool Health Clinic has a health fair. You can get a medical <u>exam</u> at one <u>booth</u>. The nurses check your blood pressure and <u>check</u> your <u>pulse</u>. At another booth, you can get a free eye exam. And an <u>acupuncture</u> treatment is only $5.00.

You can learn a lot at the fair. This month a doctor <u>is giving a lecture</u> on <u>nutrition labels</u>. There is also a <u>demonstration</u> on <u>sugar-free</u> cooking. You can learn to do <u>aerobic exercise</u> and <u>yoga</u>, too.

Do you want to get healthy and stay healthy? Then come to the Fadool Health Clinic Fair! We want to see you there!

Reread the article.

1. Who wrote this article? How do you know?
2. What information in the picture is *not* in the article?

What do you think?

3. Which booths at this fair look interesting to you? Why?
4. Do you read nutrition labels? Why or why not?

Downtown 市中心

1. parking garage
   停車場

2. office building
   辦公樓

3. hotel
   旅館

4. driver licensing office
   駕照發放處

5. bank
   銀行

6. police station
   警察局

7. bus station
   公車站

8. city hall
   市政廳

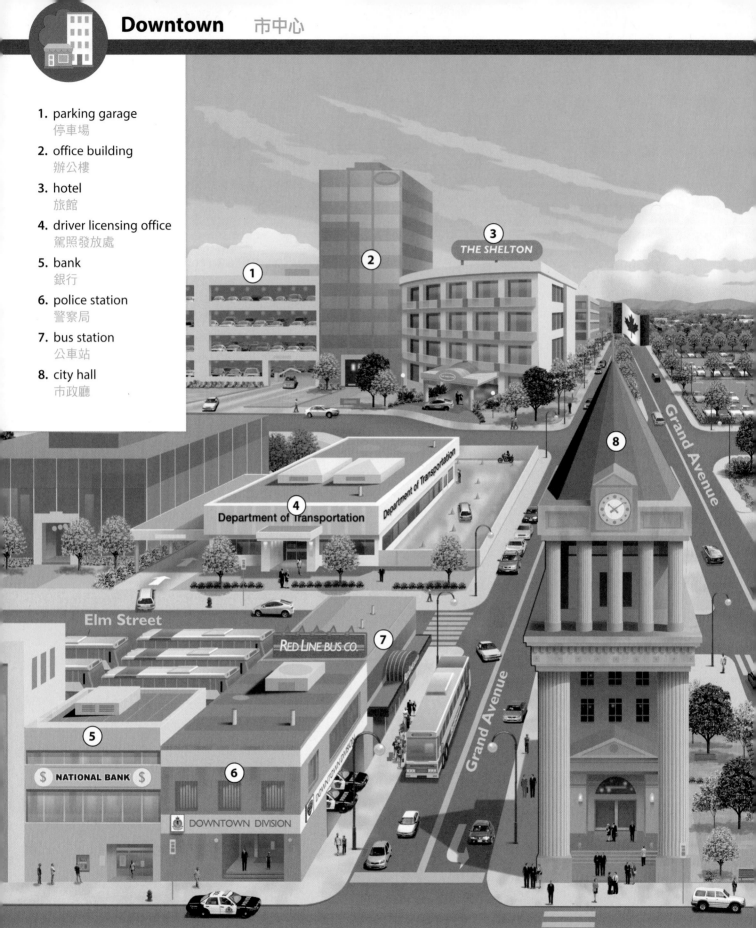

THE SHELTON

Department of Transportation

Grand Avenue

Elm Street

RED LINE BUS CO.

$ NATIONAL BANK $

DOWNTOWN DIVISION

Listen and point. Take turns.

A: *Point to the bank.*
B: *Point to the hotel.*
A: *Point to the restaurant.*

Dictate to your partner. Take turns.

A: *Write bank.*
B: *Is that spelled b-a-n-k?*
A: *Yes, that's right.*

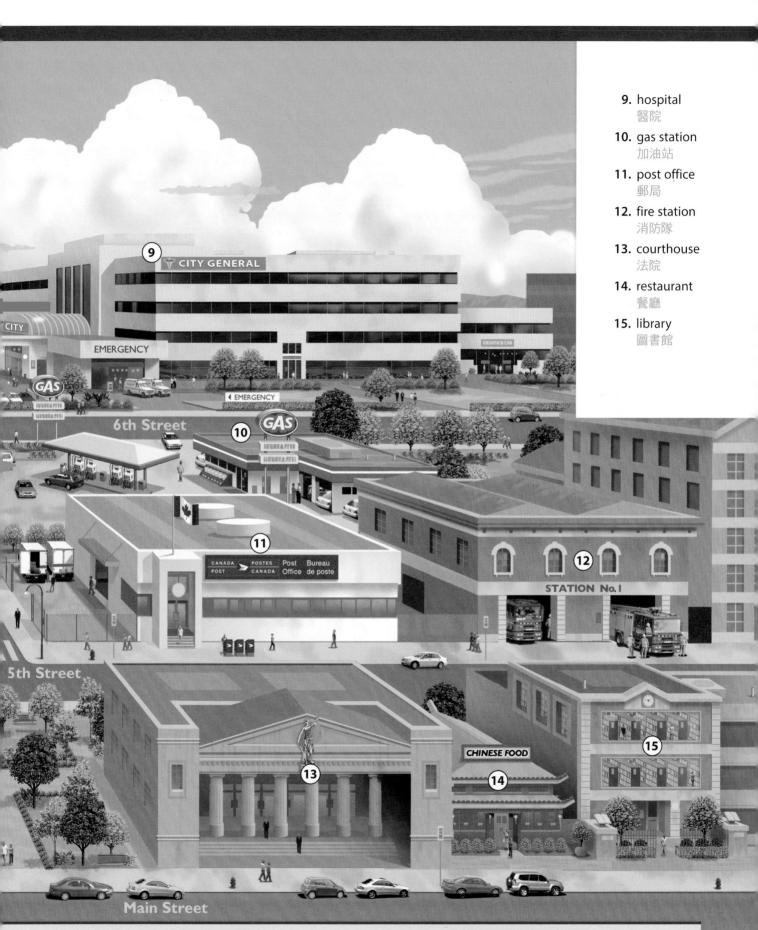

9. hospital
醫院

10. gas station
加油站

11. post office
郵局

12. fire station
消防隊

13. courthouse
法院

14. restaurant
餐廳

15. library
圖書館

Grammar Point: *in* and *at* with locations

Use *in* when you are inside the building. *I am in (inside) the bank.* Use *at* to describe your general location. *I am at the bank.*

Pair practice. Make new conversations.

A: *I'm in the <u>bank</u>. Where are you?*

B: *I'm at the <u>bank</u>, too, but I'm outside.*

A: *OK. I'll meet you there.*

1. stadium
運動場

2. construction site
建築工地

3. factory
工廠

4. car dealership
汽車經銷商

5. mosque
清真寺

6. movie theatre
電影院

7. shopping mall
購物中心

8. furniture store
家具店

9. school
學校

10. gym
體育館

11. coffee shop
咖啡店

12. motel
汽車旅館

Ways to state your destination using *to* and *to the*

Use *to* for schools, churches, and synagogues.
I'm going to school.

128 Use *to the* for all other locations. *I have to go to the bakery.*

Pair practice. Make new conversations.

A: *Where are you going today?*

B: *I'm going to school. How about you?*

A: *I have to go to the bakery.*

13. skyscraper / high-rise
摩天大樓

14. church
教堂

15. cemetery
墓地

16. synagogue
猶太教堂

17. (community) college
（社區）學院

18. supermarket / grocery store
超級市場 / 雜貨店

19. bakery
麵包糕點店

20. home improvement store
住宅裝潢修繕用品店

21. office supply store
辦公用品商店

22. garbage truck
垃圾車

23. theatre
劇院

24. convention centre
會議中心

Ways to give locations

The mall is on Second Street.
The mall is on the corner of Second and Elm.
The mall is next to the movie theatre.

Survey your class. Record the responses.

1. Do you have a favourite coffee shop? Which one?
2. Which supermarkets do you go to?
Report: *Nine* out of *ten* students go to ____.

129

1. laundromat
   自助洗衣店

2. dry cleaners
   乾洗店

3. convenience store
   便利店

4. pharmacy
   藥房

5. parking space
   停車位

6. handicapped parking
   殘障人士專用停車

7. corner
   街角

8. traffic light
   交通燈

9. bus
   公車 / 巴士

10. fast-food restaurant
    速食餐館

11. drive-through window
    直駛購物窗口

12. newsstand
    報攤

13. mailbox
    郵箱

14. pedestrian
    行人

15. crosswalk
    行人穿越道 / 行人過路處

A. **cross** the street
   穿越馬路 / 過馬路

B. **wait for** the light
   等待交通燈號

C. **jaywalk**
   隨意穿越馬路 / 亂過馬路

More vocabulary

do errands: to make a short trip from your home to buy or pick up things

neighbourhood: the area close to your home

Pair practice. Make new conversations.

A: *I have a lot of errands to do today.*
B: *Me too. First, I'm going to the* <u>laundromat</u>.
A: *I'll see you there after I stop at the* <u>copy centre</u>.

130

16. bus stop 公車站	**22.** bike 腳踏車	**28.** food cart 食物販賣車
17. doughnut shop 甜甜圈餅店	**23.** pay phone 公用電話	**29.** street vendor 小販
18. copy centre 複印店	**24.** sidewalk 人行道	**30.** childcare centre 托兒所
19. barbershop 理髮店	**25.** parking meter 停車計費表	**D.** **ride** a bike 騎腳踏車
20. used book store 舊書店	**26.** street sign 街名標示牌	**E.** **park** the car 停車
21. curb 路肩	**27.** fire hydrant 消防栓	**F.** **walk** a dog 遛狗

Internet Research: finding business listings

Type "pharmacy" and your city in a search engine.
Count the pharmacy listings you see.
Report: *I found 25 pharmacies in Fredericton.*

Think about it. Discuss.

1. How many different jobs are there at this intersection?
2. Which of these businesses would you like to own? Why?

1. music store
   音樂店

2. jewellery store
   珠寶店

3. nail salon
   修指甲店

4. bookstore
   書店

5. toy store
   玩具店

6. pet store
   寵物店

7. card store
   賀卡店

8. florist
   花店

9. optician
   眼鏡店

10. shoe store
    鞋店

11. play area
    孩童遊樂區

12. guest services
    賓客服務台

More vocabulary

beauty shop: hair salon

gift shop: a store that sells T-shirts, mugs, and other small gifts

men's store: men's clothing store

Pair practice. Make new conversations.

A: *Where is the florist?*

B: *It's on the first floor, next to the optician.*

13. department store
    百貨公司

14. travel agency
    旅行社

15. food court
    餐飲區

16. ice cream shop
    冰淇淋店

17. candy store
    糖果店

18. hair salon
    美容院

19. maternity store
    孕婦用品店

20. electronics store
    電器用品店

21. elevator
    電梯

22. kiosk
    售貨亭

23. escalator
    自動扶梯

24. directory
    地點標示圖

Ways to talk about plans

Let's go to the <u>card store</u>.
I have to go to the <u>card store</u>.
I want to go to the <u>card store</u>.

Role play. Talk to a friend at the mall.

A: *Let's go to the <u>card store</u>. I need to buy <u>a card</u> for <u>Maggie's birthday</u>.*
B: *OK, but can we go to the <u>shoe store</u> next?*

133

1. teller
出納員

3. deposit
存款

5. security guard
警衛

7. safety deposit box
保管箱

2. customer
顧客

4. deposit slip
存款單

6. vault
金庫

8. valuables
貴重物品

Bank Accounts 銀行帳戶

9. account manager
帳戶經理

11. opening deposit
開戶存款

13. chequebook
支票簿

15. chequing account number
支票帳戶號碼

10. joint account
共同帳戶

12. ATM card
自動存提款卡

14. cheque
支票

16. savings account number
儲蓄帳戶號碼

17. bank statement
銀行對帳單

18. balance
餘額

A. Cash a cheque.
兌現支票。

B. Make a deposit.
存款。

The ATM (Automated Teller Machine) 自動櫃員機

C. Insert your ATM card.
插入自動存提款卡。

D. Enter your PIN.*
輸入密碼。

E. Withdraw cash.
提款。

F. Remove your card.
取出存提款卡。

*PIN = personal identification number

A. get a library card
獲取圖書卡

B. look for a book
找書

C. check out a book
借書

D. return a book
還書

E. pay a late fine
支付過期罰款

1. library clerk
圖書館職員

2. circulation desk
借書處

3. library patron
圖書館讀者

4. periodicals
期刊

5. magazine
雜誌

6. newspaper
報紙

7. headline
頭條

8. atlas
地圖集

9. reference librarian
圖書館員

10. self-checkout
自助借書

11. online catalogue
線上目錄

12. picture book
圖畫書

13. biography
人物傳記

14. title
標題

15. author
作者

16. novel
小說

17. audiobook
有聲書

18. e-book
電子書

19. DVD
DVD光碟

1. Priority Courier™
   Priority Courier™ (優先郵件)

2. Xpresspost™
   Xpresspost™ (快遞郵件)

3. Xpresspost™ bubble envelope
   Xpresspost™ (快遞郵件) 泡泡信封

4. registered mail
   掛號郵件

5. air mail
   航空信

6. surface mail / parcel post
   平郵 / 包裹郵件

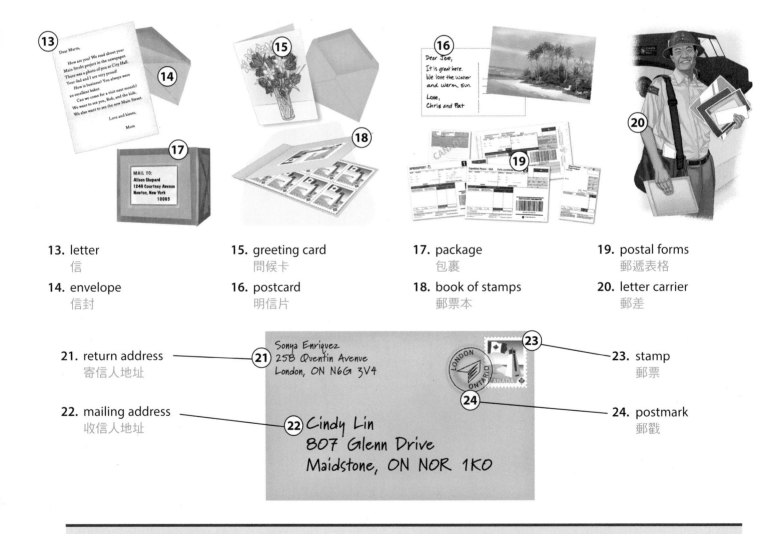

13. letter
    信

14. envelope
    信封

15. greeting card
    問候卡

16. postcard
    明信片

17. package
    包裹

18. book of stamps
    郵票本

19. postal forms
    郵遞表格

20. letter carrier
    郵差

21. return address
    寄信人地址

22. mailing address
    收信人地址

23. stamp
    郵票

24. postmark
    郵戳

Ways to talk about sending mail

This letter has to get there tomorrow. (Xpresspost™)
This letter has to arrive in two days. (Priority Courier™)
This letter can go in regular mail. (Lettermail™)

Pair practice. Make new conversations.

A: *Hi. This letter has to get there tomorrow.*
B: *You can send it by Xpresspost™ service.*
A: *OK. I need a book of stamps, too.*

7. postal clerk
　 郵局職員

8. scale
　 磅秤

9. post office box (PO box)
　 郵政信箱

10. mailbox
　 郵箱

11. online shipping
　 線上運送

Sending a Card 寄送卡片

A. Write a note in a card.
書寫卡片。

B. Address the envelope.
在信封上書寫地址。

C. Put on a stamp.
貼上郵票。

D. Mail the card.
郵寄卡片。

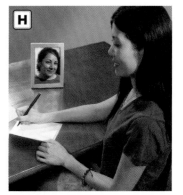

E. Deliver the card.
投遞卡片。

F. Receive the card.
收到卡片。

G. Read the card.
閱讀卡片。

H. Write back.
回信。

More vocabulary

junk mail: mail you don't want
overnight / next-day mail: Xpresspost™
postage: the cost to send mail

Survey your class. Record the responses.

1. Do you send greeting cards by mail or online?
2. Do you pay bills by mail or online?
Report: *25% of us send cards by mail.*

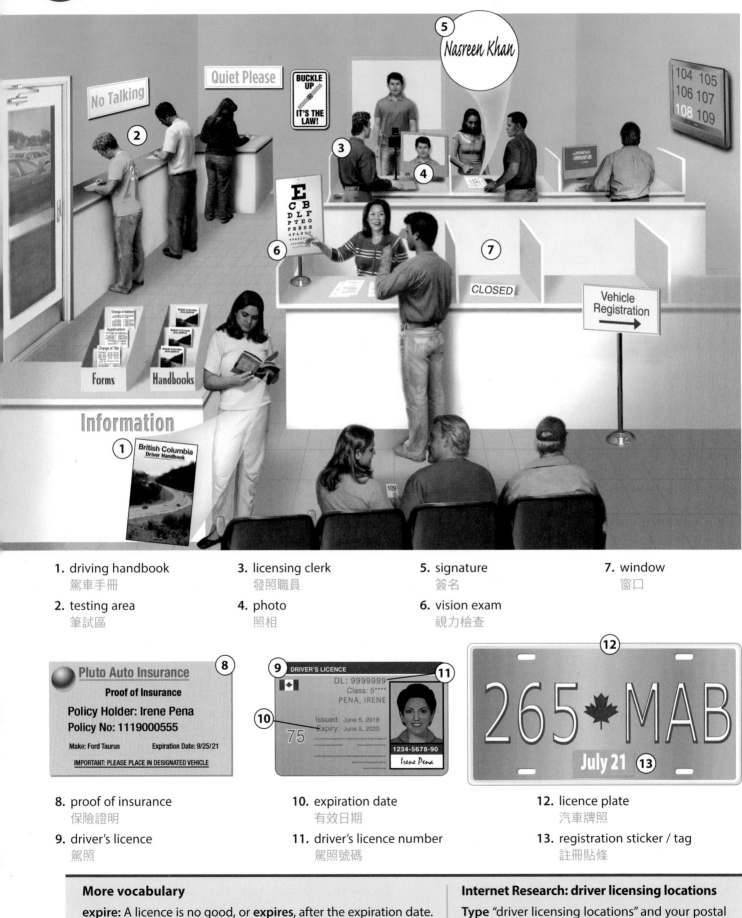

1. driving handbook
   駕車手冊

2. testing area
   筆試區

3. licensing clerk
   發照職員

4. photo
   照相

5. signature
   簽名

6. vision exam
   視力檢查

7. window
   窗口

8. proof of insurance
   保險證明

9. driver's licence
   駕照

10. expiration date
    有效日期

11. driver's licence number
    駕照號碼

12. licence plate
    汽車牌照

13. registration sticker / tag
    註冊貼條

More vocabulary

expire: A licence is no good, or **expires**, after the expiration date.
renew a licence: to apply to keep a licence before it expires
vanity plate: a more expensive, personal licence plate

Internet Research: driver licensing locations

Type "driver licensing locations" and your postal code in a search engine.
Report: *I found 2 driver licensing office(s) near me.*

Getting Your First License 第一次申請駕照

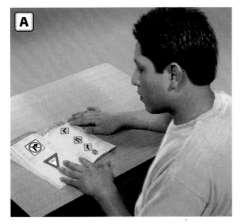

A. Study the handbook.
學習手冊。

B. Show your identification.
出示身份證明。

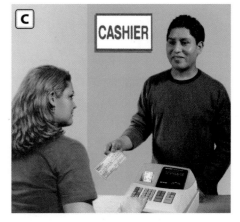

C. Pay the application fee.
交申請費。

D. Take a written test.
參加筆試。

E. Get a beginner's / learner's permit.
獲得學習執照。

F. Take a driver education and training course.
上司機教育與訓練課。

G. Pass a driving test.
通過路考。

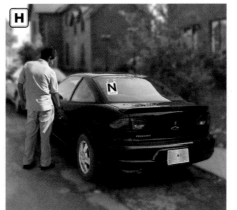

H. Get your licence.
獲得駕照。

I. Get your unrestricted licence.*
取得您的無限制執照。

*****Note:** This process will vary by province.

Ways to request more information

What do I do next?
What's the next step?
Where do I go from here?

Role play. Talk to a driver's licence office clerk.

A: *I want to apply for <u>a driver's licence</u>.*
B: *Did you <u>study the handbook</u>?*
A: *Yes, I did. <u>What do I do next</u>?*

Government and Military Service 政府和軍隊

Federal Government 聯邦政府

Head of State → Sovereign's Representative → Head of Government

1. sovereign
君主

2. Governor General
總督

3. prime minister
首相

4. cabinet
內閣

5. minister
部長

308

105

6. Parliament of Canada
加拿大聯邦議會 / 加拿大國會

7. House of Commons
眾議院

8. Senate
參議院

9. member of parliament
眾議員

10. senator
參議員

Judiciary 司法

11. Supreme Court of Canada
加拿大最高法院

12. judges
法官

13. chief justice
首席大法官

Provincial Government 省政府

14. premier
省長

15. lieutenant governor
省督

16. provincial capital
省府

17. Legislative Assembly /
House of Assembly /
National Assembly
立法院 / 議會 / 國民議會

18. member of legislative
assembly
省議員

City Government 市政府

19. mayor
市長

20. city council
市政廳

21. city councillors
市議員

The Canadian Armed Forces 加拿大武裝力量

Branches of the Armed Forces 武裝力量兵種

22. Canadian Army
加拿大陸軍

23. soldier
軍人

24. Royal Canadian Navy
皇家加拿大海軍

25. seaman / sailor
水手

26. Royal Canadian Air Force
皇家加拿大空軍

27. airman / airwoman
空軍士兵

Military Service 兵役

A. **be** a recruit
作為新兵

B. **be** on active duty
作為現役軍人

C. **be** on reserve
作為預備役軍人

D. **be** a veteran
作為退伍軍人

141

Responsibilities 義務

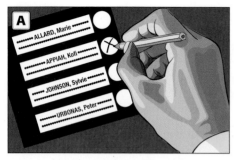

A. vote in elections
在選舉中投票

B. pay taxes
納稅

C. obey Canada's laws
遵守加拿大法律

D. care for and **protect** our heritage and environment
照顧並保護我們的遺產與環境

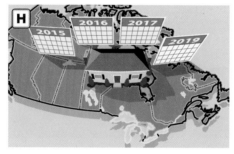

E. serve on a jury
擔任陪審員

F. be informed
關心時事

Citizenship Requirements 公民申請資格

G. be 18 or older
年滿十八歲或以上

H. live in Canada for 4 of the last 6 years
在過去六年裡於加拿大居住四年

I. take a citizenship test
參加公民考試

Rights (Fundamental Freedoms) 權利（基本自由）

1. freedom of conscience and religion
良心與宗教自由

2. freedom of thought, belief, opinion, and expression
思想、信念、看法及表達自由

3. peaceful assembly
和平集會

4. freedom of association
結社自由

5. a fair trial
公平審判

An Election 選舉

J. run for office
競選公職

6. candidate
候選人

K. campaign
競選

7. rally
集會

L. debate
辯論

8. opponent
對手

9. ballot
選票

10. voting booth /
polling booth
投票站

M. get elected
當選

11. election results
選舉結果

N. serve
服務

12. elected official
當選官員

More vocabulary

political party: a group of people with the same political goals

term: the period of time an elected official serves

Think about it. Discuss.

1. Should everyone have to vote? Why or why not?
2. Are candidates' debates important? Why or why not?
3. Would you prefer to run for city council or mayor? Why?

143

A *You are under arrest for…*

B

C *Bail is set at $20,000.*

A. arrest a suspect
逮捕嫌犯

1. police officer
警員

2. handcuffs
手銬

B. hire a lawyer / **hire** an attorney
聘雇律師

3. guard
警衛

4. defense lawyer
辯方律師

C. appear in court
出庭

5. defendant
被告

6. judge
法官

D

D. stand trial
開庭審判

7. courtroom
法庭

8. jury
陪審團

9. evidence
證據

10. Crown counsel
檢察官

11. witness
證人

12. court reporter
法庭記錄員

13. bailiff
庭警

E *Guilty.*

F *7 years*

G

H

E. convict the defendant
被告定罪

14. verdict*
判決結果

F. sentence the defendant
宣判被告刑罰

G. go to jail / **go** to prison
坐牢

15. convict / prisoner
囚犯

H. be released
釋放

*__Note:__ There are two possible verdicts, "guilty" and "not guilty."

Look at the pictures.
Describe what happened.

A: *The police officer arrested a suspect*.
B: *He put handcuffs on him*.

Think about it. Discuss.

1. Would you want to serve on a jury? Why or why not?
2. Look at the crimes on page 145. What sentence would you give for each crime? Why?

1. vandalism
   蓄意破壞
2. burglary
   竊盜
3. assault
   攻擊
4. gang violence
   幫派暴力
5. drunk driving
   酒醉駕車
6. illegal drugs
   毒品
7. arson
   縱火
8. shoplifting
   商店行竊
9. identity theft
   身份盜用
10. victim
    受害者
11. mugging
    行兇搶劫
12. murder
    謀殺
13. gun
    槍

More vocabulary

commit a crime: to do something illegal
criminal: someone who does something illegal
steal: to take money or things from someone illegally

Identify the tenants' problem. Brainstorm solutions.

The apartment tenants at 65 Elm Street are upset.
There were three burglaries on their block last month.
This month there were five burglaries and a mugging!

A. **Walk** with a friend.
與朋友一起走。

B. **Stay** on well-lit streets.
走照明良好的街道。

C. **Conceal** your PIN.
隱藏個人密碼。

D. **Protect** your purse or wallet.
保護好您的錢包。

E. **Lock** your doors.
鎖門。

F. Don't **open** your door to strangers.
不要給陌生人開門。

G. Don't **drink** and **drive**.
切勿酒後駕車。

H. **Shop** on secure websites.
在安全的網站購物。

I. **Be** aware of your surroundings.
瞭解週圍情況。

J. **Report** suspicious packages.
報告可疑的包裹。

K. **Report** crimes to the police.
向警察報告犯罪事件。

L. **Join** a neighbourhood watch.
參加鄰里守望相助。

More vocabulary

sober: not drunk

designated drivers: sober drivers who drive drunk people home safely

Survey your class. Record the responses.

1. Do you always lock your doors?
2. Do you belong to a neighbourhood watch?

Report: *75% of us always lock our doors.*

Online Dangers for Children
孩子們面對的線上危險

1. cyberbullying
网路霸凌

2. online predators
網路掠食者

3. inappropriate material
不當材料

Ways to Protect Children 保護兒童的途徑

A. **Turn on** parental controls.
啟用父母管制功能。

B. **Monitor** children's Internet use.
監視孩子的網際網路使用。

C. **Block** inappropriate sites.
阻擋不適合的網站。

Internet Crime 網際網路犯罪

4. phishing
網路釣魚

5. hacking
駭客入侵

Safety Solutions 安全解決方案

D. **Create** secure passwords.
制定安全的密碼。

E. **Update** security software.
更新安防軟體。

F. **Use** encrypted / secure sites.
使用加密或安全的網站。

G. **Delete** suspicious emails.
刪除可疑的電子郵件。

1. lost child
   孩子走失

2. car accident
   車禍

3. airplane crash
   墜機

4. explosion
   爆炸

5. earthquake
   地震

6. mudslide
   土石流

7. forest fire
   森林火災

8. fire
   火災

9. firefighter
   消防員

10. fire truck
    消防車

Ways to report an emergency

First, give your name. *My name is <u>Tim Johnson</u>.*
Then, state the emergency and give the address.
There was <u>a car accident</u> at <u>219 Elm Street</u>.

Role play. Call 911.

A: *911 emergency operator.*
B: *My name is <u>Lisa Hong</u>. There is <u>a fire</u> at <u>323 Oak Street</u>.*
Please hurry!

11. drought
旱災

12. famine
饑荒

13. blizzard
暴風雪

14. hurricane
颶風

15. tornado
龍捲風

16. volcanic eruption
火山爆發

17. tidal wave / tsunami
海嘯

18. avalanche
雪崩

19. flood
水災

20. search and rescue team
搜救隊

Survey your class. Record the responses.

1. Which natural disaster worries you the most?
2. Which natural disaster worries you the least?
Report: *Five of us are most worried about earthquakes.*

Think about it. Discuss.

1. What organizations can help you in an emergency?
2. What are some ways to prepare for natural disasters?
3. Where would you go in an emergency?

149

Before an Emergency 在發生緊急情況之前

A. Plan for an emergency.
制定應對緊急情況的計畫。

1. meeting place
集合地點

2. out-of-province contact
外省聯絡人

3. escape route
逃生路線

4. gas shut-off valve
瓦斯關閉閥門

5. evacuation route
撤離路線

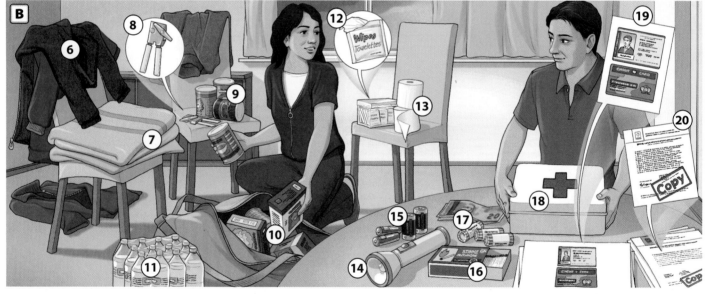

B. Make a disaster kit.
準備災難用品包。

6. warm clothes
保暖衣服

7. blankets
被毯

8. can opener
開罐器

9. canned food
罐頭食物

10. packaged food
盒裝食物

11. bottled water
瓶裝水

12. moist towelettes
濕紙巾

13. toilet paper
衛生紙

14. flashlight
手電筒

15. batteries
電池

16. matches
火柴

17. cash and coins
現金和硬幣

18. first aid kit
急救箱

19. copies of ID and credit cards
身份証和信用卡複印件

20. copies of important papers
重要文件的複印件

Pair practice. Make new conversations.

A: *What do we need for our disaster kit?*
B: *We need blankets and matches.*
A: *I think we also need batteries.*

Survey your class. Record the responses.

1. Do you have a disaster kit?
2. Do you have an out-of-province contact?
Report: *Ten of us have a disaster kit.*

During an Emergency 遇到緊急情況時

C. Watch the weather.
觀察天氣。

D. Pay attention to warnings.
注意警告。

Tornado watch

E. Remain calm.
保持冷靜。

Tornado watch

F. Follow directions.
遵循指示。

Go to a shelter.

G. Help people with disabilities.
幫助殘障人士。

Shelter

H. Seek shelter.
尋找收容所。

Shelter

I. Stay away from windows.
遠離窗戶。

J. Take cover.
找掩護。

K. Evacuate the area.
撤離該地區。

After an Emergency 在緊急情況之後

We're OK.

Great.

L. Call out-of-town contacts.
打電話給外地聯絡人。

M. Clean up debris.
清理破瓦殘礫。

N. Inspect utilities.
檢查公用事業供應。

Ways to say you're OK	Ways to say you need help	Role play. Prepare for an emergency.
I'm fine.	*We need help.*	**A:** *They just issued <u>a tornado</u> warning.*
We're OK here.	*Someone is hurt.*	**B:** *OK. We need to stay calm and follow directions.*
Everything's under control.	*I'm injured. Please get help.*	**A:** *What do we need to do first?*

1. graffiti
   街頭塗鴉

2. litter
   垃圾

3. streetlight
   街燈

4. hardware store
   五金店

5. petition
   請願

A. **give** a speech
   致詞

B. **applaud**
   鼓掌

C. **change**
   變化

What do you see in the pictures?

1. What were the problems on Main Street?
2. What was the petition for?
3. Why did the city council applaud?
4. How did the volunteers change the street?

Read the story.

Community Cleanup

Marta Lopez has a doughnut shop on Main Street. One day she looked at her street and was very upset. She saw graffiti on her doughnut shop and the other stores. Litter was everywhere. All the streetlights were broken. Marta wanted to fix the lights and clean up the street.

Marta started a petition about the streetlights. Five hundred people signed it. Then she gave a speech to the city council. The council members voted to repair the streetlights. Everyone applauded. Marta was happy, but her work wasn't finished.

Next, Marta asked for volunteers to clean up Main Street. The hardware store manager gave the volunteers free paint. Marta gave them free doughnuts and coffee. The volunteers painted and cleaned. They changed Main Street. Now Main Street is beautiful and Marta is proud.

Reread the story.

1. Find "repair" in Paragraph 2. Find another word for "repair" in the story.

What do you think?

2. What are the benefits of being a volunteer?
3. What do you think Marta said in her speech? How do you know?

1. car
   汽車

2. passenger
   乘客

3. taxi
   計程車

4. motorcycle
   摩托車

5. street
   街道

6. truck
   貨車

7. train
   火車

8. (air)plane
   飛機

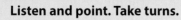

Listen and point. Take turns.

A: *Point to the motorcycle.*
B: *Point to the truck.*
A: *Point to the train.*

Dictate to your partner. Take turns.

A: *Write motorcycle.*
B: *Could you repeat that for me?*
A: *I said motorcycle.*

9. helicopter
   直升機
10. airport
    機場
11. subway station
    地鐵站
12. subway
    地鐵
13. bus stop
    公車站 / 巴士站
14. bus
    公車 / 巴士
15. bicycle (bike)
    腳踏車

Ways to talk about using transportation

Use *take* for buses, trains, subways, taxis, planes, and helicopters. Use *drive* for cars and trucks. Use *ride* for bicycles and motorcycles.

Pair practice. Make new conversations.

A: *How do you get to school?*
B: *I take the bus. How about you?*
A: *I ride a bicycle to school.*

155

Public Transportation 公共交通

A Bus Stop 公車站

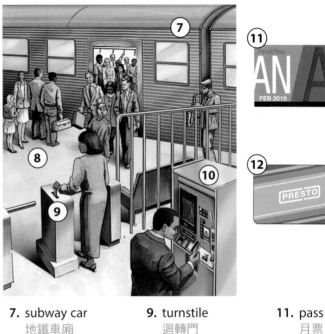

BUS 10 Northbound

Main	Elm	Oak
6:00	6:10	6:13
6:30	6:40	6:43
7:00	7:10	7:13
7:30	7:40	7:43

1. bus route
   公車路線
2. fare
   車資
3. rider
   乘客
4. schedule
   行車時間表
5. transfer
   轉車證
6. bus ticket
   公車票

A Subway Station 地鐵站

7. subway car
   地鐵車廂
8. platform
   月臺
9. turnstile
   迴轉門
10. vending machine
    自動販賣機
11. pass
    月票
12. fare card
    車票卡

A Train Station 火車站

From OTTAWA, ON
To MONTREAL, QC

Carrier 2V Train 684 Date 18FEB 3
Accom 2V COMFORT CLASS
Form of Payment AP XXXX0456791 Ax

13. ticket window
    售票窗口
14. conductor
    車長
15. track
    鐵軌
16. ticket
    車票
17. one-way trip
    單程旅行
18. round trip / return trip
    往返旅行 / 返程旅行

Airport Transportation 機場交通

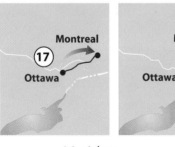

19. taxi stand
    計程車站
20. shuttle
    接駁巴士
21. town car
    豪華轎車
22. taxi driver
    計程車司機
23. taxi licence
    計程車執照
24. meter
    計費表

More vocabulary

hail a taxi: to raise your hand to get a taxi
miss the bus: to get to the bus stop after the bus leaves

Internet Research: taxi fares

Type "taxi fare finder" and your city in the search bar.
Enter a starting address and an ending address.
Report: *The fare from my house to school is $10.00.*

A. go under the bridge
穿過橋洞

B. go over the bridge
過橋

C. walk up the steps
上階梯

D. walk down the steps
下階梯

E. get into the taxi
上計程車

F. get out of the taxi
下計程車

G. run across the street
穿越馬路

H. run around the corner
轉過街角

I. get on the highway
上高速公路

J. get off the highway
下高速公路

K. drive through the tunnel
駛過隧道

Grammar Point: *into, out of, on, off*

Use *get into* for taxis and cars.
Use *get on* for buses, trains, planes, and highways.

Use *get out of* for taxis and cars.
Use *get off* for buses, trains, planes, and highways.

1. stop
停

2. do not enter / wrong way
禁止進入 / 錯行方向

3. one way
單行道

4. speed limit
速限

5. U-turn OK
可以調頭

6. no exit / dead end
此路不通 / 死路

7. right turn only
只能右轉

8. no left turn
禁止左轉

9. yield
讓路

10. merge
併道

11. no parking
禁止停車

12. handicapped parking
殘障人士專用停車

13. pedestrian crossing
行人穿越道 / 行人過路處

15. school crossing
學校穿越道

17. highway marker
公路號標誌

14. railroad crossing
鐵路平交道

16. roadwork
道路施工

18. hospital
醫院

Pair practice. Make new conversations.

A: *Watch out! The sign says <u>no left turn</u>.*
B: *Sorry, I was looking at the <u>stop</u> sign.*
A: *That's OK. Just be careful!*

Survey your class. Record the responses.

1. Which traffic signs are different in your native country?
2. Which traffic signs are similar in your native country?

Report: *The U.S. and <u>Canada</u> have similar <u>stop</u> signs.*

Directions 方向

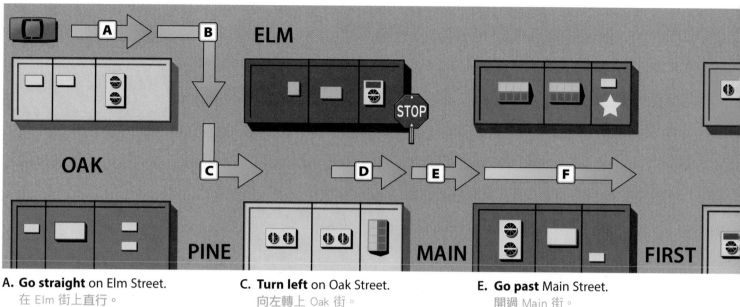

A. **Go straight** on Elm Street.
在 Elm 街上直行。

B. **Turn right** on Pine Street.
向右轉上 Pine 街。

C. **Turn left** on Oak Street.
向左轉上 Oak 街。

D. **Stop** at the corner.
在路口處停一下。

E. **Go past** Main Street.
開過 Main 街。

F. **Go** one block to First Street.
經過一個街區至 First 街。

Maps 地圖

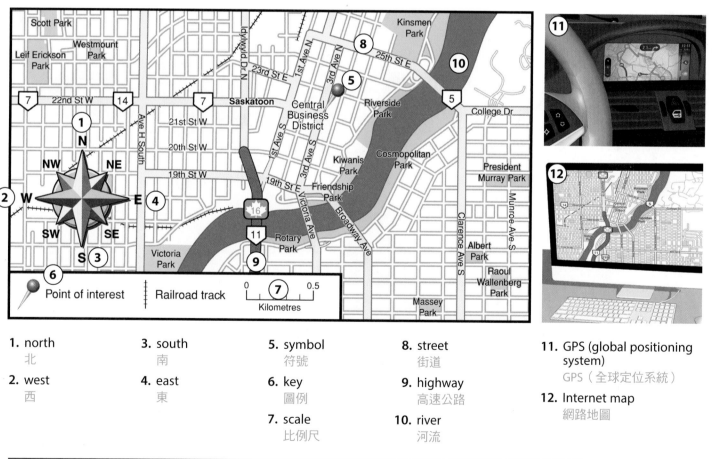

1. north
   北
2. west
   西
3. south
   南
4. east
   東
5. symbol
   符號
6. key
   圖例
7. scale
   比例尺
8. street
   街道
9. highway
   高速公路
10. river
    河流
11. GPS (global positioning system)
    GPS（全球定位系統）
12. Internet map
    網路地圖

Role play. Ask for directions.

A: *I'm lost. I need to get to <u>Elm and Pine</u>.*
B: *<u>Go straight on Oak</u> and <u>make a right on Pine</u>.*
A: *Thanks so much.*

Think about it. Discuss.

1. What are the pros and cons of using a GPS?
2. Which types of jobs require map-reading skills?

1. **hybrid**
雙動力車

2. **electric vehicle / EV**
電動車

3. **EV charging station**
電動車充電站

4. **sports car**
跑車

5. **convertible**
敞篷汽車

6. **hatchback**
掀背車

7. **SUV (sport utility vehicle)**
SUV（運動休旅車）

8. **minivan**
小型廂型車

9. **camper**
野營車

10. **RV (recreational vehicle)**
RV（野營旅遊車）

11. **limousine / limo**
加長型豪華轎車

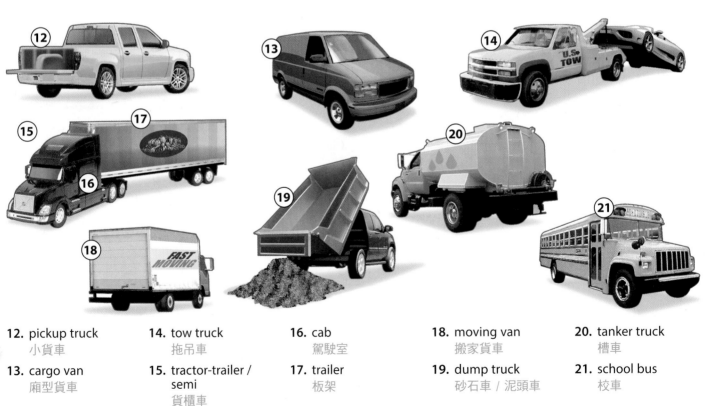

12. **pickup truck**
小貨車

13. **cargo van**
廂型貨車

14. **tow truck**
拖吊車

15. **tractor-trailer / semi**
貨櫃車

16. **cab**
駕駛室

17. **trailer**
板架

18. **moving van**
搬家貨車

19. **dump truck**
砂石車 / 泥頭車

20. **tanker truck**
槽車

21. **school bus**
校車

More vocabulary

sedan: a 4-door car
coupe: a 2-door car
make and model: the car manufacturer and style: *Ford Escape*

Pair practice. Make new conversations.

A: *I have a new car!*
B: *Did you get a hybrid?*
A: *Yes, but I really wanted a sports car.*

Buying a Used Car 購買二手車

'09 compact. Only $8,500.

'13 sedan. Must sell. Great deal!

A. **Look at** car ads.
查看汽車廣告。

How many kilometres does it have?

B. **Ask** the seller about the car.
向賣主詢問汽車情況。

It's in good condition.

C. **Take** the car to a mechanic.
請汽車技工檢查。

It's $8,500.

I can give you $8,000.

D. **Negotiate** a price.
商議價格。

E. **Get** the title from the seller.
從賣主處獲得所有權狀。

F. **Register** the car.
註冊汽車。

Taking Care of Your Car 養護汽車

G. **Fill** the tank with gas.
添加汽油。

H. **Check** the oil.
檢查機油。

I. **Put in** coolant.
添加冷卻劑。

J. **Go** for an emissions test.
去做排放測驗。

K. **Replace** the windshield wipers.
更換擋風玻璃雨刷。

L. **Fill** the tires with air.
給輪胎打氣。

Ways to request service

Please check the oil.
Could you fill the tank?
Put in coolant, please.

Think about it. Discuss.

1. What's good and bad about a used car?
2. Do you like to negotiate car prices? Why or why not?
3. Do you know any good mechanics? Why are they good?

161

At the Dealer 在汽車經銷商處

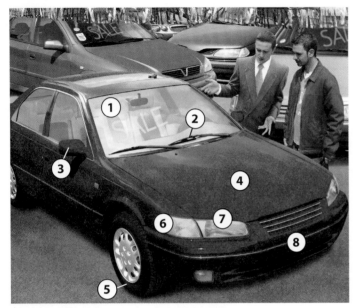

At the Mechanic 在汽車修理店

1. windshield
   擋風玻璃

2. windshield wipers
   擋風玻璃雨刷

3. side-view mirror
   車側後視鏡

4. hood
   引擎蓋

5. tire
   輪胎

6. turn signal
   轉向指示燈

7. headlight
   車前燈

8. bumper
   保險桿 / 防撞槓

9. hubcap / wheel cover
   車輪蓋

10. gas tank
    油箱

11. trunk
    後車箱

12. licence plate
    汽車牌照

13. taillight
    尾燈

14. brake light
    煞車燈

15. tailpipe
    排氣管

16. muffler
    消音器

Under the Hood 引擎蓋下面

Inside the Trunk 後車箱內

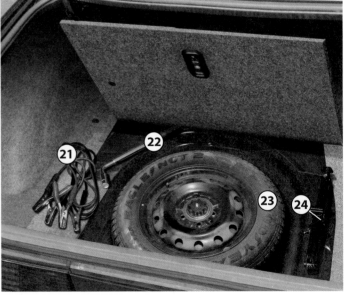

17. fuel injection system
    燃料噴射系統

18. engine
    引擎

19. radiator
    冷卻器

20. battery
    電瓶 / 電池

21. jumper cables
    充電電線

22. lug wrench
    螺母扳手

23. spare tire
    備用輪胎

24. jack
    千斤頂

The Dashboard and Instrument Panel 儀表板

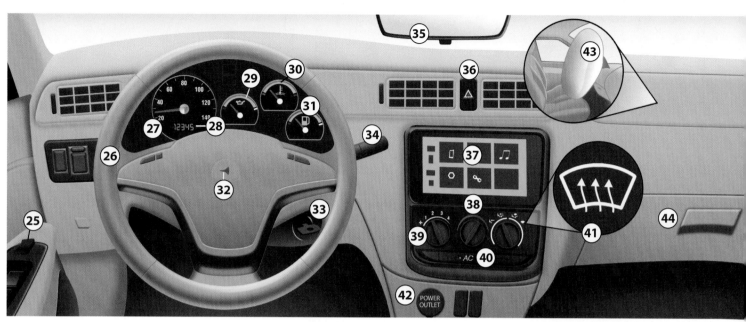

25. door lock 門鎖	**30.** temperature gauge 溫度表	**35.** rearview mirror 後視鏡	**40.** air conditioning / AC button 冷氣按鈕
26. steering wheel 方向盤	**31.** gas gauge 汽油表	**36.** hazard lights 緊急燈	**41.** defroster 除霧器
27. speedometer 速度表	**32.** horn 喇叭	**37.** touch screen / audio display 觸控式顯示幕 / 音響顯示	**42.** power outlet 電源插座
28. odometer 里程表	**33.** ignition 點火電門	**38.** temperature control dial 溫度控制旋鈕	**43.** airbag 安全氣袋
29. oil gauge 機油表	**34.** turn signal 轉向指示燈	**39.** fan speed 風扇速度	**44.** glove compartment 手套箱

An Automatic Transmission
自動變速

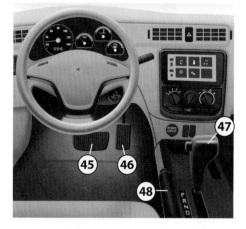

A Manual Transmission
手排變速

Inside the Car
車內

45. brake pedal 煞車踏板	**47.** gearshift 變速排檔	**49.** clutch 離合器	**51.** front seat 前座	**53.** child safety seat 孩童安全座椅
46. gas pedal / accelerator 油門踏板	**48.** handbrake 手煞車	**50.** stick shift 手排檔	**52.** seat belt 安全帶	**54.** back seat 後排座椅

 **An Airport** 機場

In the Airline Terminal 在航空公司櫃台

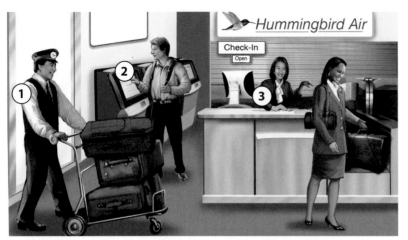

Hummingbird Air

At the Security Checkpoint
在安全檢查點

1. porter
行李搬運工人

2. check-in kiosk
登機手續自助台

3. ticket agent
售票員

4. screening area
檢查區

5. security screener
安全檢查員

6. bin
物品盛放盒

Taking a Flight 乘坐飛機

A. Check in electronically.
電子辦理登機手續。

B. Check your bags.
托運行李。

C. Show your boarding pass and ID.
出示登機證和身份證。

D. Go through security.
通過安全檢查。

E. Board the plane.
上飛機。

F. Find your seat.
找座位。

G. Stow your carry-on bag.
放好手提行李。

H. Fasten your seat belt.
繫上安全帶。

I. Put your cell phone in airplane mode.
把行動電話轉到飛航模式。

J. Take off. / Leave.
起飛。/ 離開。

K. Land. / Arrive.
著陸。/ 抵達。

L. Claim your baggage.
領取行李。

At the Gate 在登機門

On the Airplane 在飛機上

At Customs 在海關

7. arrival and departure monitors
抵達及起飛螢幕

8. gate
登機門

9. boarding area
登機區

10. cockpit
駕駛艙

11. pilot
飛行員

12. flight attendant
空服員

13. overhead compartment
上方行李箱

14. emergency exit
緊急出口

15. passenger
乘客

16. declaration form
報關表

17. customs officer
海關人員

18. luggage / bag
行李

19. e-ticket
電子機票

20. mobile boarding pass
手機登機證

21. tray table
摺疊桌

22. turbulence
亂流

23. baggage carousel
行李轉盤

24. oxygen mask
氧氣面罩

25. life vest
救生背心

26. emergency card
緊急狀況資訊卡

27. reclined seat
斜放的椅背

28. upright seat
豎起的椅背

29. on time
準時

30. delayed
延誤

FLIGHT	SCHEDULED	ARRIVAL
128	1:00 PM	1:00 PM
156	2:12 PM	2:30 PM
207	4:45 PM	4:45 PM

More vocabulary

departure time: the time the plane takes off
arrival time: the time the plane lands
nonstop flight: a trip with no stops

Pair practice. Make new conversations.

A: *Excuse me. Where do I <u>check in</u>?*
B: *At the <u>check-in kiosk</u>.*
A: *Thanks.*

A Road Trip 公路旅行

1. park warden
   公園管理員

2. wildlife
   野生動物

3. stars
   星辰

4. scenery
   風景

5. automobile club card
   汽車俱樂部卡

6. destination
   目的地

A. **pack**
   準備行李

B. **be** lost
   迷路

C. **have** a flat tire
   爆胎

D. **get** a ticket
   拿到罰單

E. **run out** of gas
   汽油用盡

F. **break down**
   汽車壞了

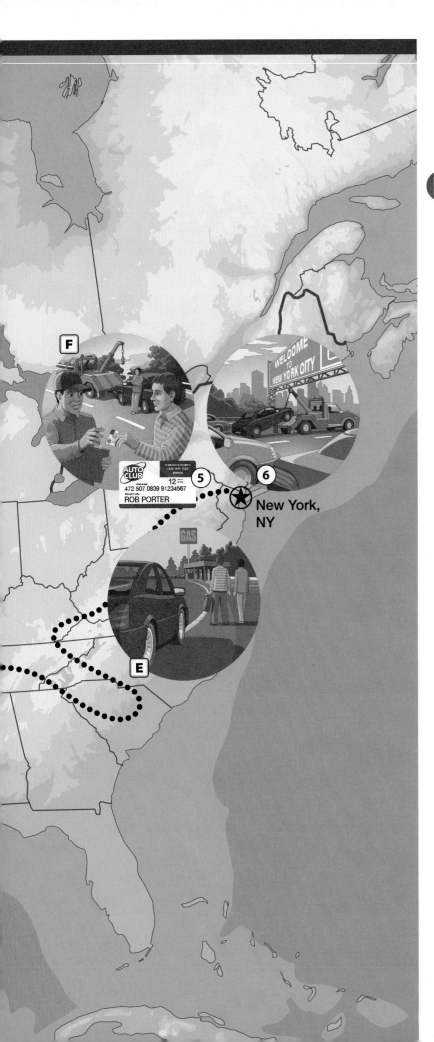

What do you see in the pictures?

1. Where are the young men from? What's their destination?

2. Do they have a good trip? How do you know?

Read the story.

A Road Trip

On July 7, Joe and Rob <u>pack</u> their bags and start their road trip to New York City.

Their first stop is Banff National Park. They listen to a <u>park warden</u> talk about the <u>wildlife</u> in the park. That night they go to bed under a sky full of <u>stars</u>, but Rob can't sleep. He's nervous about the wildlife.

The next day, their GPS breaks. "We're not going in the right direction!" Rob says. "<u>We're lost</u>!"

"No problem," says Joe. "We can take the southern route. We'll see some beautiful <u>scenery</u>."

But there are *a lot* of problems. They <u>have a flat tire</u> and later <u>get a</u> speeding <u>ticket</u>. A few days later, they <u>run out of gas</u>. Then, eight kilometres from New York City, their car <u>breaks</u> <u>down</u>. "Now, *this* is a problem," Joe says.

"No, it isn't," says Rob. He calls the number on his <u>automobile club card</u>. Help arrives in 20 minutes.

After 8,000 kilometres of problems, Joe and Rob finally reach their <u>destination</u>— by tow truck!

Reread the story.

1. Find the phrase "Help arrives." What does that phrase mean?

What do you think?

2. What is good, bad, or interesting about taking a road trip?

3. Imagine you are planning a road trip. Where will you go?

167

Job Search 求職

A. **set** a goal
設定目標

B. **write** a résumé
撰寫履歷

C. **contact** references
聯絡推薦人

D. **research** local companies
研究本地公司

E. **talk** to friends / **network**
詢問朋友 / 建立關係

F. **go** to an employment agency
造訪職業介紹所

G. **look** for help wanted signs
尋找徵人告示

H. **check** employment websites
查看求職網站

A My Goals:
Now: Get a job in a market.
2 years: Manage a market.
5 years: Get a business degree.
10 years: Own a market.

KING'S MARKET

B Dan King
1235 Oak St., Apt. 2
Charlottetown , PEI C1A 3B2
782-555-4958
Experience
Grocery clerk 2012–2014
Farmworker 2009–2011
Education
Central Technical CC 2015
Henan Hongli School 2004–2012

D #1 GROCERY COMPANY IN CANADA

SUPERMARKETS!

C May I put your number as a reference?

Of course.

E I need a job.

I think S and K is hiring.

F ABC Employment

We can get you a job!

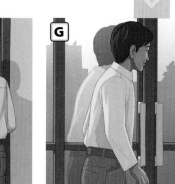

G HELP WANTED
INQUIRE WITHIN

H WORKPOWER.COM
We help YOU get the job YOU want!
1,000 Matches for Grocery

Listen and point. Take turns.

A: *Point to a résumé.*
B: *Point to a help wanted sign.*
A: *Point to an application.*

Dictate to your partner. Take turns.

A: *Write contact.*
B: *Is it spelled c-o-n-t-a-c-t?*
A: *Yes, that's right, contact.*

I. **apply** for a job
申請工作

J. **complete** an application
填寫申請表

K. **write** a cover letter
撰寫求職信

L. **submit** an application
提交申請

M. **set up** an interview
安排面試

N. **go on** an interview
前去面試

O. **get** a job / **be** hired
拿到工作 / 被聘用

P. **start** a new job
開始新工作

Ways to talk about the job search

It's important to <u>set a goal</u>.
You have to <u>write a résumé</u>.
It's a good idea to <u>network</u>.

Role play. Talk about a job search.

A: *I'm looking for a job. What should I do?*
B: *Well, it's important to <u>set a goal</u>.*
A: *Yes, and I have to <u>write a résumé</u>.*

1. accountant
會計師

2. actor
演員

3. administrative assistant
行政助理

4. appliance repair person
電器修理工

5. architect
建築師

6. artist
藝術家

7. assembler
裝配工

8. auto mechanic
汽車技工

9. babysitter
褓姆

10. baker
麵包師傅

11. business owner
業者

12. businessperson
商人

13. butcher
屠夫

14. carpenter
木匠

15. cashier
收銀員

16. childcare worker
幼教人員

Ways to ask about someone's job

What's <u>her</u> job?
What does <u>he</u> do?
What does <u>he</u> do for a living?

Pair practice. Make new conversations.

A: *What <u>does she</u> do for a living?*
B: *<u>She's an accountant</u>. What <u>do they</u> do?*
A: *<u>They're actors</u>.*

17. commercial fisher
商業捕魚者

18. computer software engineer
電腦軟體工程師

19. computer technician
電腦技師

We have that shirt in red.

20. customer service representative
客戶服務代表

21. delivery person
送貨員

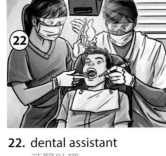

22. dental assistant
牙醫助理

23. dock worker
碼頭工人

24. electronics repair person
電子產品修理工

25. engineer
工程師

26. firefighter
消防員

27. florist
花匠

28. gardener
園丁

29. garment worker
縫衣工

30. graphic designer
平面設計師

31. hairdresser / hair stylist
美髮師

32. home health care aide
家居醫護助理

Ways to talk about jobs and occupations

Sue's <u>a garment worker</u>. She works **in** a factory.
Tom's <u>an engineer</u>. He works **for** a large company.
Luis is <u>a gardener</u>. He's self-employed.

Role play. Talk about a friend's new job.

A: Does your friend like <u>his</u> new job?
B: Yes, <u>he</u> does. <u>He's a graphic designer</u>.
A: Who does <u>he</u> work for?

33. homemaker
家庭主婦

34. housekeeper
管家

你好
He says, "Hi."

35. interpreter / translator
口譯員 / 筆譯員

36. lawyer
律師

37. machine operator
機器操作員

38. manicurist
修指甲師

39. medical records
technician
病歷保管員

40. messenger / courier
信差 / 快遞員

41. model
模特兒

42. mover
搬運工人

43. musician
音樂家

44. nurse
護士

45. occupational therapist
職業理療師

46. (house) painter
（房屋）油漆工

47. physician assistant
醫師助手

48. police officer
警員

Grammar Point: past tense of _be_

I **was** a machine operator for five years.
She **was** a model from 2010 to 2012.
Before they **were** movers, they **were** painters.

Pair practice. Make new conversations.

A: _What was your first job?_
B: _I was a musician. How about you?_
A: _I was a messenger for a small company._

49. postal worker
郵務員

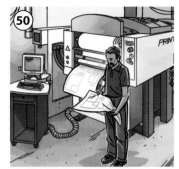

50. printer
印刷工

51. receptionist
接待員

52. reporter
記者

53. retail clerk
零售店員

54. sanitation worker
環衛工

55. security guard
警衛

56. server
侍者

Here are some programs that will help you.

57. social worker
社工

58. soldier
軍人

59. stock clerk
庫存職員

Hello. I'm calling with a very special offer.

60. telemarketer
電話行銷員

61. truck driver
貨車司機 / 貨櫃車司機

62. veterinarian
獸醫

63. welder
焊工

Norma's Story

64. writer / author
作家 / 作者

Survey your class. Record the responses.

1. What is one job you don't want to have?
2. Which jobs do you want to have?

Report: _Tom wants to be a(n) ____, but not a(n) ____._

Think about it. Discuss.

Q: What kind of person makes a good <u>interpreter</u>? Why?

A: To be a(n) ____, you need to be able to ____ and have ____, because…

Planning and Goal Setting 計劃與目標設定

A. **visit** a career planning centre
前去職業計劃中心

B. **explore** career options
探索職業選項

C. **take** an interest inventory
盤點個人興趣

D. **identify** your technical skills
確認自己的技能

E. **list** your soft skills
列出自己的軟技能

F. **consult** with a career counsellor
諮詢職業輔導員

G. **set** a long-term goal
設定長期目標

H. **set** a short-term goal
設定短期目標

I. **attend** a job fair
參加人才招募會

J. **speak** with a recruiter
與招募人員交談

Career Path 職業發展途徑

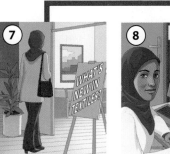

1. basic education
   基本教育
2. entry-level job
   初級工作
3. training
   訓練
4. new job
   新工作

5. college degree
   大學文憑
6. career advancement
   職業提升
7. continuing education /
   professional
   development
   專業進修教育 /
   專業發展
8. promotion
   晉升

Types of Training 培訓種類

9. career and technical
   training / vocational
   training
   職業與技術訓練 /
   專科訓練
10. apprenticeship
    學徒
11. internship
    實習
12. on-the-job training
    在職訓練
13. online course
    線上課程
14. workshop
    專題討論會

A. assemble components
裝配部件

B. assist medical patients
協助病人

C. cook
烹調

D. do manual labour
從事勞力工作

E. drive a truck
開貨車 / 開貨櫃車

F. fly a plane
開飛機

G. make furniture
製做家具

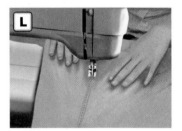

H. operate heavy machinery
操縱重型機械

I. program computers
編寫電腦程式

J. repair appliances
修理電器

K. sell cars
銷售汽車

L. sew clothes
縫製衣服

M. solve math problems
解數學題

N. speak another language
說另一種語言

O. supervise people
管理員工

P. take care of children
照顧孩童

Q. teach
教書

R. type
打字

S. use a cash register
使用收銀機

T. wait on customers
服侍顧客

Grammar Point: *can, can't*

*I am a chef. I **can** cook.*
*I'm not a pilot. I **can't** fly a plane.*
*I **can't** speak French, but I **can** speak Spanish.*

Role play. Talk to a job counselor.

A: *Let's talk about your skills. Can you <u>type</u>?*
B: *<u>No, I can't, but</u> I can <u>use a cash register</u>.*
A: *That's good. What else can you do?*

Office Skills
辦公室技能

A. **type** a letter
打信

B. **enter** data
輸入數據

C. **transcribe** notes
聽寫筆記

D. **make** copies
複印

E. **collate** papers
分揀文件

F. **staple**
裝訂

G. **fax** a document
傳真文件

H. **scan** a document
掃描文件

I. **print** a document
列印文件

J. **schedule** a meeting
安排會議時間

K. **take** notes
作筆記

L. **organize** materials
整理材料

Telephone Skills
電話技能

M. **greet** the caller
接聽來電

N. **put** the caller on hold
讓來電者等候

O. **transfer** the call
轉接來電

P. **leave** a message
留言

Q. **take** a message
記下留言

R. **check** messages
聆聽留言

177

Soft Skills 軟技能

Leadership Skills 領導技能

A. solve problems
解決問題

B. think critically
批判思考

C. make decisions
做出決策

D. manage time
管理時間

Interpersonal Skills 人際技能

E. communicate clearly
清楚溝通

F. cooperate with teammates
與同事合作

G. clarify instructions
澄清指令

H. respond well to feedback
對反饋有良好回應

Personal Qualities 個人素質

1. patient
耐心

2. positive
積極

3. willing to learn
樂於學習

4. honest
誠實

Ways to talk about your skills
I **can** <u>solve problems</u>. I <u>communicate clearly</u>.
Ways to talk about your qualities
I **am** <u>patient</u> and <u>honest</u>.

Talk about your skills and abilities.
A: *Tell me about your <u>leadership skills</u>.*
B: *I <u>can solve problems</u>. How about you?*
A: *I <u>can think critically</u>.*

178

A. **Prepare** for the interview.
準備面試。

B. **Dress** appropriately.
穿著適當。

C. **Be** neat.
乾淨整齊。

D. **Bring** your résumé and ID.
攜帶履歷表和身份證。

E. **Don't be** late.
不要遲到。

F. **Be** on time.
準時到達。

G. **Turn off** your cell phone.
關閉行動電話。

H. **Greet** the interviewer.
與面試員打招呼。

I. **Shake** hands.
握手。

J. **Make** eye contact.
眼神接觸。

K. **Listen** carefully.
認真聽。

L. **Talk** about your experience.
談論您的經驗。

M. **Ask** questions.
提出問題。

N. **Thank** the interviewer.
感謝面試員。

O. **Write** a thank-you note.
寫感謝函。

More vocabulary

benefits: health insurance, vacation pay, or other things the employer can offer an employee
inquire about benefits: to ask about benefits

Identify Dan's problem. Brainstorm solutions.

Dan has an interview tomorrow. Making eye contact with strangers is hard for him. He doesn't like to ask questions. What can he do?

179

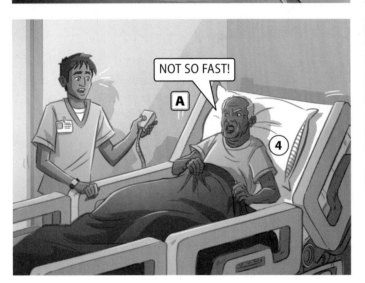

1. facility
   設施
2. staff
   工作人員
3. team player
   團隊成員
4. resident
   住客
5. co-workers
   同事
6. shift
   班次

A. **yell**
   吼叫
B. **complain**
   抱怨
C. **direct**
   指引
D. **distribute**
   分發

Not 10B, Leo! 10D – down the hall.

10B

How did it go, Leo?

I learned a lot!

FROM	TO	CNA STAFF
1ST 7:00AM	3:30PM	MARY, LIZ, LEO
2ND 3:00PM	11:30PM	BEN, SARA, TOM
3RD 11:00PM	7:30AM	MEI, KARA, JOSH

What do you see in the pictures?

1. What time does Leo arrive at the nursing home?

2. What other types of workers are on the staff?

3. Is Leo a team player? How do you know?

4. How long was Leo's shift on his first day?

Read the story.

First Day on the Job

Leo Reyes arrives at the Lakeview nursing home <u>facility</u> at 7 a.m. It's his first day as a nursing assistant. The nurse, Ms. Castro, introduces him to the <u>staff</u>. He meets Lakeview's receptionist, cook, social worker, physical therapists, and the other nursing assistants. Then it's time for work.

Leo has a positive attitude. He is a <u>team player</u>. He also makes mistakes.

One elderly <u>resident</u> <u>yells</u> at Leo. Another <u>complains</u> about him. Leo goes to the wrong room, but a <u>co-worker</u> <u>directs</u> him to the right one.

The afternoon is better. Leo listens to the residents talk about their careers. He drives the van to the mall. He helps another nursing assistant <u>distribute</u> the afternoon snacks.

At the end of his <u>shift</u>, Ms. Castro asks Leo about his day. He tells her, "I worked hard, made mistakes, and learned a lot!" Ms. Castro smiles and says, "Sounds like a good first day!"

Reread the story.

1. Highlight the word "distribute" in Paragraph 4. What other words can you use here?

2. Underline two examples of negative feedback in the story.

What do you think?

3. Should Leo respond to the residents' feedback? Why or why not?

181

1. entrance
   入口

2. customer
   顧客

3. office
   辦公室

4. employer / boss
   僱主 / 老闆

5. receptionist
   接待員

6. safety regulations
   安全規定

IRINA'S COMPUTER SERVICE

OHS

HAZARDS

SPILLS

CALL 911

SAFETY FIRST

Irina Sarkov Owner

COMPUTER NEWS

Listen and point. Take turns.

A: Point to the *front entrance*.
B: Point to the *receptionist*.
A: Point to the *time clock*.

Dictate to your partner. Take turns.

A: Can you spell *employer*?
B: I'm not sure. Is it *e-m-p-l-o-y-e-r*?
A: Yes, that's right.

7. time clock
打卡機

8. supervisor
主管人員

9. employee
員工

10. payroll clerk
發放薪資的職員

11. pay stub
薪資單

12. wages
工資

13. deductions
扣除部份

14. pay cheque
薪資支票

Ways to talk about wages

*I **earn** $800 a week.*
*He **makes** $10 an hour.*
*I'm **paid** $2,000 a month.*

Role play. Talk to an employer.

A: *Is everything correct on your pay cheque?*
B: *No, it isn't. I make $619 a week, not $519.*
A: *Let's talk to the payroll clerk. Where is she?*

183

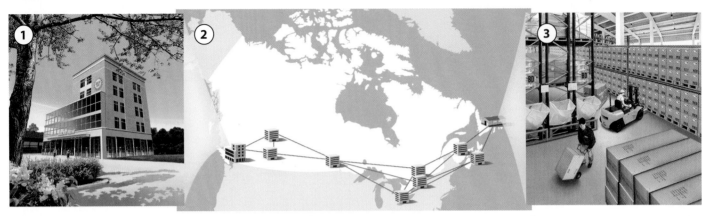

1. corporate offices / headquarters
企業辦公室 / 總部

2. branch locations
分支機構地點

3. warehouse
倉庫

4. human resources
人力資源

5. research and development
研究與開發

6. marketing
市場拓展

7. sales
銷售

8. logistics
物流

9. accounting
會計

10. IT / information technology
資訊科技

11. customer service
客戶服務

12. building maintenance
設施維護

13. security
保安

Use the new words.

Look at pages 170–173. Find jobs for each department.
A: _Accountants_ work in _accounting_.
B: _Security guards_ work in _security_.

Survey your class. Record the responses.

Which department(s) would you like to work in?
Report: _Ten_ of us would like to work in _logistics_.
_Nobody wants to work in _security_._

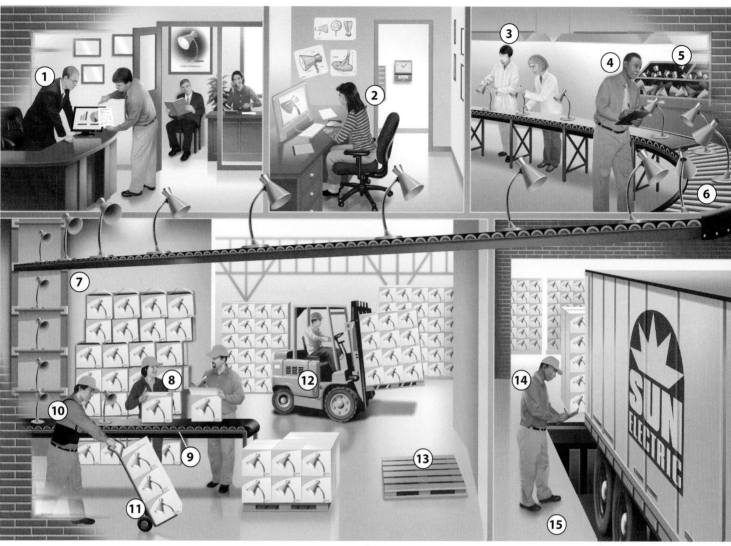

1. **factory owner**
   工廠老闆

2. **designer**
   設計師

3. **factory worker**
   工廠工人

4. **line supervisor**
   生產線主管

5. **parts**
   零件

6. **assembly line**
   裝配線

7. **warehouse**
   倉庫

8. **packer**
   包裝工人

9. **conveyor belt**
   傳送帶

10. **order picker**
    撿貨員

11. **hand truck**
    手推車

12. **forklift**
    堆高機 / 叉車

13. **pallet / skid**
    棧板

14. **shipping clerk**
    發運職員

15. **loading dock**
    裝卸平臺

A. **design**
設計

B. **manufacture**
製造

C. **assemble**
裝配

D. **ship**
發運

1. gardening crew
   園丁班組

2. leaf blower
   吹葉機

3. wheelbarrow
   獨輪車

4. gardening crew leader
   園丁班組長

5. landscape designer
   景觀設計師

6. lawn mower
   割草機

7. shovel
   鏟子

8. rake
   耙子

9. pruning shears
   修枝剪

10. trowel
    小鏟子

11. hedge clippers
    修籬剪

12. weed whacker
    雜草割草器

A. **mow** the lawn
   割草

B. **trim** the hedges
   修樹籬

C. **rake** the leaves
   耙樹葉

D. **fertilize** / **feed** the plants
   施撒肥料

E. **plant** a tree
   植樹

F. **water** the plants
   澆花

G. **weed** the flower beds
   除雜草

H. **install** a sprinkler system
   安裝灑水器

Use the new words.

Look at page 53. Name what you can do in the yard.

A: *I can mow the lawn*.

B: *I can weed the flower bed*.

Identify Inez's problem. Brainstorm solutions.

Inez works on a gardening crew. She wants to learn to install sprinklers. The crew leader has no time to teach her. What can she do?

Crops 農作物

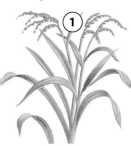

1. rice
米

2. wheat
小麥

3. soybeans
黃豆

4. corn
玉蜀黍

5. alfalfa
苜蓿

6. cotton
棉花

7. field
田地

12. farm equipment
農場設備

17. corral
畜欄

22. rancher
農場工人

8. farm worker
農場工人

13. farmer / grower
農夫 / 種植者

18. hay
乾草

A. **plant**
植物

9. tractor
拖拉機

14. vegetable garden
菜園

19. fence
圍籬

B. **harvest**
收割

10. orchard
果園

15. livestock
牲畜

20. hired hand
僱工

C. **milk**
擠奶

11. barn
穀倉

16. vineyard
葡萄園

21. cattle
牛

D. **feed**
餵食

EMPLOYEE SCHEDULE

Ben Hasler 10/11/07
Dan Green 12/11/07

GREEN ENERGY CORPORATION

1. supply cabinet	5. executive	9. desk	13. PBX
文具櫃	主管	書桌	內線交換機
2. clerk	6. presentation	10. file clerk	14. receptionist
職員	演示	檔案管理員	接待員
3. janitor	7. cubicle	11. file cabinet	15. reception area
清潔工	小隔間	檔案櫃	接待區
4. conference room	8. office manager	12. computer technician	16. waiting area
會議室	辦公室經理	電腦技師	等候區

Ways to greet a receptionist

Good <u>morning</u>. I'm here for a <u>job interview</u>.
Hello. I have a <u>9 a.m.</u> appointment with <u>Mr. Lee</u>.
Hi. I'm here to see <u>Mr. Lee</u>. <u>He's</u> expecting me.

Role play. Talk to a receptionist.

A: *Hello. How can I help you?*
B: *<u>I'm here for a job interview with Mr. Lee</u>.*
A: *OK. What is your name?*

Office Equipment 辦公室設備

17. computer
電腦

18. inkjet printer
噴墨印表機

19. laser printer
鐳射印表機

20. scanner
掃描器

21. fax machine
傳真機

22. paper cutter
切紙刀

23. photocopier
影印機

24. paper shredder
碎紙機

25. calculator
計算器

26. electric pencil sharpener
電動削鉛筆機

27. postal scale
郵件秤

Office Supplies 辦公用品

28. stapler
釘書機

29. staples
釘書針

30. clear tape
透明膠帶

31. paper clip
迴紋針

32. packing tape
包裝用膠帶

33. glue
膠水

34. rubber band
橡皮筋

35. pushpin
大頭釘

36. correction fluid
修正液

37. correction tape
修正帶

38. legal pad
長型雜記本

39. sticky notes
便利貼

40. mailer
大信封

41. mailing label
郵寄標籤

42. letterhead / stationery
信箋

43. envelope
信封

44. rotary card file
筒狀型旋轉地址錄

45. ink cartridge
墨水盒

46. ink pad
印臺

47. stamp
印章

48. appointment book
預約簿

49. organizer
行事曆 / 記事簿

50. file folder
檔案夾

1. **mainframe computer**
   大型電腦

2. **computer operations specialist**
   電腦作業專家

3. **data**
   數據

4. **cybersecurity**
   網路安全

5. **virus alert**
   病毒警告

6. **tablet**
   平板電腦

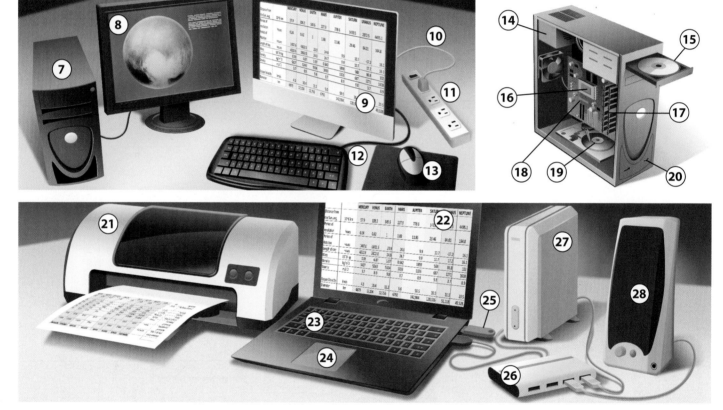

7. **tower**
   機箱

8. **monitor**
   監視器

9. **desktop computer**
   桌上型電腦

10. **power cord**
    電源線

11. **surge protector**
    電壓保護器

12. **cable**
    電線

13. **mouse**
    滑鼠

14. **power supply unit**
    電源供應器

15. **DVD and CD-ROM drive**
    DVD和CD-ROM光碟機

16. **microprocessor / CPU**
    微處理器

17. **RAM (random access memory)**
    隨機存取記憶體

18. **motherboard**
    主機板

19. **hard drive**
    硬碟機

20. **USB port**
    USB 埠

21. **printer**
    印表機

22. **laptop computer**
    膝上型電腦

23. **keyboard**
    鍵盤

24. **track pad**
    軌跡板

25. **flash drive / thumb drive**
    快閃碟 / 隨身碟

26. **hub**
    集線器

27. **external hard drive**
    外置硬碟

28. **speaker**
    揚聲器

Software / Applications 軟體 / 應用程式

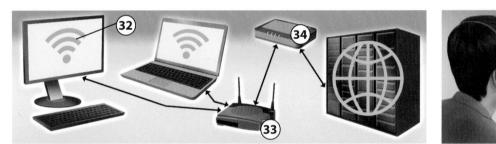

29. word processing program
文字處理程式

30. spreadsheet program
試算表程式

31. presentation program
簡報程式

Internet Connectivity 網際網路連接

32. Wi-Fi connection
Wi-Fi 無線連接

34. modem
數據機

33. router
路由器

Web Conferencing 網路會議

35. headset
頭戴收話器

37. webcam
網路鏡頭

36. mic / microphone
麥克風

A. The computer **won't start**.
電腦不啟動。

B. The screen **froze**.
螢幕凍結。

C. I **can't install** the update.
我無法安裝該更新。

D. I **can't log on**.
我無法登入。

E. It **won't print**.
它不列印。

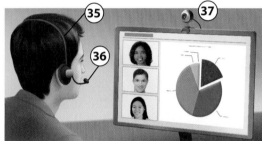

F. I **can't stream** video.
我無法串流視訊。

1. doorman
門童

2. revolving door
旋轉門

3. parking attendant
停車服務員

4. concierge
禮賓部

5. gift shop
禮品店

6. bell captain
行李總管

7. bellhop
行李服務員

8. luggage cart
行李車

9. elevator
電梯

10. guest
賓客

11. desk clerk
櫃檯職員

12. front desk
櫃檯

13. guest room
客房

14. double bed
雙人床

15. king-size bed
大雙人床

16. suite
套房

17. room service
客房用餐服務

18. hallway
走廊

19. housekeeping cart
房間清理車

20. housekeeper
房間清理工

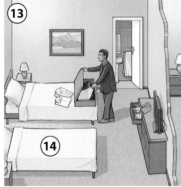

21. pool service
游泳池服務

22. pool
游泳池

23. maintenance
維護

24. gym
健身房

25. meeting room
會議室

26. ballroom
大舞廳

A Restaurant Kitchen 餐廳廚房

1. short-order cook
   快餐廚師

2. dishwasher
   洗碗工

3. walk-in freezer
   大冰庫

4. food preparation worker
   食物準備工

5. storeroom
   儲藏室

6. sous-chef
   副主廚

7. head chef / executive chef
   領班廚師 / 行政總廚

Restaurant Dining 餐廳用餐

8. server
   侍者

9. diner
   食客

10. buffet
    自助餐

11. maitre d'
    領臺員

12. headwaiter
    侍者總管

13. bus person
    侍者助手

14. banquet room
    宴會廳

15. runner
    跑堂

16. caterer
    包辦餐飲者

More vocabulary

line cook: short-order cook

wait staff: servers, headwaiters, and runners

Think about it. Discuss.

1. What is the hardest job in a hotel or restaurant? Explain.
   (*Being a _____ is hard because these workers have to _____.*)

2. Pick two jobs on these pages. Compare them.

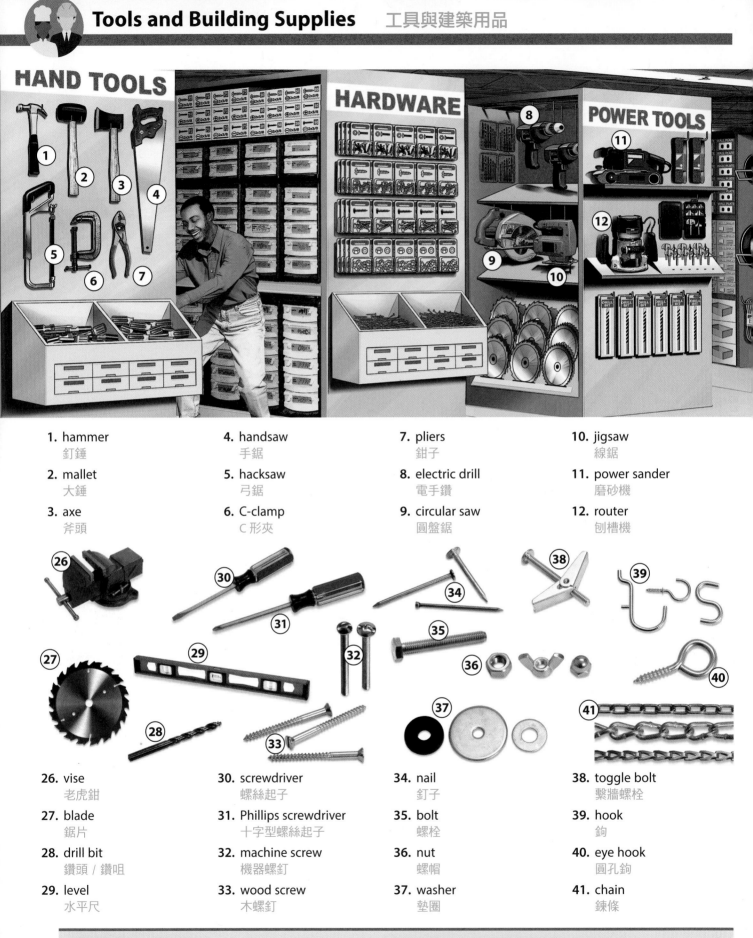

HAND TOOLS

HARDWARE

POWER TOOLS

1. hammer
釘錘

2. mallet
大錘

3. axe
斧頭

4. handsaw
手鋸

5. hacksaw
弓鋸

6. C-clamp
C 形夾

7. pliers
鉗子

8. electric drill
電手鑽

9. circular saw
圓盤鋸

10. jigsaw
線鋸

11. power sander
磨砂機

12. router
刨槽機

26. vise
老虎鉗

27. blade
鋸片

28. drill bit
鑽頭 / 鑽咀

29. level
水平尺

30. screwdriver
螺絲起子

31. Phillips screwdriver
十字型螺絲起子

32. machine screw
機器螺釘

33. wood screw
木螺釘

34. nail
釘子

35. bolt
螺栓

36. nut
螺帽

37. washer
墊圈

38. toggle bolt
繫牆螺栓

39. hook
鉤

40. eye hook
圓孔鉤

41. chain
鍊條

Use the new words.
Look at pages 62–63. Name the tools you see.

A: *There's a hammer*.
B: *There's a pipe wrench*.

Survey your class. Record the responses.
1. Are you good with tools?
2. Which tools do you have at home?
Report: *75% of us are… Most of us have…*

194

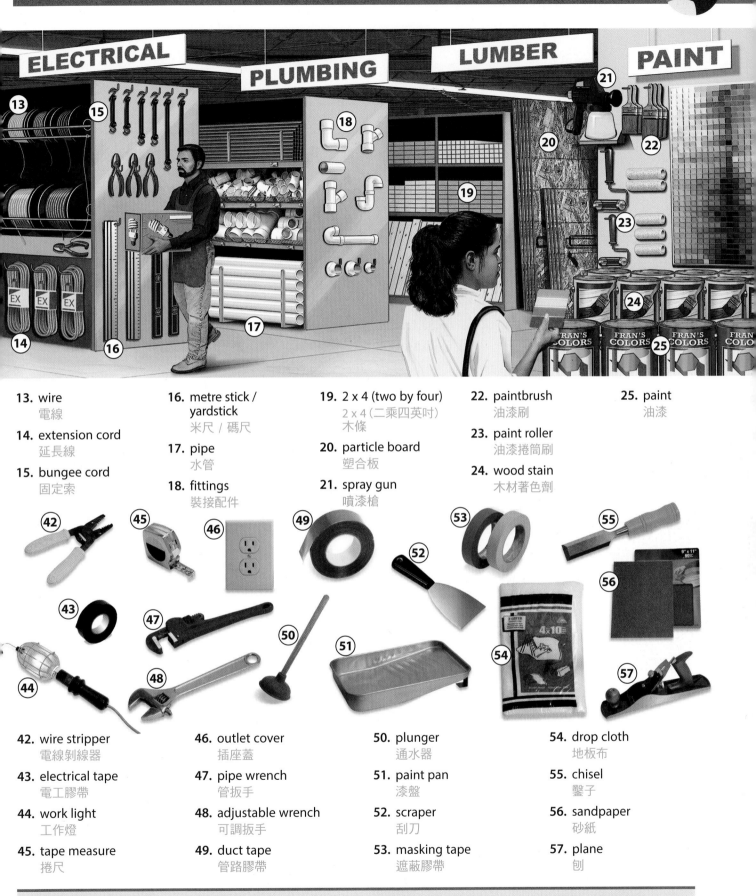

ELECTRICAL　**PLUMBING**　**LUMBER**　**PAINT**

13. wire
电线

14. extension cord
延長線

15. bungee cord
固定索

16. metre stick /
yardstick
米尺 / 碼尺

17. pipe
水管

18. fittings
裝接配件

19. 2 x 4 (two by four)
2 x 4（二乘四英吋）
木條

20. particle board
塑合板

21. spray gun
噴漆槍

22. paintbrush
油漆刷

23. paint roller
油漆捲筒刷

24. wood stain
木材著色劑

25. paint
油漆

42. wire stripper
電線剝線器

43. electrical tape
電工膠帶

44. work light
工作燈

45. tape measure
捲尺

46. outlet cover
插座蓋

47. pipe wrench
管扳手

48. adjustable wrench
可調扳手

49. duct tape
管路膠帶

50. plunger
通水器

51. paint pan
漆盤

52. scraper
刮刀

53. masking tape
遮蔽膠帶

54. drop cloth
地板布

55. chisel
鑿子

56. sandpaper
砂紙

57. plane
刨

Role play. Find an item in a building supply store.

A: *Where can I find particle board?*
B: *It's on the back wall, in the lumber section.*
A: *Great. And where are the nails?*

Identify Jean's problem. Brainstorm solutions.

Jean borrowed Jody's drill last month. Now she can't find it. She doesn't know what to do!

195

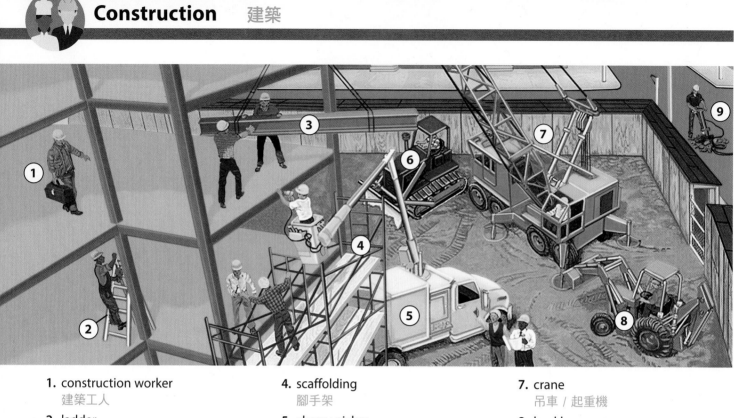

1. construction worker
建築工人

2. ladder
梯子

3. I beam / girder
房樑

4. scaffolding
腳手架

5. cherry picker
車載升降臺

6. bulldozer
推土機

7. crane
吊車 / 起重機

8. backhoe
挖土機

9. jackhammer / pneumatic drill
鑿岩機 / 風鑽

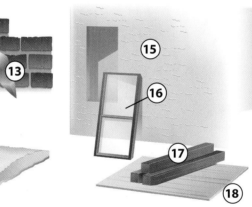

10. concrete
水泥

11. tile
瓷磚

12. bricks
磚塊

13. trowel
鏝刀 / 灰鏟

14. insulation
隔熱層

15. stucco
灰泥

16. windowpane
窗玻璃

17. wood / lumber
木材

18. plywood
夾層板

19. drywall
清水牆 / 預製牆板

20. shingles
瓦

21. pickaxe
鶴嘴鋤

22. shovel
鏟子

23. sledgehammer
大錘

A. paint
油漆

B. lay bricks
砌磚塊

C. install tile
裝瓷磚

D. hammer
錘打

Safety Hazards and Hazardous Materials 安全危害與危害性材料

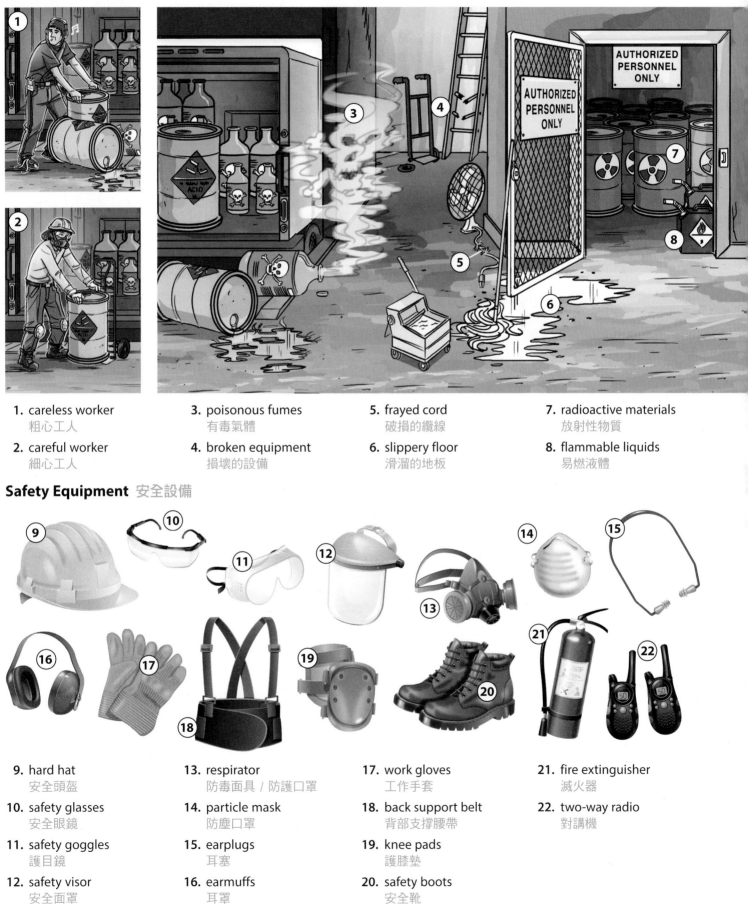

1. careless worker
粗心工人

2. careful worker
細心工人

3. poisonous fumes
有毒氣體

4. broken equipment
損壞的設備

5. frayed cord
破損的纜線

6. slippery floor
滑溜的地板

7. radioactive materials
放射性物質

8. flammable liquids
易燃液體

Safety Equipment 安全設備

9. hard hat
安全頭盔

10. safety glasses
安全眼鏡

11. safety goggles
護目鏡

12. safety visor
安全面罩

13. respirator
防毒面具 / 防護口罩

14. particle mask
防塵口罩

15. earplugs
耳塞

16. earmuffs
耳罩

17. work gloves
工作手套

18. back support belt
背部支撐腰帶

19. knee pads
護膝墊

20. safety boots
安全靴

21. fire extinguisher
滅火器

22. two-way radio
對講機

A Bad Day at Work　工作不順利的一天

1. dangerous
危險

2. clinic
診所

3. budget
預算

4. floor plan
平面圖

5. contractor
承包商

6. electrical hazard
觸電危險

7. wiring
接線

8. bricklayer
砌磚工人

A. **call in** sick
打電話請病假

What do you see in the pictures?

1. How many workers are there?
   How many are working?

2. Why did two workers call in sick?

3. What is dangerous at the construction site?

Read the story.

A Bad Day at Work

Sam Lopez is the <u>contractor</u> for a new building. He makes the schedule and supervises the <u>budget</u>. He also solves problems. Today there are a lot of problems.

Two <u>bricklayers</u> <u>called in sick</u> this morning. So Sam has only one bricklayer at work. One hour later, a construction worker fell. He had to go to the <u>clinic</u>.

Construction work is <u>dangerous</u>. Sam always tells his workers to be careful. Yesterday he told them about the new <u>wiring</u> on the site. It's an <u>electrical hazard</u>.

Right now, the building owner is in Sam's office. Her new <u>floor plan</u> has 25 more offices. Sam has a headache. Maybe he needs to call in sick tomorrow.

Reread the story.

1. Make a timeline of the events in this story. What happened first? next? last?

2. Find the sentence "He had to go to the clinic" in Paragraph 2. Is "he" the worker or Sam? How do you know?

What do you think?

3. Give examples of good reasons (or excuses) to give when you can't come in to work. Give an example of a bad excuse. Why is it bad?

4. Imagine you are Sam. What do you tell the building owner? Why?

1. preschool /
   nursery school
   學前班 / 托兒所

2. elementary school
   小學

3. middle school /
   junior high school
   初中

4. high school
   高中

5. vocational school /
   technical school
   職業學校 / 技術學校

6. (community) college /
   CEGEP
   (社區) 學院

7. university
   大學

8. adult school
   成人學校

Listen and point. Take turns.

A: *Point to the <u>preschool</u>.*
B: *Point to the <u>high school</u>.*
A: *Point to the <u>adult school</u>.*

Dictate to your partner. Take turns.

A: *Write <u>preschool</u>.*
B: *Is that <u>p-r-e-s-c-h-o-o-l</u>?*
A: *Yes, that's right.*

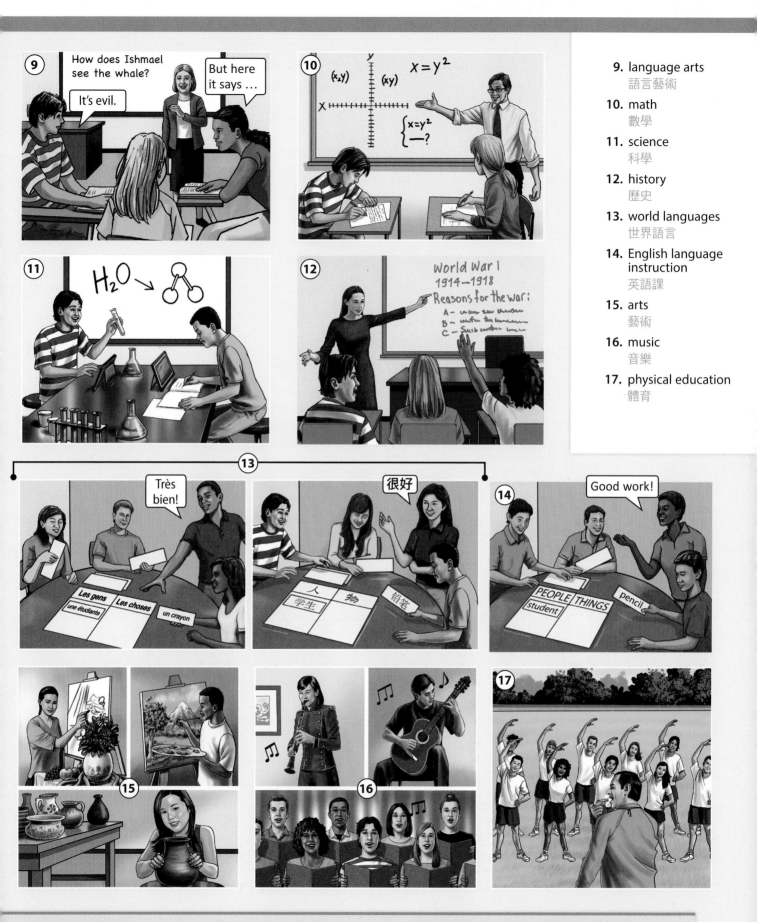

9. language arts
語言藝術

10. math
數學

11. science
科學

12. history
歷史

13. world languages
世界語言

14. English language instruction
英語課

15. arts
藝術

16. music
音樂

17. physical education
體育

More vocabulary

core course: a subject students have to take.
Math is a core course.

elective: a subject students choose to take. Art is an elective.

Pair practice. Make new conversations.

A: *I go to a community college.*
B: *What subjects are you taking?*
A: *I'm taking history and science.*

English Composition 英文寫作

1. factory

1. word
字詞

2. I worked in a factory.

2. sentence
句子

3. Little by little, work and success came to me. My first job wasn't good. I worked in a small factory. Now, I help manage two factories.

3. paragraph
段落

4.

4. essay
短文

Parts of an Essay
短文各部份

5. title
標題

6. introduction
前言

7. evidence
證據

8. body
正文

9. conclusion
結論

10. quotation
引文

11. citation
引註

12. footnote
腳註

13. source
資料來源

Erdem Koca
Eng. Comp.
10/21/16

5 Success in Canada

6 I came to Calgary from Turkey in 2006. I had no job, no friends, and no family here. I was homesick and scared, but I did not go home. I took English classes (always at night) and I studied hard. I believed in my future success!

7 According to Immigration, Refugees and Citizenship Canada, an average of more than 250,000 new immigrants come to Canada every year.[1] Most of us need to find work. During my first year here, my routine was the same: get up; look for work; go to class; go to bed. I had to take jobs with long hours and low pay. Often I had two or three jobs.

8 Little by little, work and success came to me. My first job wasn't good. I worked in a small factory. Now, I help manage two factories.

9 Hard work makes success possible, and **10** "men are born to succeed, not fail" (Thoreau, 1853). My story **11** demonstrates the truth of that statement.

12 [1] Source: www.open.gc.ca: Permanent Resident Admissions by Category **13**

Punctuation
標點符號

. 14. period
句號

? 15. question mark
問號

! 16. exclamation mark / exclamation point
感歎號

, 17. comma
逗號

" " 18. quotation marks
引號

' 19. apostrophe
撇號

: 20. colon
冒號

; 21. semicolon
分號

( ) 22. parentheses
括弧

- 23. hyphen
連字符

Writing Rules 寫作規則

A

Erdem
Turkey
Calgary

A. **Capitalize** names.
大寫專有名詞。

B

Hard work makes success possible.

B. **Capitalize** the first letter in a sentence.
大寫每句話的第一個字母。

C

I was homesick and scared, but I did not go home.

C. **Use** punctuation.
使用標點符號。

D

   I came to Calgary from Turkey in 2006. I had no job, no friends, and no family here. I was homesick and scared, but I did not go home. I took English classes (always at night) and I studied hard. I believed in my future success!

D. **Indent** the first sentence in a paragraph.
縮排每個段落的第一句話。

Ways to ask for suggestions on your compositions

What do you think of this title?
Is this paragraph OK? Is the punctuation correct?
Do you have any suggestions for the conclusion?

Pair practice. Make new conversations.

A: What do you think of this *title*?
B: *I think you need to revise it.*
A: *Thanks. How would you revise it?*

202

The Writing Process 寫作程序

E Writing assignment - Due 10/3
Write an essay about
your first year in Canada.

*my life... hmm...
what can I say...
I have one week...*

E. Think about the assignment.
考慮作業內容。

F

factory

work — 2 jobs

1st year — 2006

ESL — no family

friends — lonely

F. Brainstorm ideas.
用腦激盪法以得出大量想法。

G

I. Turkey to Calgary
  A. No family
    1. Homesick
    2. Scared
  B. No job
II. Daily routine
  A. Job search
  B. ESL class
    1. Friends
III. Success

G. Organize your ideas.
組織想法。

WRITING AND REVISING

H

I came to Calgary from Turkey in 2006...

H. Write a first draft.
寫草稿。

I

I. Edit. / Proofread.
編輯。/ 校對。

J

J. Revise. / Rewrite.
修改。/ 改寫。

SHARING AND RESPONDING

K OCTOBER 1

I like the part about your daily routine.

K. Get feedback.
徵求意見。

L

L. Write a final draft.
書寫終稿。

M OCTOBER 3

M. Turn in / Hand in your paper.
交文章。

Survey your class. Record the responses.

1. Do you prefer to write essays or read them?
2. Which is more difficult: writing a first draft or revising?

Report: *Five people I surveyed said ___.*

Think about it. Discuss.

1. What are interesting topics for essays?
2. Do you like to read quotations? Why or why not?
3. In which jobs are writing skills important?

Mathematics 數學

Integers 整數

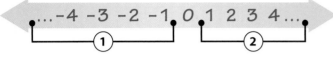

1. negative integers
負整數

2. positive integers
正整數

Fractions 分數

3 1, 3, 5, 7, 9, 11 …

4 2, 4, 6, 8, 10 …

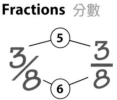

$\frac{3}{8}$ $\frac{3}{8}$

3. odd numbers
奇數

4. even numbers
偶數

5. numerator
分子

6. denominator
分母

Math Operations 數學演算

A. add 加

B. subtract 減

C. multiply 乘

D. divide 除

$$8 + 4 = 12 \qquad 8 - 4 = 4 \qquad 8 \times 4 = 32 \qquad 8 \div 4 = 2$$

7. sum
和

8. difference
差

9. product
積

10. quotient
商

A Math Problem 數學問題

11

Tom is 10 years older than Kim. Next year he will be twice as old as Kim. How old is Tom this year?

12 — x = Kim's age now
$x + 10$ = Tom's age now
$x + 1$ = Kim's age next year
$2(x + 1)$ = Tom's age next year

$x + 10 + 1 = 2(x + 1)$
$x + 11 = 2x + 2$
$11 - 2 = 2x - x$

13

$x = 9$, Kim is 9, Tom is 19 14

15

horizontal axis

vertical axis

11. word problem
文字題

12. variable
變數

13. equation
等式

14. solution
解

15. graph
圖

Types of Math 數學的種類

How much are they?

$79 NOW 40% OFF!

x = the sale price
x = 79.00 - .40 (79.00)
x = $47.40

16. algebra
代數

How many do I need?

area of path = 6 square metres
area of brick = 0.5 square metres
6/0.5 = 12 bricks

17. geometry
幾何學

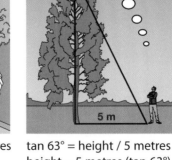

How tall is it?

5 m

tan 63° = height / 5 metres
height = 5 metres (tan 63°)
height ≃ 9.81 metres

18. trigonometry
三角學

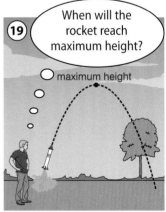

When will the rocket reach maximum height?

maximum height

$s(t) = -\frac{1}{2} gt^2 + V_0 t + h$
$s^{I}(t) = -gt + V_0 = 0$
$t = V_0 / g$

19. calculus
微積分

Lines 線

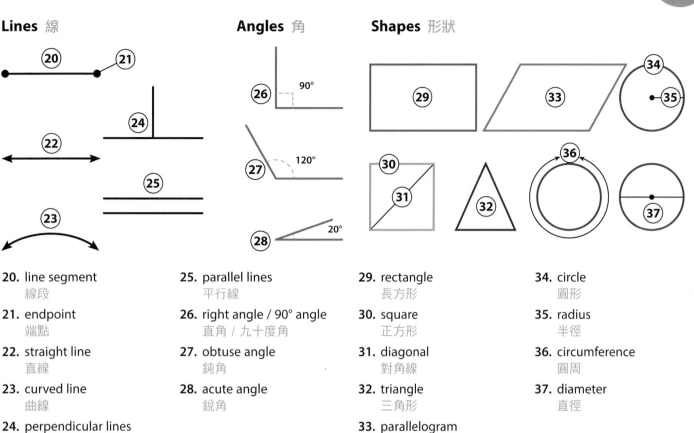

Angles 角

Shapes 形狀

20. line segment
線段

21. endpoint
端點

22. straight line
直線

23. curved line
曲線

24. perpendicular lines
垂直線

25. parallel lines
平行線

26. right angle / 90° angle
直角 / 九十度角

27. obtuse angle
鈍角

28. acute angle
銳角

29. rectangle
長方形

30. square
正方形

31. diagonal
對角線

32. triangle
三角形

33. parallelogram
平行四邊形

34. circle
圓形

35. radius
半徑

36. circumference
圓周

37. diameter
直徑

Geometric Solids 幾何體

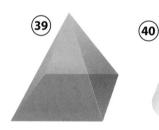

38. cube
正方體

39. pyramid
角錐體

40. cone
圓錐體

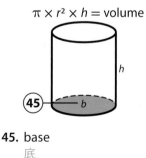

41. cylinder
圓柱體

42. sphere
球體

Measuring Area and Volume
測量面積和體積

$\ell \times w = \text{area}$

w

ℓ

$6 \times f = \text{surface area}$

f

43. perimeter
週長

44. face
面

$\pi \times r^2 \times h = \text{volume}$

h

b

$\frac{4}{3} \times \pi \times r^3 = \text{volume}$

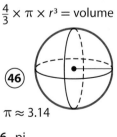

$\pi \approx 3.14$

45. base
底

46. pi
圓週率

Survey your class. Record the responses.

1. Is division easy or difficult?

2. Is algebra easy or difficult?

Report: _50% of the class thinks ____ is difficult._

Think about it. Discuss.

1. What's the best way to learn mathematics?

2. How can you find the area of your classroom?

3. Which jobs use math? Which don't?

Biology 生物學

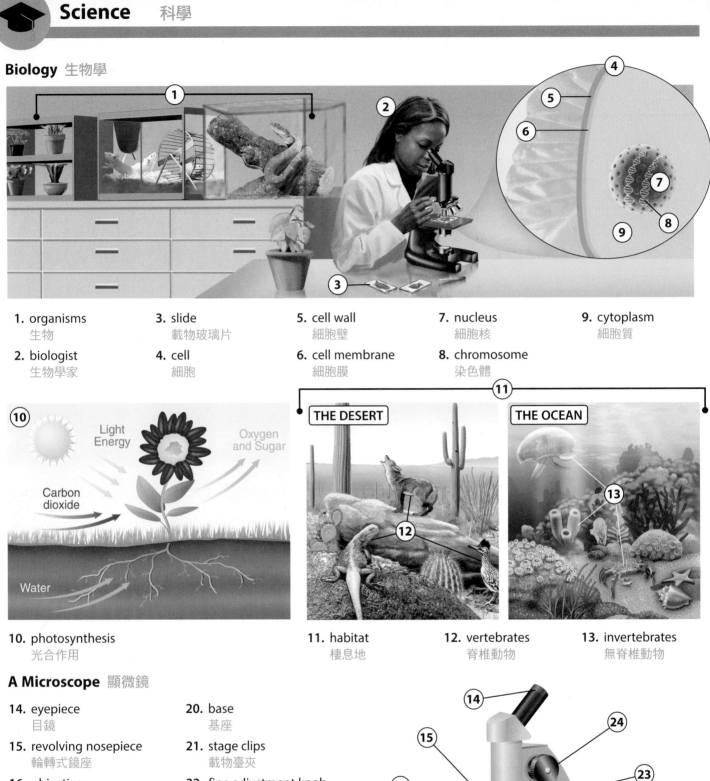

1. organisms
   生物
2. biologist
   生物學家
3. slide
   載物玻璃片
4. cell
   細胞
5. cell wall
   細胞壁
6. cell membrane
   細胞膜
7. nucleus
   細胞核
8. chromosome
   染色體
9. cytoplasm
   細胞質

10. photosynthesis
    光合作用

11. habitat
    棲息地
12. vertebrates
    脊椎動物
13. invertebrates
    無脊椎動物

A Microscope 顯微鏡

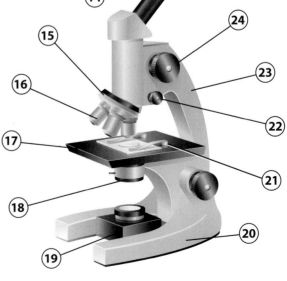

14. eyepiece
    目鏡
15. revolving nosepiece
    輪轉式鏡座
16. objective
    物鏡
17. stage
    載物臺
18. diaphragm
    光圈
19. light source
    光源

20. base
    基座
21. stage clips
    載物臺夾
22. fine adjustment knob
    微調旋鈕
23. arm
    臂
24. coarse adjustment knob
    粗調旋鈕

Chemistry 化學

Physics 物理

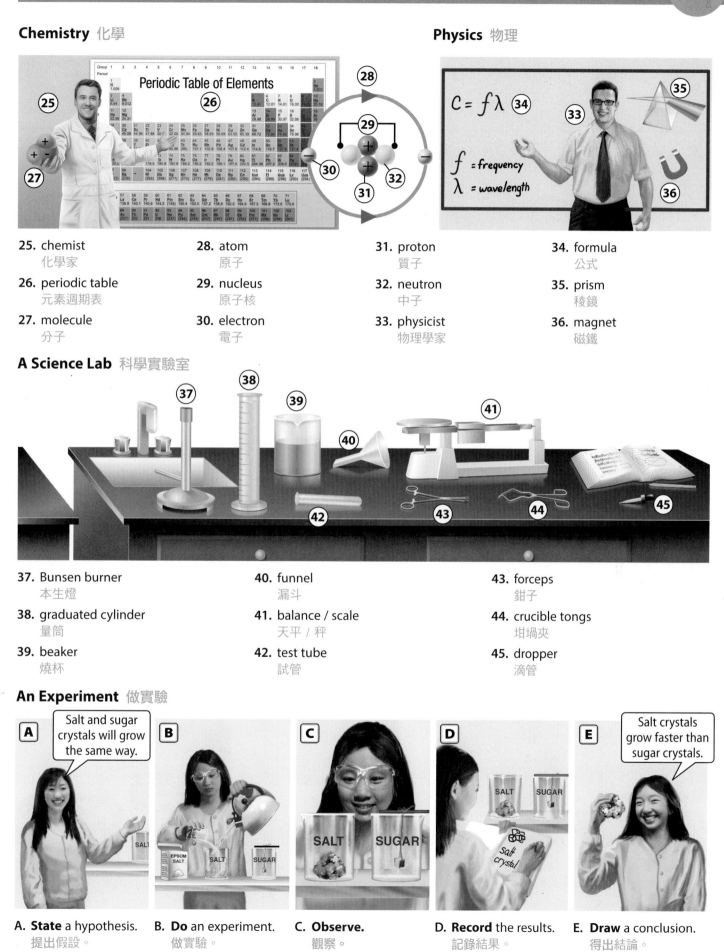

25. chemist
化學家

26. periodic table
元素週期表

27. molecule
分子

28. atom
原子

29. nucleus
原子核

30. electron
電子

31. proton
質子

32. neutron
中子

33. physicist
物理學家

34. formula
公式

35. prism
稜鏡

36. magnet
磁鐵

A Science Lab 科學實驗室

37. Bunsen burner
本生燈

38. graduated cylinder
量筒

39. beaker
燒杯

40. funnel
漏斗

41. balance / scale
天平 / 秤

42. test tube
試管

43. forceps
鉗子

44. crucible tongs
坩堝夾

45. dropper
滴管

An Experiment 做實驗

A. **State** a hypothesis.
提出假設。

B. **Do** an experiment.
做實驗。

C. **Observe.**
觀察。

D. **Record** the results.
記錄結果。

E. **Draw** a conclusion.
得出結論。

Salt and sugar crystals will grow the same way.

Salt crystals grow faster than sugar crystals.

Confederation 邦聯

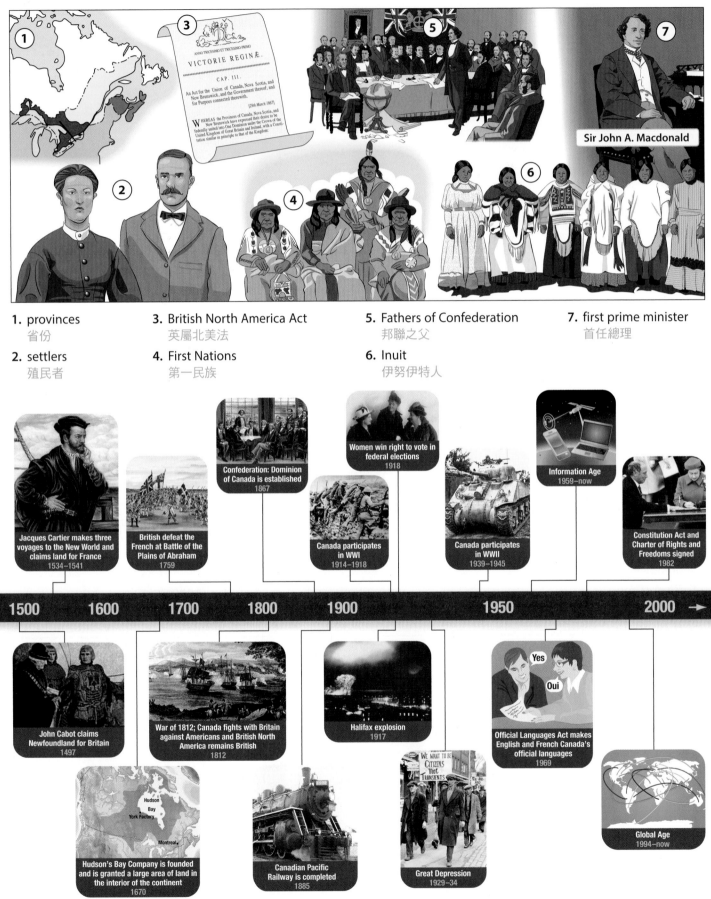

1. provinces
   省份

2. settlers
   殖民者

3. British North America Act
   英屬北美法

4. First Nations
   第一民族

5. Fathers of Confederation
   邦聯之父

6. Inuit
   伊努伊特人

7. first prime minister
   首任總理

Sir John A. Macdonald

Jacques Cartier makes three voyages to the New World and claims land for France
1534–1541

British defeat the French at Battle of the Plains of Abraham
1759

Confederation: Dominion of Canada is established
1867

Women win right to vote in federal elections
1918

Canada participates in WWI
1914–1918

Information Age
1959–now

Constitution Act and Charter of Rights and Freedoms signed
1982

Canada participates in WWII
1939–1945

1500   1600   1700   1800   1900   1950   2000 →

John Cabot claims Newfoundland for Britain
1497

War of 1812; Canada fights with Britain against Americans and British North America remains British
1812

Halifax explosion
1917

Official Languages Act makes English and French Canada's official languages
1969

Yes
Oui

Hudson's Bay Company is founded and is granted a large area of land in the interior of the continent
1670

Hudson Bay
York Factory
Montreal

Canadian Pacific Railway is completed
1885

WE WANT TO BE CITIZENS NOT TRANSIENTS

Great Depression
1929–34

Global Age
1994–now

Civilizations 文明

Pyramids Parthenon

Times Square

Julius Caesar

Qin Shi Huang

King Sobhuza II

Queen Elizabeth I

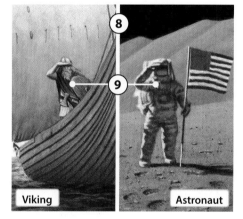

Benito Juárez

Benito Mussolini Justin Trudeau

1. ancient
   古代
2. modern
   現代

3. emperor
   皇帝
4. monarch
   君主

5. president
   總統
6. dictator
   獨裁者

7. prime minister
   首相

Historical Terms 歷史辭彙

Viking Astronaut

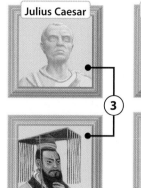

8. exploration
   探險
9. explorer
   探險者

10. war
    戰爭
11. army
    軍隊

12. immigration
    移民
13. immigrant
    移民者

Wolfgang Mozart Duke Ellington

Susan B. Anthony César Chávez

Thomas Edison Guillermo Camarena

14. composer
    作曲家
15. composition
    作曲

16. political movement
    政治運動
17. activist
    活躍分子

18. inventor
    發明家
19. invention
    發明

Digital Literacy 數位知識

Creating a Document 建立文件

A. **open** the program
開啟程式

B. **create** a new document
建立新文件

C. **type**
打字

D. **save** the document
儲存文件

E. **close** the document
關閉文件

F. **quit** the program
結束程式

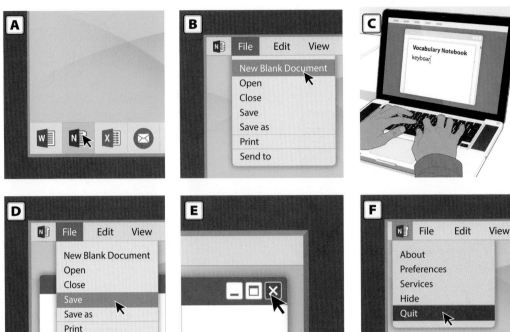

Selecting and Changing Text 選擇並更改文字

G. **click** on the screen
按一下螢幕

H. **double-click** to select a word
連按兩下選一個字詞

I. **delete** a word
刪除詞

J. **drag** to select text
拖曳以選取文字

K. **copy** text
複製文字

L. **paste** text
貼上文字

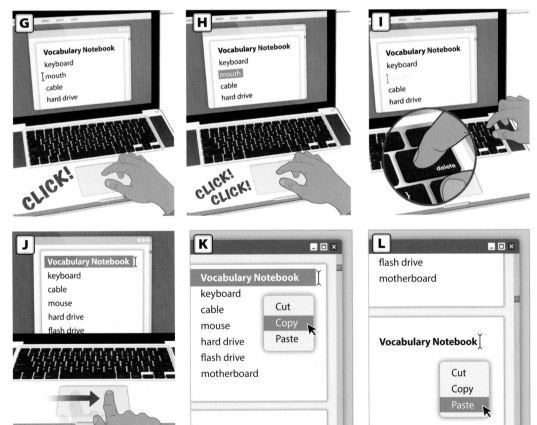

More vocabulary

keyboard shortcut: use of the keys on the keyboard to cut, copy, paste, etc. For example, press "control" on a PC ("command" on a Mac) and "C" to copy text.

Identify Diego's problem. Brainstorm solutions.

Diego is nervous around computers. He needs to complete an online job application. His brother, Luis, offers to apply for him. What could Diego do?

Moving around the Screen 在螢幕上移動

M. scroll
捲動

N. use the arrow keys
使用方向鍵

O. create a username
建立使用者名稱

Registering an Account 註冊帳戶

Registration

Username	JoshuaA	O
Password	********	P
Confirm password	********	Q

JEAN Jersey

JEAN Jersey R

SUBMIT S

P. create a password
建立密碼

Q. reenter the password /
type the password again
重新輸入密碼 / 再次鍵入密碼

R. type the verification code
鍵入驗證碼

S. click submit
按一下提交

Sending Email 發送電子郵件

T. log in to your account
登入您的帳戶

U. address the email
輸入電子郵件地址

V. type the subject
輸入主題

W. compose / **write** the message
撰寫訊息

X. check your spelling
檢查拼寫

Y. attach a file
附加檔案

Z. send the email
發送電子郵件

1. research question
   研究問題

2. search engine
   搜索引擎

3. search box
   搜索方框

4. keywords
   關鍵字

5. search results
   搜索結果

6. links
   連結

> What are the top jobs in Canada right now?

Search!   top jobs Canada

Canada's Best **Jobs** in 2016: The Top 25 Best Jobs in Canada
www.**canadian**business.com /lists-and...**jobs**/2016-**top**-25-jobs-in-**canada**/ ▾
April 21, 2016 - Our annual ranking of the best **jobs** in **Canada** returns— the highest salaries, the best career prospects and the most opportunity. Where is your …

http://www.**canadian**business.com/lists-and-rankings/best**jobs**/best-employers-ranking-2016/
Home/ Lists & Rankings /Best **Jobs** / Best Employers 2016: top companies people love working for... Our second annual ranking of Canada's Best Employers … companies where people can't wait to get to work— Nov 5, 2015 CB Staff Rigorous methodology … identify highly engaged workforces ...Leadership insights from Canada's Best Employers 2016: How they get every employee to innovate | How they hang on to their best employees | How small companies provide big perks | How they thrive in the face of crisis

Canada's Best **Jobs** 2016: The The Complete Top 100 - Canadian…
www.**canadian**business.com /lists-and…**jobs**/2016-full ranking-**canada**-100-best-**jobs**

100+ items- This is the list of Canada's 100 Best Jobs for 2016 as determined by our …

Rank	Job Title	Median Salary	5-Year Wage Growth
1	Mining or Forestry Manager	$97, 074	21%
2	Urban Planner	$85,010	15%

Public Administration Director - Primary Production Manager - Health Care Manager

Conducting Research　進行研究

A. **select** a search engine
   選擇搜索引擎

B. **type** in a phrase
   鍵入短語

C. **type** in a question
   鍵入問題

D. **click** the search icon /
   search
   按一下搜索圖示 / 搜索

E. **look** at the results
   查看結果

F. **click** on a link
   按一下連結

G. **bookmark** a site
   給網站加書籤

H. **keep** a record of sources
   記錄資料來源

I. **cite** sources
   引用資料來源

Search　**A** About　Co
Ask.com
Google
Info.com

B "top jobs in Canada"　**Search**
D
C What are the top jobs in Canada?

Search! "top jobs in Canada"

| All | Images | Shopping | Videos | News |

E Canada's Best **Jobs** 2016: The Top 25 Best **Jobs** in Canada
www.**canadian**business.com/ **F** and … **jobs**/2016-**top**-25-job
Apr 21, 2016 - Our annual ranking of the best **jobs** in **Canada** re
salaries, the best career prospects and the most opportunity. Wh

www.**canadian**business.com/lists-and-rankings/best-**jobs**/best
2016/Home/ Lists & Rankings /Best **Jobs** / Best Employers 2016:
people love working for... Our second annual 2016: top compa
working for … companies where people can't wait to get to wo
Nov 5, 2015 CB Staff Rigorous methodology … identify highly e
… Leadership insights from Canada's Best Employers 2016: Ho
employee to innovate | How they hang on to their best employ
companies provide big perks | How they thrive in the face of cris

.com/lists-and-rankings/best-jobs/2016-top-25-jobs-in-canada/ ★ **G**

The 25 Best **Jobs** for the Year|WorldWide News
www.money.wwnews.org /.../jobs/25-**job**s-for- Money
The **top jobs** for the year were announced on O*Net and
DOL Oc

The Top
career.d
January
the job y
goals. D

100 Bes
blog.the
The late
pay mo
DOL ca

H
BOOKS
Jobs for the Future – Brown
Classic Careers – Vega
Careers to Count On – Kim

SITES
blog.thepaycheck.com
www.money.wwnews.org
career.daily.com

I
WORKS CITED

Brown, L. (2015) *Jobs for the Future.*
New York, NY: Oxford University Press.
Retrieved from http://jobsfutureBrown/sitebasedbooks

Kim, M. (2012) *Careers to Count On.*
New York, NY: Oxford University Press.
Retrieved from http://careerstocounton.com

Vega, A. (2017) *Classic Careers.*

More vocabulary

research: to search for and record information that answers a question

investigate: to research a problem or situation

Ways to talk about your research

My research shows _____.
According to my research, _____.
These are the results of my research: _____.

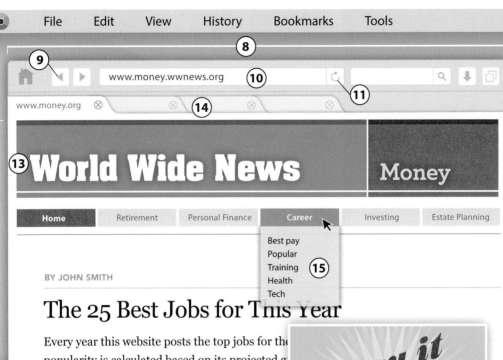

File   Edit   View   History   Bookmarks   Tools

www.money.wwnews.org

www.money.org

World Wide News   Money

Home   Retirement   Personal Finance   Career   Investing   Estate Planning

Best pay
Popular
Training
Health
Tech

BY JOHN SMITH

The 25 Best Jobs for This Year

Every year this website posts the top jobs for the
popularity is calculated based on its projected g
next five years, associated salary, number of yea
tion and training required, and a satisfaction su
Tristan Mathes & Associates.

While it is tempting to make career decisions ba
100 list, it is important to remember that these
only part of the picture.

Click to continue reading

Buy it NOW!!

JANUARY 8, 2017 7:00 PM EST

7. menu bar
功能表列

8. browser window
瀏覽器視窗

9. back button
返回按鈕

10. URL / website address
URL / 網址

11. refresh button
重新整理按鈕

12. web page
網頁

13. source
資料來源

14. tab
分頁

15. drop-down menu
下拉功能表單

16. content
內容

17. pop-up ad
彈出式廣告

18. video player
視訊播放器

19. social media links
社群媒體連結

20. date
日期

Internet Research: online practice

Type "practice" in a search engine. Add more keywords. ("ESL vocabulary," etc.)

Report: *I found vocabulary practice on a site called _____.*

Think about it. Discuss.

1. Which is better for Internet research: searching with a question, a phrase, or keywords? Explain.

2. Do you enjoy research? Why or why not?

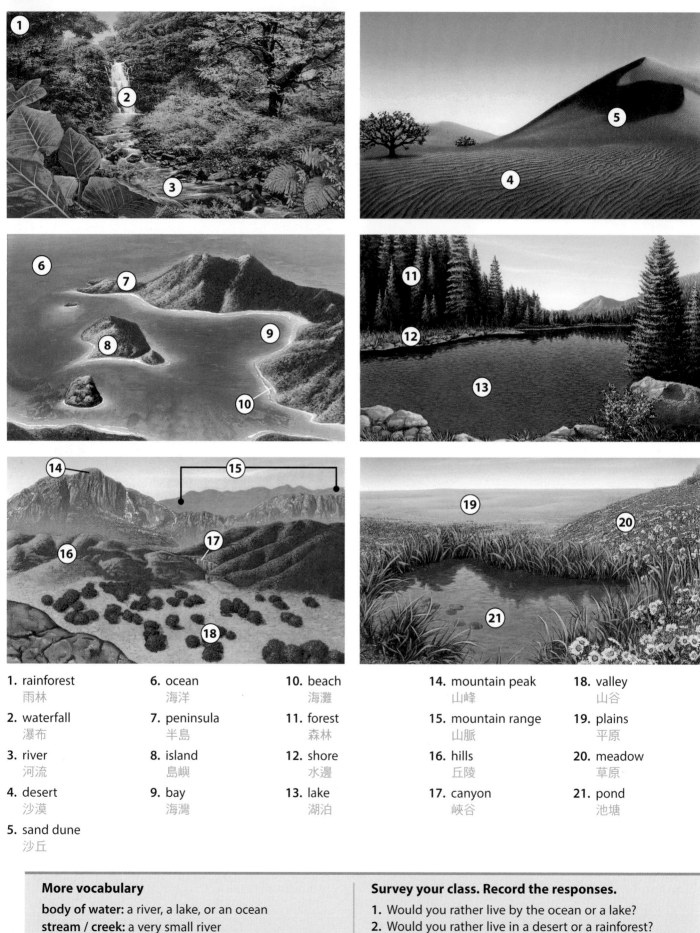

1. rainforest
雨林

2. waterfall
瀑布

3. river
河流

4. desert
沙漠

5. sand dune
沙丘

6. ocean
海洋

7. peninsula
半島

8. island
島嶼

9. bay
海灣

10. beach
海灘

11. forest
森林

12. shore
水邊

13. lake
湖泊

14. mountain peak
山峰

15. mountain range
山脈

16. hills
丘陵

17. canyon
峽谷

18. valley
山谷

19. plains
平原

20. meadow
草原

21. pond
池塘

More vocabulary

body of water: a river, a lake, or an ocean
stream / creek: a very small river
inhabitants: the people and animals living in a habitat

Survey your class. Record the responses.

1. Would you rather live by the ocean or a lake?
2. Would you rather live in a desert or a rainforest?
Report: *Fifteen of us would rather ____ than ____.*

The Solar System and the Planets 太陽系和行星

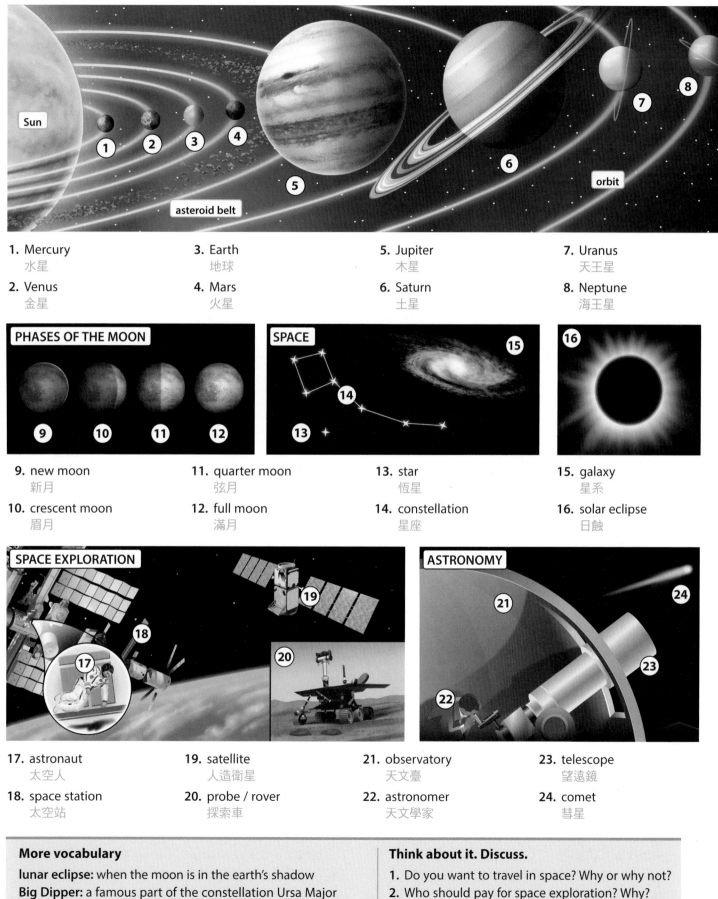

1. Mercury
水星

2. Venus
金星

3. Earth
地球

4. Mars
火星

5. Jupiter
木星

6. Saturn
土星

7. Uranus
天王星

8. Neptune
海王星

PHASES OF THE MOON

9. new moon
新月

10. crescent moon
眉月

11. quarter moon
弦月

12. full moon
滿月

SPACE

13. star
恆星

14. constellation
星座

15. galaxy
星系

16. solar eclipse
日蝕

SPACE EXPLORATION

17. astronaut
太空人

18. space station
太空站

19. satellite
人造衛星

20. probe / rover
探索車

ASTRONOMY

21. observatory
天文臺

22. astronomer
天文學家

23. telescope
望遠鏡

24. comet
彗星

More vocabulary

lunar eclipse: when the moon is in the earth's shadow
Big Dipper: a famous part of the constellation Ursa Major
Sirius: the brightest star in the night sky

Think about it. Discuss.

1. Do you want to travel in space? Why or why not?
2. Who should pay for space exploration? Why?
3. What do you like best about the night sky?

215

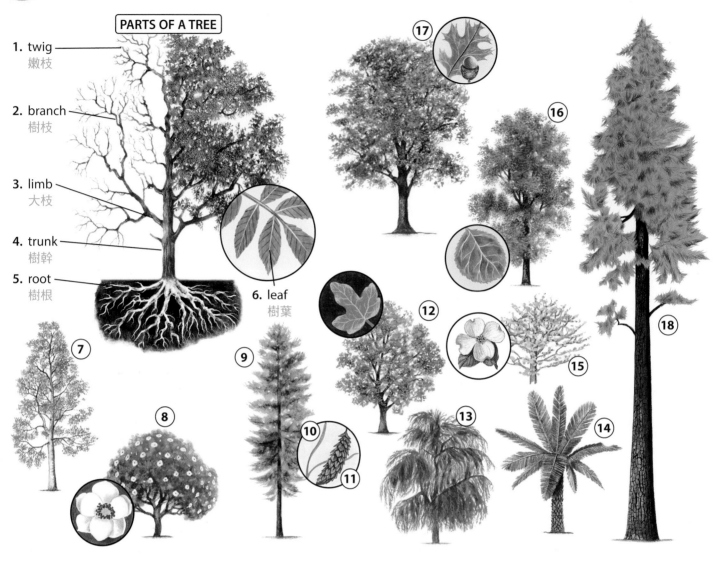

PARTS OF A TREE

1. twig
   嫩枝
2. branch
   樹枝
3. limb
   大枝
4. trunk
   樹幹
5. root
   樹根
6. leaf
   樹葉

7. birch 樺木	**10.** needle 松針	**13.** willow 柳樹	**16.** elm 榆樹
8. magnolia 木蘭	**11.** pine cone 松果	**14.** palm 棕櫚	**17.** oak 橡樹
9. pine 松樹	**12.** maple 楓樹	**15.** dogwood 山茱萸	**18.** redwood 紅杉

Plants 植物

19. holly 冬青屬灌木	**21.** cactus 仙人掌	**23.** poison sumac 毒膚楊	**25.** poison ivy 毒葛
20. berries 漿果	**22.** vine 藤蔓	**24.** poison oak 毒漆樹	

Parts of a Flower 花的各部份名稱

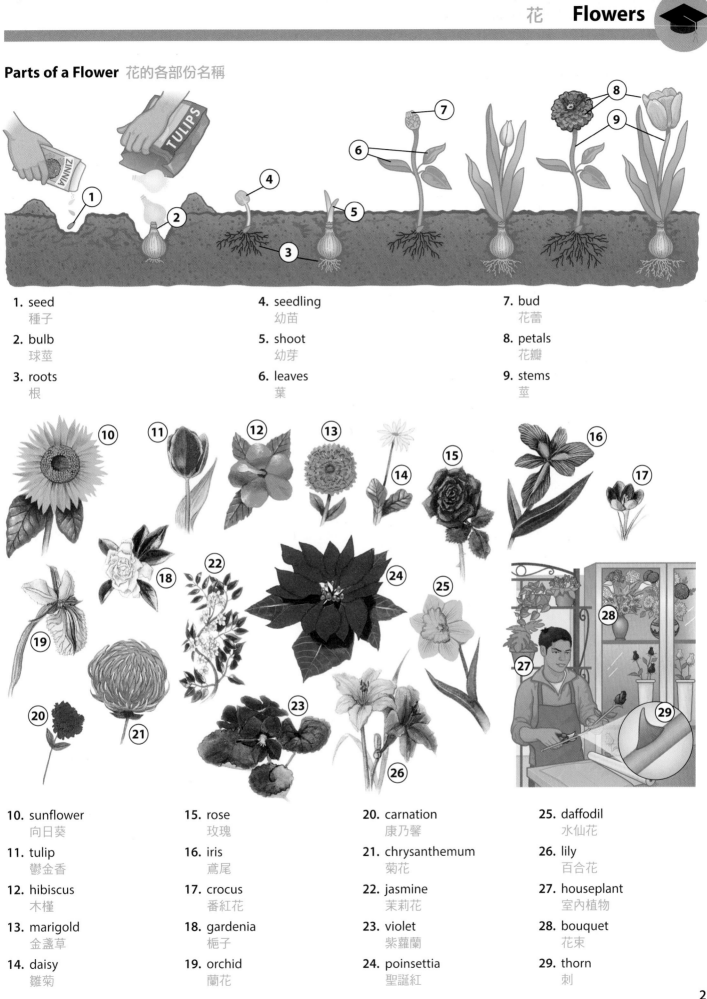

1. seed
   種子

2. bulb
   球莖

3. roots
   根

4. seedling
   幼苗

5. shoot
   幼芽

6. leaves
   葉

7. bud
   花蕾

8. petals
   花瓣

9. stems
   莖

10. sunflower
    向日葵

11. tulip
    鬱金香

12. hibiscus
    木槿

13. marigold
    金盞草

14. daisy
    雛菊

15. rose
    玫瑰

16. iris
    鳶尾

17. crocus
    番紅花

18. gardenia
    梔子

19. orchid
    蘭花

20. carnation
    康乃馨

21. chrysanthemum
    菊花

22. jasmine
    茉莉花

23. violet
    紫蘿蘭

24. poinsettia
    聖誕紅

25. daffodil
    水仙花

26. lily
    百合花

27. houseplant
    室內植物

28. bouquet
    花束

29. thorn
    刺

Sea Animals 海洋動物

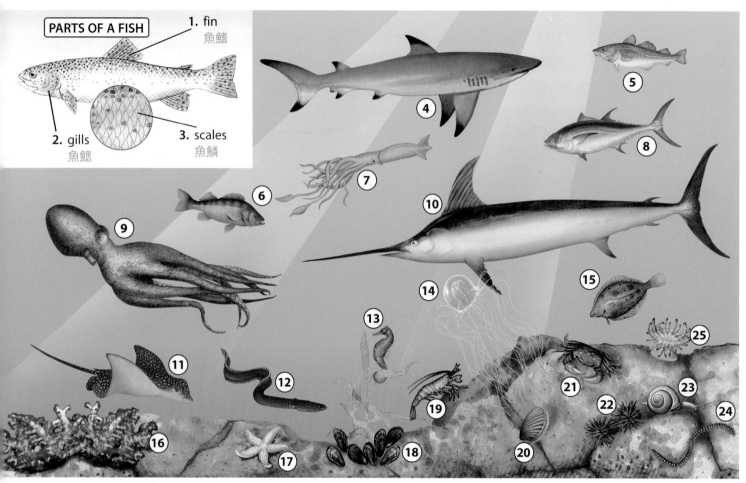

PARTS OF A FISH

1. fin
魚鰭

2. gills
魚鰓

3. scales
魚鱗

4. shark 鯊魚	9. octopus 章魚	14. jellyfish 水母	19. shrimp 蝦	24. worm 蟲
5. cod 鱈魚	10. swordfish 旗魚	15. flounder 比目魚	20. scallop 扇貝	25. sea anemone 海葵
6. bass 鱸魚	11. ray 魟魚	16. coral 珊瑚	21. crab 螃蟹	
7. squid 魷魚	12. eel 鰻魚	17. sea star 海星	22. sea urchin 海膽	
8. tuna 鮪魚	13. seahorse 海馬	18. mussel 貽貝	23. snail 蝸牛	

Amphibians 兩棲動物

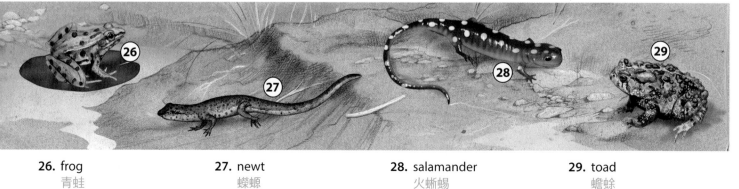

26. frog 青蛙	27. newt 蠑螈	28. salamander 火蜥蜴	29. toad 蟾蜍

218

Sea Mammals 海洋哺乳動物

30. water
水

31. dolphin
海豚

32. porpoise
鼠海豚

33. whale
鯨魚

34. walrus
海象

35. sea lion
海獅

36. seal
海豹

37. sea otter
海獺

38. rock
岩石

Reptiles 爬蟲類

39. alligator
短吻鱷

40. crocodile
鱷魚

41. tortoise
陸龜

42. turtle
烏龜

43. lizard
蜥蜴

44. cobra
眼鏡蛇

45. rattlesnake
響尾蛇

46. garter snake
束帶蛇

PARTS OF A BIRD

1. wing
翼

2. claw
爪

3. beak / bill
鳥嘴

4. feather
羽毛

5. nest
巢

6. owl
貓頭鷹

7. blue jay
冠藍鴉

8. sparrow
麻雀

9. woodpecker
啄木鳥

10. eagle
鷹

11. hummingbird
蜂鳥

12. penguin
企鵝

13. duck
鴨

14. goose
鵝 / 雁

15. peacock
孔雀

16. pigeon
鴿子

17. robin
知更鳥

Insects and Arachnids 昆蟲及蛛形綱動物

18. wasp
黃蜂

19. beetle
甲蟲

20. butterfly
蝴蝶

21. caterpillar
毛蟲

22. moth
蛾

23. mosquito
蚊子

24. cricket
蟋蟀

25. grasshopper
蚱蜢

26. honeybee
蜜蜂

27. ladybug
瓢蟲

28. tick
扁蝨

29. fly
蒼蠅

30. spider
蜘蛛

31. scorpion
蠍

Farm Animals / Livestock 農場動物 / 牲畜

1. cow
牛

2. pig
豬

3. donkey
驢

4. horse
馬

5. goat
山羊

6. sheep
綿羊

7. rooster
公雞

8. hen
母雞

Pets 寵物

9. cat
貓

10. kitten
小貓

11. dog
狗

12. puppy
小狗

13. rabbit
兔

14. guinea pig
天竺鼠

15. parakeet
長尾小鸚鵡

16. goldfish
金魚

Rodents 齧齒類

17. rat
大老鼠

18. mouse
小老鼠

19. gopher
地鼠

20. chipmunk
金花鼠

21. squirrel
松鼠

22. groundhog
土撥鼠

More vocabulary

Farm animals and pets are **domesticated**. They work for and/or live with people. Animals that are not domesticated are **wild**. Most rodents are wild.

Survey your class. Record the responses.

1. Have you worked with farm animals? Which ones?
2. Are you afraid of rodents? Which ones?
Report: _Lee has worked with cows. He's afraid of rats._

221

1. moose
麋鹿

2. mountain lion
山獅

3. coyote
山狗 / 郊狼

4. wolf
狼

5. buffalo / bison
水牛 / 美洲野牛

6. bat
蝙蝠

7. polar bear
北極熊

8. beaver
海狸

9. bear
熊

10. caribou
北美馴鹿

11. porcupine
豪豬

12. deer
鹿

13. opossum
負鼠

14. elk
駝鹿

15. skunk
臭鼬

16. raccoon
浣熊

17. fox
狐狸

16. antlers
鹿角

17. hooves
蹄

18. whiskers
鬚

19. coat / fur
皮 / 毛

20. paw
腳爪

21. horn
角

22. tail
尾巴

23. quill
刺

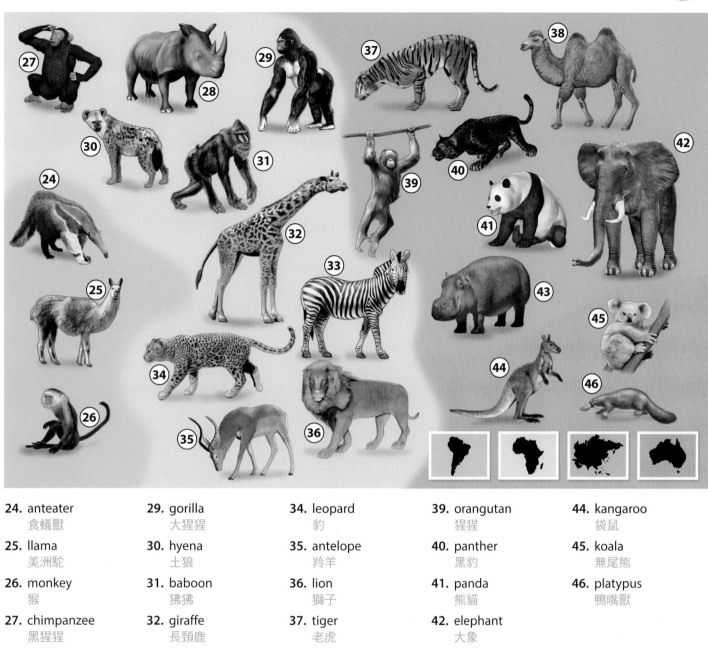

24. anteater 食蟻獸	**29.** gorilla 大猩猩	**34.** leopard 豹	**39.** orangutan 猩猩	**44.** kangaroo 袋鼠
25. llama 美洲駝	**30.** hyena 土狼	**35.** antelope 羚羊	**40.** panther 黑豹	**45.** koala 無尾熊
26. monkey 猴	**31.** baboon 狒狒	**36.** lion 獅子	**41.** panda 熊貓	**46.** platypus 鴨嘴獸
27. chimpanzee 黑猩猩	**32.** giraffe 長頸鹿	**37.** tiger 老虎	**42.** elephant 大象	
28. rhinoceros 犀牛	**33.** zebra 斑馬	**38.** camel 駱駝	**43.** hippopotamus 河馬	

47. trunk 象鼻	**48.** tusk 象牙	**49.** mane 鬃	**50.** pouch 肚袋	**51.** hump 駝峰

223

Energy and the Environment 能源與環境

Energy Sources 能源

1. solar energy
太陽能

2. wind power
風能

3. natural gas
天然氣

4. coal
煤

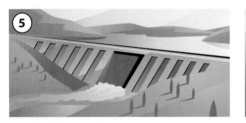

5. hydroelectric power
水力發電

6. oil / petroleum
石油

7. geothermal energy
地熱

8. nuclear energy
核電

9. biomass / bioenergy
生物能

10. fusion
核融合

Pollution 汙染

11. air pollution / smog
空氣汙染 / 霧霾

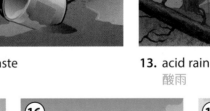

12. hazardous waste
危害性廢棄物

13. acid rain
酸雨

14. water pollution
水汙染

15. radiation
輻射汙染

16. pesticide poisoning
殺蟲劑毒害

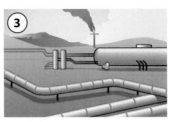

17. oil spill
石油外溢

More vocabulary

National Environmental Emergencies Centre (NEEC): federal group that supports, recommends, or directs the clean-up actions in environmental emergencies

Internet Research: recycling

Type "recycle" and your city in a search engine. Look for information on local recycling centers.
Report: *You can recycle cans at ____.*

Ways to Conserve Energy and Resources 節能與節約資源的方式

A. reduce trash
減少垃圾

B. reuse shopping bags
重新利用購物袋

C. recycle
回收

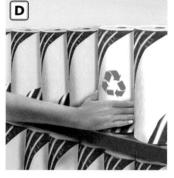

D. buy recycled products
買回收再生產品

E. save water
節約用水

F. fix leaky faucets
修理漏水的水龍頭

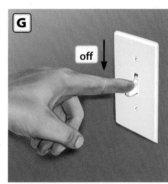

G. turn off lights
關燈

H. use energy-efficient bulbs
使用節能燈泡

I. carpool
共乘

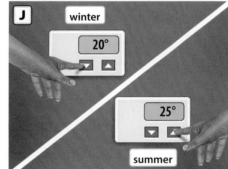

J. adjust the thermostat
調節溫控器

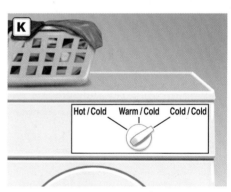

K. wash clothes in cold water
用冷水洗衣

L. don't litter
不亂扔垃圾

M. compost food scraps
廚餘堆肥

N. plant a tree
植樹

225

A Graduation 畢業

I loved Art History.

My last economics lesson

Marching Band is great!

The photographer was upset.

We look good!

I get my diploma.

Dad and his digital camera

1. photographer
攝影師

2. funny photo
滑稽照片

3. serious photo
嚴肅照片

4. guest speaker
來賓致詞人

5. podium
講台

6. ceremony
儀式

7. cap
畢業帽

8. gown
畢業服

A. **take** a picture
照相

B. **cry**
哭

C. **celebrate**
慶祝

People	Comments	
Sara	June 29th 8:19 p.m. Great pictures! What a day!	Delete
Zannie baby	June 30th 10 a.m. Love the funny photo.	Delete

I'm behind the mayor.

We're all very happy.

What do you see in the pictures?

1. Which classes are Adelia's favourites?
2. Do you prefer the funny or the serious graduation photo? Why?
3. Who is standing at the podium?
4. What are the graduates throwing in the air? Why?

Read the story.

A Graduation

Look at these great photos on my web page! The first three are from my favourite classes, but the other pictures are from graduation day.

There are two pictures of my classmates in <u>caps</u> and <u>gowns</u>. In the first picture, we're laughing and the <u>photographer</u> is upset. In the second photo, we're serious. I like the <u>serious photo</u>, but I love the <u>funny photo</u>!

There's also a picture of our <u>guest speaker</u>, the mayor. She is standing at the <u>podium</u>. Next, you can see me at the graduation <u>ceremony</u>. My dad wanted to <u>take a picture</u> of me with my diploma. That's my mom next to him. She <u>cries</u> when she's happy.

After the ceremony, everyone was happy, but no one cried. We wanted to <u>celebrate</u> and we did!

Reread the story.

1. Which events happened before the graduation? After?
2. Why does the author say, "but no one cried" in Paragraph 4?

What do you think?

3. What kinds of ceremonies are important for children? for teens? for adults?

227

Places to Go 去處

1. zoo
   動物園
2. movies
   電影
3. botanical garden
   植物園
4. bowling alley
   保齡球館
5. rock concert
   搖滾音樂會
6. swap meet /
   flea market
   露天市集 / 跳蚤市場
7. aquarium
   水族館

Places to Go in Our City

Listen and point. Take turns.

A: *Point to the zoo.*
B: *Point to the flea market.*
A: *Point to the rock concert.*

Dictate to your partner. Take turns.

A: *Write these words: zoo, movies, aquarium.*
B: *Zoo, movies, and what?*
A: *And aquarium.*

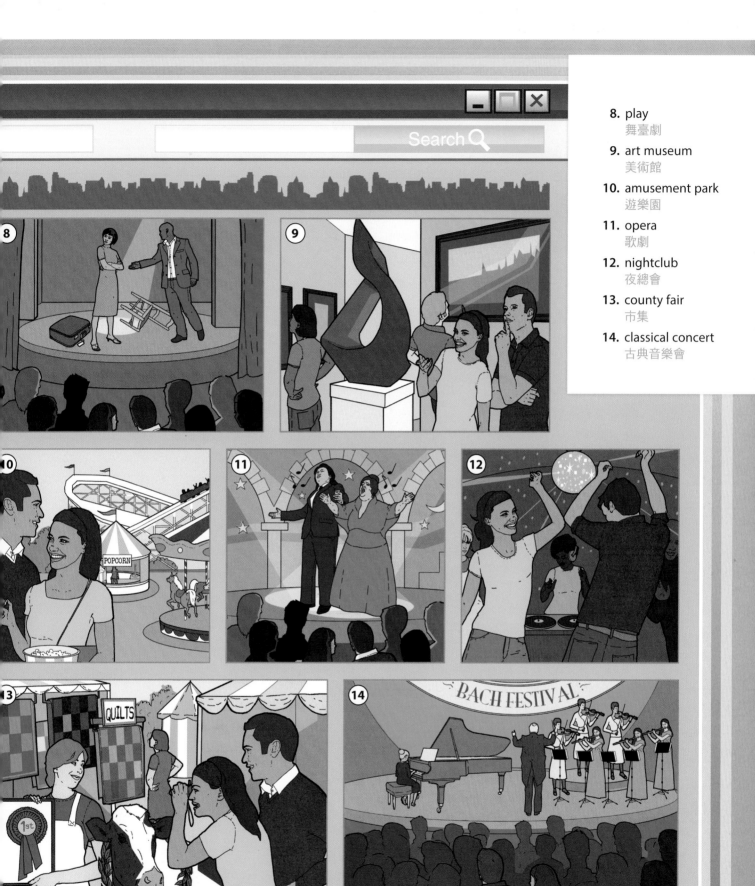

8. play
舞臺劇

9. art museum
美術館

10. amusement park
遊樂園

11. opera
歌劇

12. nightclub
夜總會

13. county fair
市集

14. classical concert
古典音樂會

Ways to make plans using *Let's go*

Let's go to <u>the amusement park</u> tomorrow.
Let's go to <u>the opera</u> on Saturday.
Let's go to <u>the movies</u> tonight.

Pair practice. Make new conversations.

A: <u>Let's go to the zoo this afternoon</u>.
B: *OK. And let's go to* <u>the movies tonight</u>.
A: *That sounds like a good plan.*

229

The Park and Playground 公園及遊樂場

1. ball field
   球場

2. cyclist
   騎腳踏車者

3. bike path
   腳踏車道 / 單車徑

4. jump rope
   跳繩

5. fountain
   噴水池

6. tennis court
   網球場

7. skateboard
   滑板

8. picnic table
   野餐桌

9. water fountain
   飲水器

10. bench
    長板凳

11. swings
    鞦韆

12. tricycle
    三輪車

13. slide
    滑梯

14. climbing apparatus
    攀爬設施

15. sandbox
    沙坑

16. outdoor grill
    室外燒烤爐

A. pull the wagon
拉四輪車

B. push the swing
推鞦韆

C. climb the bars
爬架

D. picnic / have a picnic
野餐

1. ocean / water 海洋 / 海水 / 湖水	**7.** diving mask 潛水面罩	**13.** shade 蔭	**19.** lifeguard 救生員
2. sailboat 帆船	**8.** fins 蛙鞋	**14.** beach umbrella 海灘遮陽傘	**20.** life preserver 救生圈
3. kite 風箏	**9.** cooler 保溫箱	**15.** surfer 衝浪	**21.** lifeguard station 救生站
4. sky 天空	**10.** sunscreen / sunblock 防曬油	**16.** surfboard 衝浪板	**22.** beach chair 海灘椅
5. wetsuit 潛水服	**11.** blanket 被毯	**17.** wave 波浪	**23.** sand 沙子
6. scuba tank 潛水氣瓶	**12.** sandcastle 沙堡	**18.** pier 碼頭	**24.** seashell 貝殼

More vocabulary

seaweed: a plant that grows in the ocean
tide: the level of the ocean. The tide goes in and out every 12 hours.

Grammar Point: prepositions *in, on, under*

*Where are the little kids? They're **under** the umbrella.*
*Where's the cooler? It's **on** the blanket.*
*Where's the kite? It's **in** the sky.*

1. boating
   開船
2. rafting
   划橡皮艇
3. canoeing
   划獨木舟
4. fishing
   釣魚
5. camping
   露營
6. backpacking
   背包旅行
7. hiking
   健行 / 遠足
8. mountain biking
   騎越野腳踏車
9. horseback riding
   騎馬

10. tent
    帳篷
11. campfire
    營火
12. sleeping bag
    睡袋
13. foam pad
    泡沫墊
14. life vest / PFD
    救生背心
15. backpack
    背包
16. camping stove
    野營用火爐
17. fishing net
    魚網
18. fishing pole
    魚桿
19. rope
    繩
20. multi-use knife
    多用途小刀
21. matches
    火柴
22. lantern
    燈籠
23. insect repellent
    驅蟲劑
24. canteen
    水壺

1. downhill skiing
下坡滑雪

2. snowboarding
滑雪板

3. cross-country skiing
越野滑雪

4. ice skating
溜冰

5. figure skating
花式溜冰

6. sledding
滑雪橇

7. water skiing
滑水

8. sailing
玩風帆

9. surfing
衝浪

10. windsurfing
風浪板 / 滑浪風帆

11. snorkeling
浮潛

12. scuba diving
水肺潛水

More vocabulary

speed skating: racing while ice skating
kitesurfing: surfing with a small surfboard and a kite

Internet Research: popular winter sports

Type "popular winter sports" in a search engine.
Compare the information on two sites.
Report: *Two sites said _____ is a popular winter sport.*

233

1. archery
射箭

2. billiards / pool
撞球 / 桌球

3. bowling
保齡球

4. boxing
拳擊

5. cycling / biking
騎腳踏車

6. badminton
羽毛球

7. fencing
擊劍

8. golf
高爾夫球

9. gymnastics
體操

10. inline skating
直排輪溜冰 /
單線滾軸溜冰

11. martial arts
武術

12. racquetball
回力球

13. skateboarding
滑板

14. table tennis
乒乓球

15. tennis
網球

16. weightlifting
舉重

17. wrestling
角力

18. track and field
田徑

19. horse racing
賽馬

Pair practice. Make new conversations.

A: *What sports do you like?*
B: *I like <u>bowling</u>. What do you like?*
A: *I like <u>gymnastics</u>.*

Internet Research: dangerous sports

Type "most dangerous sports" in a search engine.
Look for information on two or more sites.
Report: *According to my research, ____ is dangerous.*

| **1.** score 分數 | **3.** team 球隊 | **5.** player 球員 | **7.** basketball court 籃球場 |
| **2.** coach 教練 | **4.** fan 球迷 | **6.** official / referee 裁判 | **8.** basketball hoop 籃球框 |

9. basketball
籃球

10. baseball
棒球

11. softball
壘球

12. football
美式足球

13. soccer
足球

14. ice hockey
冰上曲棍球

15. volleyball
排球

16. water polo
水球

More vocabulary

win: to have the best score
lose: the opposite of win
tie: to have the same score

captain: the team leader
goalie: the team member who protects the goal in soccer, ice hockey, and water polo
umpire: the referee in baseball
Little League: a baseball and softball program for children

A. **pitch**
投

B. **hit**
擊

C. **throw**
擲

D. **catch**
接

E. **kick**
踢

F. **tackle**
擒抱

G. **pass**
傳球

H. **shoot**
投籃

I. **jump**
跳

J. **dribble**
運球

K. **dive**
跳水

L. **swim**
游泳

M. **stretch**
伸拉

N. **exercise / work out**
鍛鍊

O. **bend**
彎腰

P. **serve**
發球

Q. **swing**
揮桿

R. **start**
起跑

S. **race**
賽跑

T. **finish**
衝刺

U. **skate**
溜冰

V. **ski**
滑雪

Use the new words.
Look at page 235. Name the actions you see.

A: He's _throwing_.
B: She's _jumping_.

Ways to talk about your sports skills

I can _throw_, but I can't _catch_.
I _swim_ well, but I don't _dive_ well.
I'm good at _skating_, but I'm terrible at _skiing_.

1. golf club
   高爾夫球桿

2. tennis racket
   網球拍

3. volleyball
   排球

4. basketball
   籃球

5. bowling ball
   保齡球

6. bow
   弓

7. target
   靶

8. arrows
   箭

9. ice skates
   冰刀鞋

10. inline skates
    直排輪溜冰鞋 /
    單線滾軸溜冰鞋

11. hockey stick
    曲棍球桿

12. soccer ball
    足球

13. shin guards
    脛護墊

14. baseball bat
    棒球棒

15. catcher's mask
    接球員面具

16. uniform
    制服

17. glove
    手套

18. baseball
    棒球

19. football helmet
    美式足球頭盔

20. shoulder pads
    肩墊

21. football
    美式足球

22. weights
    啞鈴

23. snowboard
    雪板

24. skis
    雪屐

25. ski poles
    滑雪杖

26. ski boots
    滑雪靴

27. flying disc*
    飛盤 / 飛碟

* **Note:** one brand is
  Frisbee®, of Wham-O, Inc.

Use the new words.
Look at pages 234–235. Name the sports equipment you see.

A: *Those are ice skates*.
B: *That's a football*.

Survey your class. Record the responses.

1. What sports equipment do you own?
2. What sports stores do you recommend?
Report: *Sam* owns a ____. *He recommends* ____.

237

A. collect things
收藏東西

B. play games
玩遊戲

C. quilt
縫被

D. do crafts
做手工藝品

Collectibles

1. figurine	5. board game	9. model kit	13. construction paper
小雕像	棋盤遊戲	模型套件	美工紙
2. baseball cards	6. dice	10. acrylic paint	14. woodworking kit
棒球卡	骰子	壓克力顏料 / 膠彩	木工套件
3. video game console	7. checkers	11. glue stick	15. quilt block
電玩遊戲系統	西洋跳棋	膠棒	被塊
4. video game controller	8. chess	12. glue gun	16. rotary cutter
電玩遊戲控制器	西洋象棋	熱熔膠槍	滑輪美工刀

Grammar Point: *used to*

When I was a kid, I **used to** play cards every day.
Now, I don't play very often.

Pair practice. Make new conversations.

A: *What were your hobbies when you were a kid?*
B: *I used to <u>collect baseball cards</u>. And you?*
A: *I used to <u>play video games</u>.*

238

E. paint
畫油畫

F. knit
編織

G. pretend
模仿假裝

H. play cards
玩牌

17. canvas
畫布

18. easel
畫架

19. oil paint
油畫

20. paintbrush
畫筆

21. watercolours
水彩

22. yarn
紗線

23. knitting needles
織針

24. embroidery
刺繡

25. crochet
鉤針編織

26. action figure
動作人物

27. model train
模型火車

28. dolls
玩偶

29. diamonds
紅方塊

30. spades
黑桃

31. hearts
紅心

32. clubs
黑梅花

Ways to talk about hobbies and games

This <u>board game</u> is **interesting**. It makes me think.
That <u>video game</u> is **boring**. Nothing happens.
I love to <u>play cards</u>. It's **fun** to play with my friends.

Internet Research: popular hobbies

Type "most popular hobbies" in a search engine.
Look for information on one or more sites.
Report: I read that _____ is a popular hobby.

239

1. boom box
   攜帶式音響

2. video MP3 player
   影音播放機

3. dock / charging station
   擴展 / 充電塢

4. lightweight headphones
   輕型頭戴式耳機

5. earbuds / in-ear headphones
   耳塞式耳機

6. noise-cancelling headphones
   降噪頭戴式耳機

7. personal CD player
   個人 CD 碟播放機

8. flat-screen TV / flat-panel TV
   平面螢幕電視機 / 平板螢幕電視機

9. Blu-ray player
   Blu-ray（藍光）碟播放機

10. universal remote
    通用遙控器

11. DVD player
    DVD 碟播放機

12. turntable
    電唱機

13. tuner
    收音機

14. speakers
    喇叭

15. portable charger
    攜帶式充電器

16. microphone
    麥克風

17. digital camera
數碼相機

18. memory card
記憶卡

19. zoom lens
變焦鏡頭

20. tripod
三腳架

21. camcorder
攝影機 / 攝錄機

22. camera case / bag
照相機包

23. battery pack
電池組

24. battery charger
充電器

25. plug
插頭

26. international power adapter
國際電源轉接器

27. LCD projector
液晶投影機

28. screen
投影幕

29. photo album
相簿

30. digital photo album
數碼相簿

31. out of focus
聚焦不良

32. overexposed
曝光過度

33. underexposed
曝光不夠

A. **record**
錄影

B. **play**
回放

C. **rewind**
快速倒轉

D. **fast forward**
快速前轉

E. **pause**
暫停

Types of TV Programs 電視節目種類

1. news program
新聞

2. sitcom (situation comedy)
情境喜劇片、影集

3. cartoon
卡通

4. talk show
脫口秀

5. soap opera
肥皂劇

6. reality show
實境節目

7. nature program
大自然節目

8. game show
遊戲節目

9. children's program
孩童節目

10. shopping program
購物節目

11. sports program
體育節目

12. drama
戲劇

Types of Movies 電影種類

13. comedy
喜劇

14. tragedy
悲劇

15. western
西部片

16. romance
愛情片

17. horror story
恐怖片

18. science fiction story
科幻片

19. action story / adventure story
動作片 / 冒險片

20. mystery / suspense
懸疑片

Types of Music 音樂種類

21. classical
古典樂

22. blues
藍調樂

23. rock
搖滾樂

24. jazz
爵士樂

25. pop
流行樂

26. hip-hop
嘻哈樂

27. country
鄉村音樂

28. R&B / soul
節奏藍調 / 靈魂樂

29. folk
民樂

30. gospel
福音音樂

31. reggae
雷鬼搖滾樂

32. world music
世界音樂

A. play an instrument
演奏樂器

B. sing a song
唱歌

C. conduct an orchestra
指揮管絃樂團

D. be in a rock band
參加搖滾樂隊

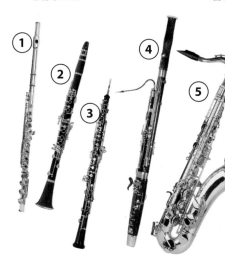

Woodwinds 管樂器

1. flute
   笛子
2. clarinet
   單簧管
3. oboe
   雙簧管
4. bassoon
   巴松管
5. saxophone
   薩克斯風

Strings 弦樂器

6. violin
   小提琴
7. cello
   大提琴
8. bass
   低音提琴
9. guitar
   吉他

Brass 銅管樂器

10. trombone
    長號
11. trumpet / horn
    小號
12. tuba
    大號
13. French horn
    法國號

Percussion 打擊樂器

14. piano
    鋼琴
15. xylophone
    木琴
16. drums
    鼓
17. tambourine
    鈴鼓 / 搖鼓

Other Instruments 其它樂器

18. electric keyboard
    電子琴
19. accordion
    手風琴
20. organ
    風琴
21. harmonica
    口琴

1. parade 遊行	**6.** heart 紅心	**11.** mask 面具	**15.** ornament 掛飾品
2. float 花車	**7.** fireworks 煙花	**12.** jack-o'-lantern 南瓜燈	**16.** Christmas tree 聖誕樹
3. confetti 五彩碎紙	**8.** flag 旗幟	**13.** costume 服裝	**17.** candy cane 糖果杖
4. couple 情侶 /夫婦	**9.** feast 盛宴	**14.** candy 糖果	**18.** string lights 串燈
5. card 賀卡 / 問候卡	**10.** turkey 火雞		

*Thanksgiving is on the second Monday in October.

A Birthday Party 生日派對

1. decorations
   裝飾

2. deck
   庭院平臺

3. present / gift
   禮品

A. **videotape**
   錄影

B. **make** a wish
   許願

C. **blow out**
   吹熄

D. **hide**
   躲藏

E. **bring**
   帶來

F. **wrap**
   包

Happy Birthday!

What do you see in the picture?

1. What kinds of decorations do you see?
2. What are people doing at this birthday party?
3. What wish did the teenager make?
4. How many presents did people bring?

Read the story.

A Birthday Party

Today is Lou and Gani Bombata's birthday barbecue. There are <u>decorations</u> around the backyard, and food and drinks on the <u>deck</u>. There are also <u>presents</u>. Everyone in the Bombata family likes to <u>bring</u> presents.

Right now, it's time for cake. Gani <u>is blowing out</u> the candles, and Lou <u>is making a wish</u>. Lou's mom wants to <u>videotape</u> everyone, but she can't find Lou's brother, Todd. Todd hates to sing, so he always <u>hides</u> for the birthday song.

Lou's sister, Amaka, has to <u>wrap</u> some <u>gifts</u>. She doesn't want Lou to see. Amaka isn't worried. She knows her family loves to sing. She can put her gifts on the present table before they finish the first song.

Reread the story.

1. Which paragraph gives you the most information about the Bombata family? Explain why.
2. Tell the story in your own words.

What do you think?

3. What wish do you think Gani made? Give your reasons.
4. Imagine you are invited to this party. You want to get one special gift for Gani **and** Lou to share. What's one gift they could both enjoy?

Verb Guide

Verbs in English are either regular or irregular in the past tense and past participle forms.

Regular Verbs
The regular verbs below are marked 1, 2, 3, or 4 according to four different spelling patterns.
(See page 250 for the irregular verbs, which do not follow any of these patterns.)

Spelling Patterns for the Past and the Past Participle	Example	
1. Add -ed to the end of the verb.	ASK	ASKED
2. Add -d to the end of the verb.	LIVE	LIVED
3. Double the final consonant and add -ed to the end of the verb.	DROP	DROPPED
4. Drop the final y and add -ied to the end of the verb.	CRY	CRIED

The Oxford Picture Dictionary List of Regular Verbs

accept (1)
add (1)
address (1)
adjust (1)
agree (2)
answer (1)
apologize (2)
appear (1)
applaud (1)
apply (4)
arrange (2)
arrest (1)
arrive (2)
ask (1)
assemble (2)
assist (1)
attach (1)
attend (1)
bake (2)
bargain (1)
bathe (2)
block (1)
board (1)
boil (1)
bookmark (1)
borrow (1)
bow (1)
brainstorm (1)
breathe (2)
browse (2)
brush (1)
buckle (2)
burn (1)
bus (1)
calculate (2)
call (1)
capitalize (2)

carpool (1)
carry (4)
cash (1)
celebrate (2)
change (2)
check (1)
chill (1)
choke (2)
chop (3)
circle (2)
cite (2)
claim (1)
clarify (4)
clean (1)
clear (1)
click (1)
climb (1)
close (2)
collate (2)
collect (1)
colour (1)
comb (1)
comfort (1)
commit (3)
compare (2)
complain (1)
complete (2)
compliment (1)
compose (2)
compost (1)
conceal (1)
conduct (1)
consult (1)
contact (1)
convert (1)
convict (1)
cook (1)

cooperate (2)
copy (4)
correct (1)
cough (1)
count (1)
create (2)
cross (1)
cry (4)
dance (2)
debate (2)
decline (2)
delete (2)
deliver (1)
design (1)
dial (1)
dice (2)
dictate (2)
die (2)
direct (1)
disagree (2)
discipline (2)
discuss (1)
disinfect (1)
distribute (2)
dive (2)
divide (2)
double-click (1)
drag (3)
dress (1)
dribble (2)
drill (1)
drop (3)
drown (1)
dry (4)
dust (1)
dye (2)
earn (1)

edit (1)
empty (4)
end (1)
enter (1)
erase (2)
evacuate (2)
examine (2)
exchange (2)
exercise (2)
expire (2)
explain (1)
explore (2)
exterminate (2)
fast forward (1)
fasten (1)
fax (1)
fertilize (2)
fill (1)
finish (1)
fix (1)
floss (1)
fold (1)
follow (1)
garden (1)
gargle (2)
graduate (2)
grate (2)
grease (2)
greet (1)
hail (1)
hammer (1)
hand (1)
harvest (1)
help (1)
hire (2)
hug (3)
identify (4)

immigrate (2)
indent (1)
inquire (2)
insert (1)
inspect (1)
install (1)
introduce (2)
investigate (2)
invite (2)
iron (1)
jaywalk (1)
join (1)
jump (1)
kick (1)
kiss (1)
knit (3)
label (3)
land (1)
laugh (1)
learn (1)
lengthen (1)
lift (1)
list (1)
listen (1)
litter (1)
live (2)
load (1)
lock (1)
log (3)
look (1)
mail (1)
manufacture (2)
match (1)
measure (2)
microwave (2)
milk (1)
misbehave (2)
miss (1)
mix (1)
monitor (1)
mop (3)
move (2)
mow (1)
multiply (4)
negotiate (2)
network (1)
numb (1)
nurse (2)
obey (1)

observe (2)
offer (1)
open (1)
operate (2)
order (1)
organize (2)
overdose (2)
pack (1)
paint (1)
park (1)
participate (2)
pass (1)
paste (2)
pause (2)
peel (1)
perm (1)
pick (1)
pitch (1)
plan (3)
plant (1)
play (1)
polish (1)
pour (1)
praise (2)
preheat (1)
prepare (2)
prescribe (2)
press (1)
pretend (1)
print (1)
program (3)
protect (1)
pull (1)
purchase (2)
push (1)
quilt (1)
race (2)
raise (2)
rake (2)
receive (2)
record (1)
recycle (2)
redecorate (2)
reduce (2)
reenter (1)
refuse (2)
register (1)
relax (1)
remain (1)

remove (2)
renew (1)
repair (1)
replace (2)
report (1)
request (1)
research (1)
respond (1)
retire (2)
return (1)
reuse (2)
revise (2)
rinse (2)
rock (1)
sauté (1)
save (2)
scan (3)
schedule (2)
scroll (1)
scrub (3)
search (1)
seat (1)
select (1)
sentence (2)
separate (2)
serve (2)
share (2)
shave (2)
ship (3)
shop (3)
shorten (1)
shower (1)
sign (1)
simmer (1)
skate (2)
ski (1)
slice (2)
smell (1)
smile (2)
smoke (2)
solve (2)
sort (1)
spell (1)
spoon (1)
staple (2)
start (1)
state (2)
stay (1)
steam (1)

stir (3)
stop (3)
stow (1)
stretch (1)
study (4)
submit (3)
subtract (1)
supervise (2)
swallow (1)
tackle (2)
talk (1)
taste (2)
thank (1)
tie (2)
touch (1)
transcribe (2)
transfer (3)
translate (2)
travel (3)
trim (3)
try (4)
turn (1)
type (2)
underline (2)
undress (1)
unload (1)
unpack (1)
unscramble (2)
update (2)
use (2)
vacuum (1)
videotape (2)
visit (1)
volunteer (1)
vomit (1)
vote (2)
wait (1)
walk (1)
wash (1)
watch (1)
water (1)
wave (2)
weed (1)
weigh (1)
wipe (2)
work (1)
wrap (3)
yell (1)

Verb Guide

Irregular Verbs
These verbs have irregular endings in the past and/or the past participle.

The Oxford Picture Dictionary List of Irregular Verbs

simple	past	past participle	simple	past	past participle
be	was	been	make	made	made
beat	beat	beaten	meet	met	met
become	became	become	pay	paid	paid
bend	bent	bent	picnic	picnicked	picnicked
bleed	bled	bled	proofread	proofread	proofread
blow	blew	blown	put	put	put
break	broke	broken	quit	quit	quit
bring	brought	brought	read	read	read
buy	bought	bought	rewind	rewound	rewound
catch	caught	caught	rewrite	rewrote	rewritten
choose	chose	chosen	ride	rode	ridden
come	came	come	run	ran	run
cut	cut	cut	say	said	said
do	did	done	see	saw	seen
draw	drew	drawn	seek	sought	sought
drink	drank	drunk	sell	sold	sold
drive	drove	driven	send	sent	sent
eat	ate	eaten	set	set	set
fall	fell	fallen	sew	sewed	sewn
feed	fed	fed	shake	shook	shaken
feel	felt	felt	shoot	shot	shot
find	found	found	show	showed	shown
fly	flew	flown	sing	sang	sung
freeze	froze	frozen	sit	sat	sat
get	got	gotten	speak	spoke	spoken
give	gave	given	stand	stood	stood
go	went	gone	steal	stole	stolen
hang	hung	hung	sweep	swept	swept
have	had	had	swim	swam	swum
hear	heard	heard	swing	swung	swung
hide	hid	hidden	take	took	taken
hit	hit	hit	teach	taught	taught
hold	held	held	think	thought	thought
keep	kept	kept	throw	threw	thrown
lay	laid	laid	wake	woke	woken
leave	left	left	win	won	won
lend	lent	lent	withdraw	withdrew	withdrawn
let	let	let	write	wrote	written
lose	lost	lost			

Index

Index Key

fast **23**–3

 fast food restaurant **130**–10

FAST FOOD RESTAURANT **79**

fast forward 241–D

fasten 164–H

fastener **99**–29

fat / heavy 32–7

father **34**–4, **35**–23

 father-in-law **34**–11

 grandfather **34**–2

 stepfather **35**–25

Fathers of Confederation **208**–5

faucet **57**–8

fax 177–G

fax machine **189**–21

feast **245**–9

feather **220**–4

 feather duster **61**–1

February **21**–26

Federal Government **140** AWL

feed 36–C, **186**–D, **187**–D

feed dog / feed bar **98**–20

feedback

 respond well to feedback **178**–H

feel 110–A, **110**–B

FEELINGS **42**–43

female **4**–18

fence **187**–19

fencing **234**–7

fertilize 186–D

fever **110**–7

fiction **243**–18

field **5**–2, **187**–7

 ball field **230**–1

 track and field **234**–18

fifteen **16**

fifteenth **16**

fifth **16**

fiftieth **16**

fifty **16**

 fifty dollars **26**–9

 50 percent **17**–10

fighter

 firefighter **148**–9, **171**–26

figs **68**–27

figure **239**–26

 figure skating **233**–5

figurine **238**–1

file **189**–44 AWL

 attach a file **211**–Y AWL

 file cabinet **188**–11 AWL

 file clerk **188**–10 AWL

 file folder **189**–50

fill

 fill a cavity **120**–E

 fill in 9–O, **10**–K

 fill prescriptions **114** ✦

 fill the tank **161**–G

 fill the tires **161**–L

filling **120**–9

Filling Out a Form **4**

fin **218**–1

find 164–F

FINDING A HOME **48**–49

fine adjustment knob **206**–22

finger **105**–16

 fingernail **106**–18

 swollen finger **110**–16

Fingers **106**

finish 236–T

 finish all medication **114**–C

fins **231**–8

fire **148**–7, **148**–8

 campfire **232**–11

 fire escape **50**–2

 fire exit **51** ✦

 fire extinguisher **197**–21

 fire hydrant **131**–27

 fire screen **56**–12

 fire station **127**–12

 fire truck **148**–10

 firefighter **148**–9, **171**–26

 fireplace **56**–13

 fireworks **245**–7

first **16**

 first aid kit **119**–1, **150**–18

 first aid manual **119**–2 AWL

 first name **4**–2

 First Nations **208**–4

 first prime minister **208**–7

FIRST AID **119**

First Aid **119**

First Aid Procedures **119** AWL

FIRST DAY ON THE JOB **180**–181

First Floor **50**

First Licence **139** AWL

fish **66**–1, **81**–29

 catfish **71**–2

 goldfish **221**–16

 jellyfish **218**–14

 sea star **218**–17

 swordfish **71**–5, **218**–10

Fish **71, 218**

fisher **171**–17

fishing **232**–4

 fishing net **232**–17

 fishing pole **232**–18

fitted sheet **58**–12

fittings **195**–18

five **16**

 five after one **18**–7

 five dollars **26**–6

fix 62 ✦, **225**–F

fixture **55**–18

flag **245**–8

flammable liquids **197**–8

flash drive / thumb drive **190**–25

flashlight **150**–14

flat

 flat sheet **58**–13

 flat-panel TV **240**–8

 flat-screen TV **240**–8

 have a flat tire **166**–C

flats **95**–27

fleas **63**–25

 flea market **228**–6

flight

 flight attendant **165**–12

 nonstop flight **165** ✦

Flight **164**

float **245**–2

flood **149**–19

floor **46**–7, **58**–21, **197**–6

 floor lamp **56**–15

 floor plan **198**–4

Floor **50**

floral **96**–25

florist **132**–8, **171**–27

floss **109**–24

floss 109–K

flounder **218**–15

flour **73**–29

Flower **217**

flowers

 flower bed **53**–20

FLOWERS **217**

flu **112**–2

fluid

 correction fluid **189**–36

 fluid ounce **75**–1

flute **244**–1

fly **220**–29

fly 176–F

flyer **102**–1

flying disc **237**–27

foam pad **232**–13

focus **241**–31 AWL

foggy **13**–22

foil **72**–23

fold 101–F

folder **189**–50

folding

 folding card table **102**–4

 folding chair **102**–5

folk **243**–29

follow 116–J, **151**–F

Following Directions **9**

food

 baby food **37**–4

 canned food **150**–9

 fast food restaurant **130**–10

 food court **133**–15

 food preparation worker **193**–4

 food processor **54**–26

 packaged food **150**–10

 pet food **72**–6

FOOD **79**

FOOD PREPARATION AND SAFETY **76**–77

Food Processor **92**

Food Safety **76**

FOOD SERVICE **193**

Foods **72, 73**

foot **104**–8

 football **235**–12, **237**–21

 football helmet **237**–19

 footless tights **91**–17

letter carrier **136**–20
letterhead **189**–42
lettuce **69**–1
level **175**–2, **194**–29 🔑
librarian **135**–9
library **5**–17, **127**–15 🔑
   library clerk **135**–1 🔑
   library patron **135**–3
LIBRARY **135** 🔑
licence 🔑 AWL
   driver's licence **40**–4, **138**–9 🔑 AWL
   driver's licence number **138**–11 🔑
   licence plate **138**–12, **162**–12 🔑 AWL
   marriage licence **41**–8 🔑 AWL
   renew a licence **138** ✦ 🔑
   taxi licence **156**–23 🔑
   unrestricted licence **139**–I
Licence **139** 🔑 AWL
licensing office **126**–4, **138**–**139**
lid **78**–24 🔑
lieutenant governor **141**–15 🔑
life 🔑
   life preserver **231**–20 🔑 AWL
   life vest **165**–25, **232**–14
   lifeguard **231**–19 🔑
   lifeguard station **231**–21 🔑
   wildlife **166**–2 🔑
LIFE **218**–**219** 🔑
LIFE EVENTS AND DOCUMENTS
   40–**41** 🔑 AWL
lift **11**–E 🔑
light **23**–14, **97**–28 🔑
   brake light **162**–14
   daylight saving time **19**–25 🔑
   flashlight **150**–14
   hazard lights **163**–36
   headlight **162**–7
   light blue **24**–11 🔑
   light bulb **56** ✦
   light fixture **55**–18
   light source **206**–19 🔑 AWL
   light switch **58**–27 🔑
   night light **37**–28 🔑
   porch light **53**–13
   streetlight **152**–3
   string lights **245**–18 🔑
   taillight **162**–13
   traffic light **130**–8 🔑
   work light **195**–44 🔑
lightning **13**–19
lily **217**–26
limbs **106** ✦, **216**–3
limes **68**–8
limit **158**–4 🔑
limo / limousine **160**–11
line **73**–11 🔑
   assembly line **185**–6 🔑 AWL
   clothesline **101**–9
   curved line **205**–23 🔑
   headline **135**–7
   line cook **93**, **193** ✦ 🔑
   line segment **205**–20

line supervisor **185**–4
   parallel lines **205**–25 🔑 AWL
   perpendicular lines **205**–24
   phone line **14**–1 🔑
   straight line **205**–22 🔑
linen **98**–2
   linen closet **57** ✦
liner
   eyeliner **109**–36
Lines **205** 🔑
lingerie **91** ✦
links **212**–6, **213**–19 🔑 AWL
lion **219**–35, **222**–2, **223**–36
lip **106**–5 🔑
   lipstick **109**–38
Liquid Measures **75** 🔑
liquids **61**–21, **197**–8 🔑
list 🔑
   contact list **14**–15 🔑 AWL
   list your soft skills **174**–E
   shopping list **67**–14 🔑
listen **6**–C, **111**–C, **179**–K 🔑
listing **48**–2
litre
   4 litre jug **75**–5
   litre of milk **75**–4
litter **152**–2
litter **225**–L
little **23**–1 🔑
Little League **235** ✦
LIVE **52**
live **142**–H 🔑
live music **84**–1 🔑
liver **70**–7, **107**–40
livestock **187**–15
Livestock **221**
living room **47**–13 🔑
LIVING ROOM **56** 🔑
lizard **219**–43
llama **223**–25
load **101**–C
loading dock **185**–15
loaf **74**–22
   meatloaf **81**–31
loafers **95**–30
loaves **74**–10
Lobby **50**
lobster **71**–10
local call **15**–33 🔑
lock **51**–35, **163**–25 🔑
   locksmith **62**–11
lock **146**–E 🔑
locker **5**–11, **50**–17
locket **95**–35
log in to your account **211**–T
logistics **184**–8
lonely **42**–17 🔑
long **96**–18 🔑
   long hair **33**–3 🔑
   long underwear **91**–3 🔑
   long-distance call **15**–34 🔑
   long-sleeved **96**–14 🔑

look 🔑
   look at **49**–H, **161**–A, **212**–E 🔑
   look for **135**–B, **168**–G 🔑
   look up **8**–A 🔑
loonie / a dollar **26**–4
loop **99**–29
loose **97**–30 🔑
lose **235** ✦ 🔑
loss **117**–2 🔑
lost child **148**–1 🔑
lotion **37**–13, **108**–9
loud **23**–11 🔑
loungewear **91** ✦
love **40**–H, **42**–18 🔑
   loveseat **56**–1 🔑
low **97**–31 🔑
   low-cut socks **91**–10 🔑
   low-fat milk **81**–42 🔑
lower back **107**–29 🔑
lozenges **115**–30
lug wrench **162**–22
luggage **165**–18
   luggage cart **192**–8
lumber **196**–17
lunar eclipse **215** ✦
Lunch **80** 🔑
lung **107**–39 🔑

machine 🔑
   fax machine **189**–21
   machine operator **172**–37
   machine screw **194**–32 🔑
   sewing machine **98**–13
   sewing machine operator **98**–14
   vending machine **156**–10
Machine **98**, **134** 🔑
magazine **135**–5 🔑
   magazine rack **56** ✦
magnet **207**–36
magnolia **216**–8
mail 🔑
   air mail **136**–5
   junk mail **137** ✦
   mailbox **50**–11, **53**–1, **130**–13, **137**–10
   next-day mail / overnight **137** ✦ 🔑
   registered mail **136**–4
   surface mail **136**–6
   voice mail **14**–17 🔑
mail **137**–D
mailer **189**–40
mailing
   mailing address **136**–22
   mailing label **189**–41
main office **5**–12 🔑
mainframe computer **190**–1
MAINTAINING A CAR **161** 🔑 AWL
maintenance **184**–12, **192**–23
maitre d' **193**–11
make 🔑
   make a deposit **134**–B 🔑
   make a disaster kit **150**–B 🔑
   make a mortgage payment **49**–L 🔑

beauty shop **132**–✦ 🔑
coffee shop **128**–11 🔑
doughnut shop **131**–17
gift shop **132**–✦, **192**–5 🔑
ice cream shop **133**–16 🔑
shop 28–A, **146**–H
SHOP **80–81** 🔑
Shop **100**
shoplifting **145**–8
shopping 🔑
   shopping bag **67**–13 🔑
   shopping basket **73**–9
   shopping list **67**–14 🔑
   shopping mall **128**–7 🔑
   shopping program **242**–10
SHOPPING **27** 🔑
shore **214**–12
short **32**–6, **96**–16 🔑
   short hair **33**–1 🔑
   short-order cook **193**–1 🔑
   short-sleeved **96**–12 🔑
shorten 100–B
shorts **89**–25, **91**–4
shoulder **105**–13 🔑
   shoulder bag **94**–17 🔑
   shoulder blade **107**–28 🔑
   shoulder pads **237**–20
   shoulder-length hair **33**–2
shovel **186**–7, **196**–22
show **242**–4, **242**–6, **242**–8
show 139–B, **164**–C 🔑
shower 🔑
   shower cap **108**–1 🔑
   shower curtain **57**–14 🔑
   shower gel **108**–2
   showerhead **57**–13
   stall shower **57**–✦
   take a shower **38**–C, **108**–A 🔑
shredder **189**–24
shrimp **71**–11, **218**–19
shut-off **150**–4 🔑
shuttle **156**–20
sick **42**–12 🔑
   homesick **43**–20
side 🔑
   sideburns **33**–7
   side-view mirror **162**–3
   sunny-side up **76**–10
Side Salads **80** 🔑
sidewalk **131**–24
sign 🔑
   street sign **131**–26 🔑
   vacancy sign **50**–7
   vital signs monitor **123**–26 🔑 AWL
sign 4–E, **48**–D
signal 🔑
   strong signal **14**–11 🔑
   turn signal **162**–6, **163**–34 🔑
   weak signal **14**–12 🔑
signature **4**–20, **138**–5 🔑
SIGNS **158** 🔑
silk **98**–5 🔑

simmer **77**–P
sing 36–O, **244**–B 🔑
single 🔑
   single father **35**–23 🔑
   single mother **35**–22 🔑
sink **54**–4, **57**–25
Sirius **215**–✦
sister **34**–5 🔑
   half sister **35**–27 🔑
   sister-in-law **34**–16
   stepsister **35**–29
sit down 6–F 🔑
sitcom (situation comedy) **242**–2 🔑
site **128**–2 🔑 AWL
sitter **170**–9
situation comedy (sitcom) **242**–2 🔑
six **16**
   six-pack **74**–9, **74**–21
   6-year-old boy **31**–9 🔑
sixteen **16**
sixteenth **16**
sixth **16**
sixtieth **16**
sixty **16**
Sizes **96** 🔑
skate 236–U
skates **237**–9, **237**–10
   skateboard **230**–7
   skateboarding **234**–13
skating **233**–4, **233**–5, **234**–10
Skeleton **107**
ski 236–V
skiing **233**–1, **233**–3
   waterskiing **233**–7
SKILLS **176–179** 🔑
Skills **177**, **178** 🔑
skin **107**–31 🔑
   skinless **70**–✦
skirt **87**–10 🔑
skis **237**–24
   ski boots **237**–26
   ski hat **90**–11
   ski mask **90**–15
   ski poles **237**–25
SKU number **27**–5
skull **107**–47
skunk **222**–15
sky **231**–4 🔑
   skyscraper **129**–13
slacks **87**–12
sledding **233**–6
sledgehammer **196**–23
sleeper **91**–26
sleeping bag **232**–12 🔑
SLEEPWEAR **91**
Sleepwear **91**
sleepy **42**–3 🔑
sleeve **100**–6 🔑
   long-sleeved **96**–14 🔑
   short-sleeved **96**–12 🔑
   sleeveless **96**–11
   3/4 sleeved **96**–13 🔑

slender **32**–9
slice 77–C
slide **206**–3, **230**–13
   mudslide **148**–6
sliding glass door **53**–18 🔑
sling **115**–19
slip **91**–21, **91**–22, **134**–4
slip-ons **95**–30
slippers **91**–25
slippery floor **197**–6 🔑
slow **23**–4 🔑
small **96**–1, **96**–2, **97**–37 🔑
   small town **52**–3 🔑
smartphone **15**–25
smell 106–C 🔑
smile 2–E 🔑
smock **93**–26
smog **224**–11
smoggy **13**–16
smoke 116–G
smoke detector **51**–30 🔑 AWL
smoked turkey **71**–25
Snack Foods **73**
snail **218**–23
snake 🔑
   garter snake **219**–46
   rattlesnake **219**–45
snap **99**–26
sneezing **113**–12
snorkeling **233**–11
snow **13**–12 🔑
   snowboard **237**–23
   snowboarding **233**–2
   snowstorm **13**–25
soap **57**–4, **61**–5, **108**–3 🔑
   soap dish **57**–3 🔑
   soap opera **242**–5
sober **146**–✦
soccer **235**–13
   soccer ball **237**–12
social 🔑
   Social Insurance Number **4**–19
   Social Insurance Number card
      40–5
   social worker **173**–57 🔑
social media links **213**–19 🔑 AWL
socks **86**–6 🔑
   ankle socks **91**–7 🔑
   crew socks **91**–8
   dress socks **91**–9 🔑
   low-cut socks **91**–10 🔑
Socks **91** 🔑
sofa **56**–18
sofa cushions **56**–✦
soft **23**–6 🔑
   softball **235**–11
   soft drink **73**–34
soft skills **174**–E 🔑
SOFT SKILLS **178** 🔑
softener **101**–6
software **171**–18 🔑
Software / Applications **191** 🔑

Index 索引

298

Research Bibliography

The authors and publisher wish to acknowledge the contribution of the following educators for their research on vocabulary development, which has helped inform the principles underlying *OPD*.

Burt, M., J. K. Peyton, and R. Adams. *Reading and Adult English Language Learners: A Review of the Research.* Washington, DC: Center for Applied Linguistics, 2003.

Coady, J. "Research on ESL/EFL Vocabulary Acquisition: Putting it in Context." In *Second Language Reading and Vocabulary Learning,* edited by T. Huckin, M. Haynes, and J. Coady. Norwood, NJ: Ablex, 1993.

de la Fuente, M. J. "Negotiation and Oral Acquisition of L2 Vocabulary: The Roles of Input and Output in the Receptive and Productive Acquisition of Words." *Studies in Second Language Acquisition* 24 (2002): 81–112.

DeCarrico, J. "Vocabulary learning and teaching." In *Teaching English as a Second or Foreign Language,* edited by M. Celcia-Murcia. 3rd ed. Boston: Heinle & Heinle, 2001.

Ellis, R. *The Study of Second Language Acquisition.* Oxford: Oxford University Press, 1994.

Folse, K. *Vocabulary Myths: Applying Second Language Research to Classroom Teaching.* Ann Arbor, MI: University of Michigan Press, 2004.

Gairns, R. and S. Redman. *Working with Words: A Guide to Teaching and Learning Vocabulary.* Cambridge: Cambridge University Press, 1986.

Gass, S. M. and M. J. A. Torres. "Attention When?: An Investigation of the Ordering Effect of Input and Interaction." *Studies in Second Language Acquisition* 27 (Mar 2005): 1–31.

Henriksen, Birgit. "Three Dimensions of Vocabulary Development." *Studies in Second Language Acquisition* 21 (1999): 303–317.

Koprowski, Mark. "Investigating the Usefulness of Lexical Phrases in Contemporary Coursebooks." *Oxford ELT Journal* 59(4) (2005): 322–332.

McCrostie, James. "Examining Learner Vocabulary Notebooks." *Oxford ELT Journal* 61 (July 2007): 246–255.

Nation, P. *Learning Vocabulary in Another Language.* Cambridge: Cambridge University Press, 2001.

National Center for ESL Literacy Education Staff. *Adult English Language Instruction in the 21st Century.* Washington, DC: Center for Applied Linguistics, 2003.

National Reading Panel. *Teaching Children to Read: An Evidenced-Based Assessment of the Scientific Research Literature on Reading and its Implications on Reading Instruction.* 2000. https://www.nichd.nih.gov/publications/pubs/nrp/documents/report.pdf.

Newton, J. "Options for Vocabulary Learning through Communication Tasks." *Oxford ELT Journal* 55(1) (2001): 30–37.

Prince, P. "Second Language Vocabulary Learning: The Role of Context Versus Translations as a Function of Proficiency." *Modern Language Journal* 80(4) (1996): 478–493.

Savage, K. L., ed. *Teacher Training Through Video - ESL Techniques: Early Production.* White Plains, NY: Longman Publishing Group, 1992.

Schmitt, N. *Vocabulary in Language Teaching.* Cambridge: Cambridge University Press, 2000.

Smith, C. B. *Vocabulary Instruction and Reading Comprehension.* Bloomington, IN: ERIC Clearinghouse on Reading English and Communication, 1997.

Wood, K. and J. Josefina Tinajero. "Using Pictures to Teach Content to Second Language Learners." *Middle School Journal* 33 (2002): 47–51.